The Lady
from Vermont

Books by Elizabeth Yates

For Young People

QUEST IN THE NORTHLAND

HAVEN FOR THE BRAVE

UNDER THE LITTLE FIR

PATTERNS ON THE WALL

MOUNTAIN BORN

ONCE IN THE YEAR

A PLACE FOR PETER

CHILDREN OF THE BIBLE

THE YOUNG TRAVELLER IN THE U. S. A.

AMOS FORTUNE, FREE MAN

PRUDENCE CRANDALL, WOMAN OF COURAGE

RAINBOW ROUND THE WORLD

PEBBLE IN A POOL, THE WIDENING CIRCLES OF
DOROTHY CANFIELD FISHER'S LIFE

JOSEPH

THE CHRISTMAS STORY

YOUR PRAYERS AND MINE

Novels

WIND OF SPRING

NEARBY

BELOVED BONDAGE

GUARDIAN HEART

BRAVE INTERVAL

HUE AND CRY

THE CAREY GIRL

Dorothy and John Fisher

The Lady
from Vermont

Dorothy Canfield Fisher's

Life and World

By ELIZABETH YATES

The Stephen Greene Press
Brattleboro, Vermont

Published by The Stephen Greene Press, Brattleboro, Vt. 05301
First published under the title *Pebble in a Pool*
by E. P. Dutton & Company, 1958.

Library of Congress Card Number: 74–148629
International Standard Book Number: 0–8289–0127–9

Contents

Illustrations

Foreword

Most everybody thinks of Dorothy Canfield Fisher as a loyal Vermonter, but I think of her not only as a loyal Vermonter but as a loyal friend and political ally. To the best of my recollection the first, last and only time she ever became involved in politics was in my behalf.

Leaving politics aside, her home in the hills outside of Arlington where I used to visit her and her husband, John, spoke almost divinely of her love of Vermont.

Although Dorothy was better known because of her writings, John Fisher was also a Vermont citizen of whom we could well be proud. I had the privilege while I was Governor of appointing him to our State Board of Education where he served the State well.

There isn't much more I can say about this couple except to express the regret that John and Dorothy are no longer with us and the wish that we could have people like the Fishers, loyal, sympathetic and dedicated, in each community of the State of Vermont to which they were so devoted.

George D. Aiken

A Word to the Reader

When Dorothy Canfield was a little girl, her Uncle Zed said, "If you want to learn something about a man or a woman, Dolly, and the town they live in, don't ask them direct questions. Listen while they think they are talking about something else."

I have been listening—while reading the many books Dorothy Canfield Fisher has written, while studying the massive files of her correspondence in the Wilbur Library at the University of Vermont, and during many visits at her home.

This book is the result of that listening. It is not an evaluation of her accomplishments but an attempt to follow the thread of her life and her work through the greater part of a century, and that thread is a strong and shining one in the fabric of our American life. She has written most often of Vermont, but she is not a regional writer unless her region may be considered to be that of the human spirit. Her influence as a writer has been one with her influence as a person for more than three generations. Her books have become household words. Her letters are friendly treasures. And people express their gratitude to her by telling her how much they love her. Ideals and principles which she has held have changed no more through the years than her handwriting, except, like it, they have become more vigorous.

Often when reading the story of another's life, the question arises, "What is there here for me? What is there in this person's way of living to help my own?" With this particular person there is a very great deal for she has had a genius for people, embracing them as comrades on life's way; and she has a richness of loving-kindness which has grown as it has been dispensed.

Find her, as I found her the first time I met her, in her study. Her small quick-motioned hands were still, her firm clear voice was warm with welcome. There was a look of restful alertness on her face. "We don't inherit our expressions," she said to me once, "they are the signature of the years." A sense of deeply-grounded peace put me at ease. She gave her complete attention, really listening to me, really looking at me.

Later, when I was talking with Dr. Russell, he told me that he had often acted in community plays with Dorothy. "She's a trump to play with. If you forget your lines just start talking with her and she'll keep the conversation going until it's time for something else to happen."

And she kept our conversation going, easily as talk between friends. When my visit was over, she turned instantly to something else, as quick in movement as she was unhurried.

Laughingly she has said that her besetting sin is to spin yet another metaphor. It is difficult to write of her without sharing her sin. She is like a bright flame in a sturdy iron lamp. She is like the elm in the hill pasture at Arlington. She is a result of the influences around her as well as a standing up to them. Hers has been a richly triumphant life, rounded and realized as a work of art. To cover nearly a century and find the story of Dorothy Canfield Fisher is to find not only day-to-day happenings and a writer's steady development, but a whole way of living—vibrant, gay, heartening, gloriously natural.

Often in these pages she speaks in her own words, through her writings, in her letters with their sparkle and warmth. And she says to you, as she has said to me, "My hope for all of us is that we may meet all of life with courage and some of it with joy."

Elizabeth Yates

Peterborough, N.H.
February 1958

Chapter 1

A Pebble Is Cast

THE wind blew cold across the Kansas plains. It swept through the streets of Lawrence, swirled over the heights of Mount Oread and whistled around the buildings of the State University. Snow that had fallen three days before still covered the ground. The river, sheeted with ice, sparkled in the sunlight.

It was Monday, February 17, 1879. For young Professor Canfield it was a day like no other. The child whose arrival had been so eagerly awaited had been born. He walked briskly home to make acquaintance with his little daughter.

Five-year-old James met him at the door. "A baby sister, Papa! Come and see."

Up the stairs they went and into Flavia's room. James Hulme Canfield smiled happily at his wife, then he gazed at the minute piece of humanity that was his daughter. The baby stirred and stretched in her cocoon of blankets, and stared up at her father.

"Dorothea Frances," Flavia murmured.

"Dolly," young James exclaimed.

Neither the Canfields nor the Camps had had a Dorothea among their near or remote ancestors, but ever since Flavia had read *Middlemarch* no name had seemed so appealing to her as that of the heroine of George Eliot's broad canvas of middle-class, middle-century life. Perhaps a name could not shape the destiny of a child, but Flavia hoped that her daughter would become as great-souled as Dorothea Brooke, whose life was a widening influence of love. She had recently reread several of her favorite passages:

> In Dorothea's mind there was a current into which all thought and feeling were apt sooner or later to flow—the reaching forward of the whole consciousness toward the fullest truth, the least partial good. . . . A human being is a very wonderful whole, the slow creation of long interchanging influences; and charm is a result of the two such wholes, the one loving and the one loved. . . . Her full nature . . . spent itself in channels which had no great name on the earth. But the effect of her being on those around her was incalculably diffusive.

During those first weeks when his daughter was making herself at home in the world, James Canfield would find himself thinking deep thoughts as he watched her. He knew that this child had been born at a time when the social pattern was undergoing great and rapid changes. She would accept her sex as she would the color of her eyes and hair, but there would no longer be the necessity to fit herself into a tightly prescribed role because she was a girl. Those days were past. The challenge of a new order was at hand and, whether she wanted to or not, this daughter of his would have to face it. He was a teacher, through long preparation and recent application, and he was determined to do all he could to equip his daughter to meet the challenge of the world she had inherited.

Little James rocked the cradle gently and studied the tiny, mobile face of his sister. He was conscious of a sense of happy relief. Here at last was someone to play with, someone to share things with. He was tired of being an only child. Mama was always occupied with her paintpots and brushes, studying painting and thinking about art; Papa had his teaching and his books. Of course, the baby was very small, James realized as he reached down and touched her hand. It might be a little while before her fingers could hold a ball, or her legs run a race, but he hoped she would grow up fast. If Papa had anything to do with teaching her, James thought, she'd grow fast enough!

As the baby's eyes began to focus, she returned the gaze of the three faces that came most often to her cradle with something humorous and uncompromising in her glance. "Just you wait," she as much as said to each one in turn—father, mother, brother—"until these hands can do things for me, these legs can take me where I want to go. Just you wait—"

Family traditions were strong and Dolly heard tales of her forebears as other babies heard lullabies. Her mother's parents had both been born in Vermont, but they had left farming for frontier life, and Flavia had been born in a small Wisconsin settlement. Her early years had been filled with danger and hardship, but freedom was the air she had breathed and courage had always meant more than comfort. Grandfather Canfield had been born in Arlington, Vermont, though as a minister in a New York parish he had lived away from it for many years. Now he lived in Arlington with his sister Mary Ann, his brother Zadock, and his daughter Mattie. All were waiting eagerly for the time when the newest member of the family would be brought home on a visit. Canfield roots went deep into Vermont soil and none of the old people doubted that Arlington would be home to the child who had been born in Kansas.

College and European travel had taken Dolly's father far from Arlington. Wanting rugged experience to complete his education, he had gone west. There, with an enormous capacity for hard work and a genius for making friends, he had worked in lumber camps, on railroads, and begun to read law when he met Flavia Camp. They met in Iowa, but they had Vermont in common, and the same kind of uncompromising ideals. Soon after their marriage, James commenced the teaching that would be his life work. More than anything else, he wanted to help young men and women to think vigorously and independently. Such thinking was needed as the rich sprawling area that was the West became integrated with the rest of the country and the United States prepared itself to take a place in the world.

Dolly liked hearing stories. The words might not yet have meaning for her, but the sound of familiar voices was a happy, comforting sound. It mattered little if the stories were of her family or of the town in which she had been born. Lawrence, on the banks of the Kaw River, had been settled a few years before the Civil War by a group of New England men and women who were ardent abolitionists. They were ready to undergo anything so that the Territory of Kansas might be admitted to the Union as a Free State. Through struggle and bloodshed they succeeded. Lawrence became the center of the Free State cause and a station on the Underground Railway. Now, twenty-five years later, the countryside was rich with fertile farms and growing orchards, and Kansas was a member of the Union of States.

The abolition of slavery in the United States was one of the many evidences of the changing pattern that was part of the world of the late nineteenth century. Machinery had begun to take over much of the necessary toil; a tide of immigration was pouring into the New World from the Old; the continent had been spanned and trains now ran from the Atlantic Ocean to the Pacific; communication had become easily possible between distant points; an unfamiliar bell could be heard ringing in one house after another as people picked up the telephone to talk with other people distant by a city block or a state. On the threshold of the twentieth century one fact stood out clearly: in the new age, everyone would have a chance, even a little girl.

Dolly, wriggling her feet and reaching out with her hands, was impatient for the skills that would enable her to move forward in her world. Her brother's hope that she would grow fast was fulfilled, although at times the process seemed discouragingly slow to the small boy. He watched each new stage of her development with an eager, personal interest. And when finally Dolly was able to creep around the house, James followed at her heels, to see that she stayed out of trouble. Mama's paints and brushes were not to be touched, and James would head his sister toward Papa's study, where experience had taught him that books could be dragged from the shelves. Together they would sit on the floor using the books for blocks to build houses. Dolly learned to love the smell of her father's study, with its shelves and shelves of books.

There was endless conversation going on around Dolly, and she soon learned to mimic the sounds. Words grew in meaning, and it was not long before she realized that printed words had meaning, too. Tense with excitement at the discovery, she pored over the pages of the books which such a short time before she had considered only playthings. Some she dipped into and tasted, but others she swallowed whole. There was an endless supply. In time she would sample Thackeray, Fielding, Hakluyt, Dickens . . . rich food for a growing mind. There was Ruskin, too, and Defoe, Cervantes and Shakespeare.

For her sixth birthday, James gave her a copy of *Ivanhoe*. She read it, though she often yawned with boredom. The words presented no difficulty, but some of the people did, and there were too many. It was like a room full of visiting aunts and uncles.

When Dolly discovered the Pilgrims in her history primer, she became absorbed in their story, sitting on the edge of her chair, swinging her feet and chewing her tongue, as her eager mind raced ahead of her eyes' capacity to follow the words. Here was a story worth reading of a small group of people who were willing to sacrifice comfort and dare the unknown, rather than submit to the tyranny that tried to control their thinking. She closed the book in a daze of hero-worship. Opening it later to the next story, she read about Roger Williams and the Quakers in Rhode Island and what they suffered at the hands of the Pilgrims. The unfairness of the first settlers of the Massachusetts Bay Colony infuriated Dolly, and she strained hotly after each word. Stunned by disappointment, unable to understand or accept the inconsistency of human behavior, she finished the story and ran out of the house to the woods. Standing alone among the sheltering trees, she shouted at the top of her voice, "Looky-here, looky-here! You're doing just what you left England for, so people wouldn't do it to you. Stop it! Stop, stop—oh, *please* don't."

Still troubled that night, she asked her father about it. His answer, dry with adult cynicism, brought a club of reality down on her young ideals. "Oh, shucks, Dolly, the Pilgrim Fathers wanted the same sort of 'freedom of thought' that everybody wants—freedom to bully everybody else into thinking as they do."

It was not a satisfying answer, but it was the only one he would give her. She poked it into a corner of her mind.

School widened the horizon of Dolly's world and her teachers helped her develop the ability to express herself and to follow the thoughts of others. But there were equally important lessons that she sometimes learned in unexpected ways. One day on her way home from school, Dolly saw a tall Indian step down from the streetcar. Fascinated by his unusual height and his towering war bonnet, Dolly stood rooted to the sidewalk, staring. She realized that he had probably come to visit one of the children at Haskell Institute, a boarding school for the sons and daughters of Indians. He had scarcely planted his feet on the ground, when the streetcar conductor whipped up his horses. The car rattled on down the street. A woman wheeling a baby carriage, turned quickly at sight of the Indian and pushed the carriage into a convenient back yard. Two elderly ladies whispered to each other and disappeared down a side street. Dolly found herself alone on the street with the tall Indian. What on earth ailed everyone? People in Lawrence were used to Indians. It couldn't be fear that had prompted them to turn away. Then why had they avoided him? Could they think that he was not as good as they were?

As Dolly stood and puzzled, the Indian crossed the street, and walked toward her, giving no sign that he had noticed the fleeing backs of the people. Dolly could see that he was very old. His brown face was deeply lined, his strong hands wrinkled. He stopped beside her and smiled. As Dolly looked up into his face, she was shocked by the sadness in his deep-set eyes shadowed by the boldly beautiful headdress.

The Indian reached out and touched her head gently with his hand, then he turned away. Dolly wished there were something she could say to him, but she was silent as she watched him go down the empty street, treading noiselessly in his embroidered moccasins, his head held high. When he had gone from sight, she turned and hurried home; but the shadow he had cast as he stood beside her was to stay with her always.

Once a week the horse was hitched to the family surrey and Dolly and her mother drove out to the Burt's farm to buy vegetables and eggs. In early summer these trips held all the excitement of an excursion. Verbena and wild strawberries grew in profusion along the roadside, phlox made a blue splash in the woodlands, a pink haze on the prairie. Meadow larks and redbirds filled the air with their song, and when the trotting horse was drawn in to a walk, quail could be heard piping in the thickets.

There was always a warm greeting for Dolly and her mother at the farm. Sometimes Mr. Burt was there to load the baskets of vegetables into the wagon, but often Mrs. Burt was there alone, doing the work with quiet efficiency. There was one time that Dolly would never forget. She and her mother had driven along the familiar road, only to find the farmhouse deserted, the doors and windows tightly closed. "Well, never mind," her mother said, as they drove back to town. "It does seem as if they might have sent word, though, and saved us a trip."

"Where can they have gone?" Dolly asked.

Her mother, holding the reins slack in her hands, stared off across the prairie. "Heaven only knows, child," she said, "with that man of hers as given to wandering as he is."

In the weeks that followed, Dolly overheard snatches of conversation that at least explained what had happened to the Burts. It might seem queer to grownups, but to Dolly it was vastly exciting that two seemingly settled people would just suddenly pack the few things they needed in their one-horse wagon, close the door of their house and go off for a "bit of wandering."

When word reached the Canfield house that the Burts were back, Dolly and her mother drove out to see them. There was a warm friendliness about the sparkling kitchen, and the Burts seemed happier than Dolly had ever seen them before. There was a new family of kittens and Dolly sat on the kitchen floor playing with them. Once she glanced up and was puzzled to notice her mother wiping her eyes. Dolly heard her say, "Mrs. Burt, you do your duty way beyond anyone else." Was doing your duty something to cry about, Dolly wondered. She waited for Mrs. Burt's reply, hoping it would explain what her mother had said. When it came, it was calm and comforting. "Well, I married him, didn't I?" So that was it, Dolly thought. Marriage meant doing one's duty, but duty could be more than keeping a house and taking care of children. It could be accepting people as they were, and going off for a "bit of wandering" if that's what your husband wanted.

Turning this new idea in her mind as they drove back to town, Dolly felt more than ever aware of the dramatic beauty of the sunset. People's lives were dramatic, too, and sometimes held unsuspected beauty. Pondering the many reasons why people acted as they did and how their actions affected each other, Dolly stared off across the prairie to the mass of color piled up in the west. She felt overwhelmed by the vastness of the world around her, the limitless sky pressing down on the rolling land, the hidden thoughts behind the simple everyday things that people said.

The sound of horse's hoofs was muffled as they drove past a grove of cottonwoods. The wind sang through the trees with a sound like the sea, a gentle soughing which held secrets for those who would listen. Without warning, a meadow lark spiraled up from the grass beside the road, high, high, singing as it rose. Dolly clapped her hands at the sudden gaiety, the soaring aliveness that broke the spell of her brooding mood. But even as she turned her shining eyes to her mother, she knew that the meaning of Mrs. Burt's words would stay with her, shaping her own feelings and thoughts.

Her mother looked down at her and smiled. "Look at that sky," she said, slapping the reins over the horse's back. "It will be hot tomorrow."

A feeling of joy welled up inside Dolly. She had been waiting for those words. Since her sickness last summer, hot weather had taken on a new meaning for her. It was something to be avoided. Ever since she had heard her parents say that this year she was to be sent to Vermont, she had waited impatiently for the hot weather to come. The prospect filled her with a tingling anticipation. Dolly breathed deeply into her lungs the prairie wind that had the sea in its sound. She could imagine what the sea was like, although she had never seen it. She knew mountains, though. Their air had been a part of her ever since her first visit to Arlington when she was six months old.

She moved closer to her mother. "Tell me about the time you didn't go to the circus," she demanded.

Looking down at her daughter, Flavia wondered why, of all the stories she told, Dolly preferred that particular one. There was little to it but the recounting of an episode, how she had once been promised that she would be taken to the circus "tomorrow . . . but the circus did not come. Something happened . . . and 'tomorrow' never came." The horse's hoofs clopped along the road. Dolly waited for her mother's voice to continue. "I suppose," she said, "there are no tomorrows in a child's world. Everything is now."

Not always, Dolly thought, snuggling against the back of the padded seat, with its smell of horse and hay and dust. Tomorrow would come, and tomorrow meant Arlington for her.

Dolly had wispy brown hair and slate-blue eyes. Except for being so small, she was as like all the other little girls of that time as a percale dress, long cotton stockings and stout buttoned shoes could make her. Her hands were calloused from climbing trees and swinging a baseball bat, but her fingers were supple and already beginning to find their way over the keys of a piano.

Each day when classes were over at the public school in Lawrence, the university campus became Dolly's playground. Racing, tumbling, shouting, she urged her playmates to hurl themselves with her own passionate intensity into games of "Red Rover, Come Over," "Run Sheep, Run," or "Duck on the Rock, Still Pond No More Moving." Sometimes she would sit silent and absorbed over mumblety-peg or marbles, intent on every move, determined to win, but accepting defeat, if it came, with a cheerful word of praise for the winner. On her way home, she was never too tired to "skin the cat" on any iron railing she passed, never too hurried to accept a challenge with a wild shout, and stop to climb a tree as high as its branches would hold her.

Quick and active as a cricket, it seemed to her parents that Dolly was never still. And her mind kept pace with her body, moving agilely from one interest to another. To see a page of type was to read it, whatever the subject. It was easy to read, and she found that it was equally easy to memorize passages or poems, when she wanted to keep them with her. At night before sleep claimed her, she would lie in the dark and study the pictures that filled her mind . . . pictures of the day that was behind her, the games she had played, the people she had met, the fascinating sequence of events.

Like the slow appearance of rain clouds in the sky, Dolly began to be aware of a growing tension between her parents. Often she had sensed that they did not think alike; now her realization went deeper. Her mother, absorbed in her interest in art, felt the confinement of a regulated life and yearned for a more sympathetic audience for her radical ideas. Her father, finding all the stimulation he needed in the hours spent in study or classroom, longed only for a well-ordered household that would leave him free to read the books he loved. Dolly was puzzled as she looked from one to the other across the dining room table, flooded with warm lamplight. Beginning to understand something of the differences bound to exist between scholarly exactness and artistic irresponsibility, she tried to think of something she could do or say that would smooth things over; but rarely was there anything.

Music was her escape, her resource. Now that she had begun to study the violin she found that its swelling current of sound could often carry her away from a world where personalities clashed to airy spaces. Even a Mozart minuet, rising and falling within her, left space for nothing else. When she went to bed at night she lived the music again and her room became like a great sea shell echoing tones that thrilled her and stilled any troubling thoughts.

Chapter 2

Good Growing Weather

THE long-awaited "tomorrow" came, summer after summer, and Dolly was sent to Vermont, sometimes with her brother, often alone. It did not matter what had been troubling her or how hot the winds were that swept across the prairies, in Arlington the wind flowed cool and sweet down a gentle green valley, following the course of the Battenkill River.

Grandfather would be waiting for her at the station. Dolly flattened her nose against the train window, trying to see him. There he was, as she had known he would be, ready to help her down the steps. She put her hand in his.

"Haven't grown much bigger, have you?" he said. "Guess you'll always be just a half-pint."

Dolly grinned, knowing he didn't expect an answer.

Hand in hand they walked down the hill, along the village street with its low friendly homes under tall elms, past St. James' and its quiet churchyard, past the Town Hall toward the Brick House where three generations of Canfields had lived. Plain and substantial, the sight of the house filled Dolly with joy. Before they turned off the marble sidewalk, Dolly glanced back at the Town Hall.

"Grandfather, is the curtain still up on the stage?"

"Why yes, child. Where else would it be?"

Dolly sighed happily. She had a special feeling for the curtain that had been painted years ago by an itinerant artist. It was an

Italian scene of lake and mountains and cheerful peasants. Whenever Dolly looked at it she wondered if she would ever see such faraway places. But right now, Arlington was all she wanted of the world.

At the Brick House, the old people were waiting to welcome her. The door was thrown open and, running inside, Dolly could feel the house fit around her, just as Aunt Mattie's arms did. Everything was the same. The cookie jar in the pantry was full, as Dolly had known it would be. In the back room the churn and cheese press were waiting for the next day's milk.

With the sureness of a homing pigeon, Dolly raced up the stairs to her own little room. She hung her coat on a peg and poured cold water from the pitcher on the stand into the heavy china bowl. Washing her face and hands, she rubbed them dry with the rough linen towel. Then hooking her arms over the window sill, she looked out at the dear familiar world, and one by one she felt the knots inside her slowly untie.

She was still standing there, when Aunt Mattie's cheerful voice called, "Come on, Dolly. Supper's ready."

Dolly clattered down the stairs and took her place at the table with Grandfather, Great-aunt Mary, Aunt Mattie, and Uncle Zed. A curious sense of relief settled over her, as she shared the fried ham and scrambled eggs, the fresh-baked rolls and the cherry pie. When the table was cleared and the dishes done, the evening glowed with warm circles of lamplight. The conversation about village doings and people, and what had been happening since Dolly had last been there, was punctuated by the friendly creaking of rocking chairs.

It was comforting to know that her room was waiting for her at the head of the stairs. It was tiny, but with its cot bed, chest of drawers, washstand and hooks for her clothes, it was all that she needed. Tired from her trip, Dolly went up to her room early. She closed the door softly and let the room's indefinable, protective atmosphere settle around her. This was her own, always there, always ready for her, no matter how far away she had been. Her trunk had been brought from the station and Dolly knelt beside it and unpacked her gingham dresses, her underwear and black cotton stockings and high buttoned shoes. Slipping into her long nightgown, she padded in bare feet to look out the window once more before climbing into bed.

The next afternoon Grandfather hitched the team of horses to the three-seater. Dolly scrambled up on to the seat beside him. He put the reins into her small but knowing hands and they drove through the shaded village and along a white dusty road that wound through the sunlit valley. Dolly slowed the horses when they came to the bridge that spanned the Battenkill. Raising herself as high as she could on the wagon seat, she peered down into the glass-clear water and turned her head to listen to the sound it was making.

"Cat got your tongue?" Grandfather asked.

Dolly shook her head. There was nothing she could say, no way she knew to tell Grandfather of the joy of rediscovery.

At the Brick Farm House, Uncle 'Niram Canfield greeted her warmly and started to tell her about the farm and the kind of weather they had been having. Dolly liked to look into the shining kindness of his face. Years of devoted caring for a sick wife had made him eager to help people who were in trouble and his household was always comfortably filled with elderly relatives needing some kind of care. At Uncle 'Niram's there was never the feeling of respectability and order that there was at the Brick House, but Dolly was aware of something else—a quiet heroism.

As soon as she could without being rude, she slipped out of the house and climbed up to the hill pasture, walking slowly at first in case anyone was watching, then running faster and faster. At the old elm, she stopped to pay her respects to the tree that had grown against such odds. A century ago when a seed had fallen on the rocky ledge it had sprouted in a crack;

the roots fighting for life spilt the rock and pushed two great boulders to either side. Between them the tree had grown. It made a perfect place to play house and Dolly often did, but not this time. She hurried on to a favorite place of hers beside a brook where a pool was partly hidden by the branches of a great maple. When she reached it, she threw herself flat on the ground beside the pool. Burying her head in her hands, she lay very still.

As Dolly lay there, breathing in the damp smell of the earth, something sure slowly took possession of her. A jay scolded from the branches of the tree above her; a chipmunk watched her from a nearby stone, his tail twitching. Finally she raised her head and sat up, rubbing her eyes.

There had been something she had needed to figure out for herself, fighting her way through a maze she did not understand. Why did grownups so often hurt each other, not just with deeds but with words? Why did they? Watching the long golden shafts of light the westering sun was sending across the pasture, Dolly realized that there was little she could do to change other people. But she could do something about herself. She felt a surge of hope that she would never hurt anyone—not ever, as long as she lived. She hugged her knees up under her chin, feeling a joyful wonder spread through her, as if she had discovered a sort of secret that no one else knew.

Looking down from the hill, Dolly could see toy-like houses and barns. The cattle were small and the road was a narrow ribbon along the valley. She could see so much more than she had been able to see when she was driving along the road with Grandfather. But still, everything was in proportion. That was worth remembering. Maybe the next time things hurt inside her and the knots tied tight, if she could get above them she would be able to see them in proportion. She shut her eyes tight, and there was the view in her mind, in sharp detail, all bathed in the golden light of the late afternoon sun. Dolly realized that whenever she wanted to, wherever she might be, she could shut her eyes and be on the hill again.

With a feeling of happiness bubbling inside her, Dolly jumped up and raced down the hill, bursting into the kitchen bright-eyed and hungry.

The teakettle was humming on the gleaming black stove and behind it the big water boiler was rumbling. Dolly looked at the table in the middle of the room set for supper with the familiar checked cloth and white china. Beyond it she could see the other table, covered, as it always was, with an old dark red cashmere shawl, a large oil lamp placed exactly in its center. Near it was the bookcase and three rocking chairs. And then Dolly noticed that her own small chair had been brought down from the attic and she knew that it was especially for her visit, to make her feel at home.

Another call was made the next day to Great-uncle Malcolm Canfield's in Manchester, seven miles north. There were three older cousins and a house full of books and always much lively talk. Uncle Malcolm was not the farmer Uncle 'Niram was, but he had traveled and he was a great reader. There was a breath of the world about his house which charmed Dolly. Returning to the Brick House in Arlington, she felt that she could launch into the summer, for she had seen all the relatives. They were all the same. Some things in the world were safe and sure, some things could be counted on.

A few days later she wrote her parents, "Dear People, Everyone is exactly the same and so is everything. . . . Arlington is exactly the same, only more beautiful. I haven't had a cold since I've been here and my feet have been wet every day."

Dolly never tired of listening to the stories the old people told, and they never tired of telling them. It was Uncle Zed's stories she loved the best, stories of earlier Canfields, brave or crotchety or humorous. She delighted in hearing about Uncle

Zed's grandfather, Israel Canfield, who had first come to Arlington from Connecticut. It was Israel's wife who had carried a piece of homemade soap in the pocket of her riding skirt for testing the water in every creek, insisting she would not settle where the water was hard and risk spoiling all the household linen she had so laboriously woven. She washed her way northward, mile by mile, until at last she found a soft-water creek. It was near the northern boundary line of Arlington and there Canfields had lived ever since. Dolly always waited for the end of the story, even though she knew it well. "That was your great-great-grandmother, Dolly," Uncle Zed would say, "and when they unsaddled the horses, she stuck her willow riding switch into the deep sand beside the water—that's the big tree you see leaning across the brook."

Dolly and Uncle Zed were spending one of their long days together. Stooped and wizened, he stumped along on two canes; while Dolly, tousleheaded and spry as a chickadee, tagged along beside him, drinking in every word he uttered. Arlington folk called them "The Heavenly Twins."

Uncle Zed had a brilliant, sharp-faceted mind with cutting edges and hard corners, but he had a warm fellow-feeling for his little grandniece.

She skipped along beside him, as they followed a familiar path.

"See there, those stones by the brook," he said. Dolly stopped, tingling with the foreknowledge of what was to come. "They're what's left of the foundations of the carding mill. The overshot water wheel was there, where the banks are higher. You do remember, don't you, Dolly, what a carding mill was?"

"Yes, but tell me what the boys did when they saw the bear," she begged.

And Uncle Zed told her about the boys, one of whom had been her grandfather, as if he were telling the story for the first time. The boys had been taking wool to the carding mill, when suddenly right in front of them they saw a huge black bear. It wasn't that the boys were not mortally scared when they found their road blocked by that enormous bear, but that they didn't run away—that was what mattered, as Uncle Zed told it. They went right on about their business and only skedaddled for home when they had done their errand. "That kind of thing's good growing weather," Uncle Zed commented. "A young 'un turns a corner he'll never have to turn again, once he's had a chance to find out he can go on and get his business done, even if he is scared."

They walked along in silence for a while. "Tell me now about my great-grandfather and the sheep," Dolly said.

Uncle Zed chuckled. "Taught him something, that did, though I guess he didn't see it right at first. Never get the idea, Dolly, that loyalty means following anybody or anything blindly, without knowing why you're doing it. Your great-grandfather learned that from sheep."

As if she had never heard it before, Dolly listened to the story of the boy who went to the barn one morning to let the sheep out to pasture. Standing aside, he watched the flock led by the ancient ram file sedately toward the door. Their pattering feet stirred up the dust, which rose in a cloud. Suddenly the old ram stopped, halting the flock behind him. He stood uncertainly and no amount of urging would persuade him to go on. At first the boy could see nothing, and then he noticed that a beam of early sunlight, shining through a knothole, caught the particles of dust in the air and formed what seemed to be a solid golden bar across the opening of the door. The ram backed a few steps, gathered his haunches under him and launched himself into the air, clearing the bar of sunlight. Doubled over with laughter, the boy watched as one by one each sheep in the flock sprang high in the air to clear a barrier that didn't exist.

Walking along beside Uncle Zed, Dolly decided that though

Dorothy Canfield at the age
of six. Inscribed on the back
"To Uncle Zed from Dolly."

At thirteen years

A senior at college, 1899.

In 1907 Dorothy and John Fisher were married.

At home in Arlington, Vermont.

some people might be like sheep, she would not. She would think and question first, never just follow the flock.

Uncle Zed was not too old and crippled to teach Dolly new skills. She wanted to learn how to use a scythe. Guiding her small hands, he showed her first how to sharpen the long thin blade, then how to move the scythe before her in easy rhythmic sweeps. Delighting in the clean falling of the grass before her, Dolly found fully as much pleasure in the response of her muscles to a new activity.

"I never could abide a fool and I don't like a fool any better for being a woman," Uncle Zed said one afternoon as they sat rocking on the porch.

"Why?" Dolly asked.

He told her of the woman who wanted to chide her son's teacher for having given the boy a scolding. "I gave her my advice—tie a string around his neck and throw him in the river, you might's well, for you've done for him. I tell you that boy's mother never forgot that lesson." As he finished speaking, Uncle Zed looked longingly at his favorite chair in which the cat was still sleeping.

"Why don't you wake her up and send her away?" Dolly asked.

Uncle Zed shook his head. "A cat has so few pleasures compared with those open to me."

A neighbor came running down the street. "Zed, Zed," he called as he neared the Brick House, "those young folks you let your house to have just packed up all their belongings and are driving toward the York State line."

Uncle Zed got up slowly, a little stiffly, but it didn't take him long to decide what to do. He went to the barn for the horse and buggy and drove off over the road to Cambridge. Dolly waited on the porch with Aunt Mattie and Great-aunt Mary. Grandfather Eli joined them.

"Those young folks owe Zed months of payments," Grandfather said, "but if they reach the state line no law can be put on them for unpaid rent."

Two hours later Uncle Zed got back to Arlington and told them what he had done. When he caught up to the farm wagon with its occupants and belongings, he drove ahead, then turned and blocked the road. Calling out from his buggy, he ordered them to pay their debts. There he stayed until the younger man turned his horses and started back to Arlington.

"Twan't so much that he owed *me* money," Zed said, "but there just isn't any backbone to hold things together if you let folks get away with things like that."

Grandfather Eli was a great teller of stories, too, and when Dolly played checkers with him in the evening a move could always wait if there was a story to tell. Working with him in the vegetable garden, she was ready to drop whatever she was doing to listen if a story came to his mind.

"Remember that old apple tree up on the edge of the woods?" Grandfather asked her. "That's been growing there since the year the Declaration of Independence was signed."

Dolly's eyes opened wide as Grandfather went on talking, telling the story of the tree whose blossoms were so pink, whose fruit so tart.

"At the time of the Revolution, Dolly, many of the families in Arlington were Loyalists—loyal to King George and the Colonial governors—and they wanted to keep the old ways that had come down to them. One of the Canfield families was loyal to the King, but their son joined the American side. His parents were shocked and ashamed, but his sister wasn't. Whenever the boy could get away on furlough he'd come back to Arlington, but he didn't dare go to his home. Instead he'd meet his sister in the woods behind the house and she'd bring him bread and butter, hunks of maple sugar, slices of cold pork, and once an apple. There on the slope she'd tell her brother the news of home and he'd tell her about the army and the battles they were fighting, and about the principles of freedom and justice which meant so much to him.

"One day, when he was eating the apple, he said to his sister, 'Old England is as dead and done for as that! You'll just see!' and he flung the core down on the soft damp earth and ground it in with his heel.

"Well," Grandfather said, "the apple tree grew from a seed in that core. That's how dead England was! It all turned out differently and both England and America are as alive today as that tree. Isn't that better than anything folks back then thought of?"

Dolly nodded.

"One reason England *is* so fine a country is just because the American Revolution succeeded," Grandfather went on. "She learned a lesson from getting beaten that winning never teaches anybody. Just remember the stubborn old apple tree the next time you don't pass an examination. There's a bone to gnaw on in that story, with lots of marrow in it, if you'll take the trouble to think about it."

"What is the marrow you've got out of it, Grandfather?"

"Well, child, what I've got out of it—it took me fifty years to get it—is that 'and' is always better than 'or.' "

Dolly told the stories again in letters she wrote back to Kansas, while the past became as real to her as the present. "The reckless way these people talk of years is perpetually astonishing to me," she exclaimed in a letter to her father. " 'How long ago did that happen, Uncle Zed?' I asked him yesterday. 'Oh, a few years, fourteen or fifteen maybe.' Why, that's more than my whole life!"

Her father, replying, told her to "go over to the farm, up into the woods where I used to play and go after the cows, up the brook where we used to fish, down in the meadows and into the sap woods. I would like you to see how perfectly quiet it is there at nightfall and just as the sun is rising." Dolly did not

need to be told. She had already found out. And she had found
out there was something she could do with the quiet, and that
was think. Reasoning things out with herself, she discovered
deeper meaning in the pictures that formed in her mind, pictures
so vividly seen with her eyes that she could see them again
with all their lights and shadows whenever she brought them
to mind.

Driving through the country with grandfather or the aunts
on a summer afternoon, the houses they passed were observed
with warm human interest. Everyone seemed to be known to
the old people and conversation flowed easily on. Sometimes
Dolly puzzled over what was being said, for the elders never
thought to pass human doings through a sieve to make them
suitable for Dolly's understanding. If there was any straining to
be done, time would do it. The voices droned on, coming to
silence when they passed the house where a malicious gossip
lived, a woman who even Dolly knew was like a sliver in the
life of the community. Dolly might have asked the aunts about
her, but she didn't. It was all part of the full flood of living and
Dolly accepted it as she did the weather.

Aunt Mattie glanced approvingly at a well-kept field. "Their
corn's coming on."

"Looky-there, looky-there," Dolly cried, "sweet peas are in
flower!"

"See all that fine wood that's been split and stacked," Grandfather nodded with approval.

The surrey jogged on. Dolly, sitting between the large and
comfortable old people, saw it all and stored it away in her
mind—lilies of the valley whitely fragrant against old stone
walls, barns with hay and stock, apple trees heavy with fruit,
blue hills rising beyond field and pasture, firewood laid up
against the winter.

One cool night when they were all driving home after a late
call, a lantern could be seen twinkling on the mountainside.

"Must be Lem Warren out fussin' with his sheep," Aunt Mattie said.

Later, when they had almost reached home, they saw the lantern on the road ahead of them and stopped the horses. Dolly, half-asleep, looked out from the shawl in which she was wrapped and saw the tall figure of a man, his arms cradling something under his coat. The lantern lighted his weather-beaten face as he looked down at the small white head laid against his breast.

"You're foolish, Lem," Uncle Zed said. "The ewe won't own it if you take it away so long the first night."

"I—I—know," the man stuttered, "but it's mortal cold up on the mounting for little fellers. I'll bring him up as a cosset."

Uncle Zed clicked his teeth together and the horse moved on. "What a numskull," he muttered, "his house is so full of cossets now that you can't find your way around it."

Dolly snuggled down in her shawl. The sound of Uncle Zed's voice was like the taste of a tart apple. Sharp. But she liked it the way she liked a tart apple better than a sweet one. She leaned her head against Uncle Zed and her eyes closed.

Other girls might play with dolls, but Dolly liked living things—a chicken, a dog. The summer that she was ten years old Uncle Zed gave her a Morgan colt.

"It's a good thing Don is too big to take into the house or you'd certainly have him sleeping on the floor of your room," Uncle Zed said when Dolly had had Don a week.

Waking early in the mornings, she would saddle the little Morgan and gallop over the road from one farm to another. She liked the freshness of the air, the feel of Don's strong body under her, and the friendly exchange of greetings along the way. A farmer called to her from his barn.

"Well, you're quite a ways from home, don't you know it? Git off your horse, can't ye? I've got a new calf in here."

Dolly saw the calf, had a drink of milk, played with some

kittens, listened to the farmer's talk, then said good-by, got on her horse and rode away.

Whenever she was not needed at the Brick House, she would be off on Don, riding up the valley to call at Uncle 'Niram's or Uncle Malcolm's, exploring the back roads and the trails that were passable only for a horse and rider. One of her favorite rides was up a steep stony mountain road, dense with the shade of sugar maples and oaks. Don would be breathing hard when they reached the top but he was still good for a canter across a small upland plateau. Here, where an early settlement had flourished, there were now only abandoned farmhouses, and thickets of white birch shivering in the fields. Dolly had heard many stories of the thriving farms that had once been there. She reined Don in so he could get his wind back and as they stood still the earlier days began to live for her.

She felt sure that she could hear the sound of whetstones on scythes as the farmers mowed the fields, the lowing of cattle, the shrill cries of children. The shiver of popple leaves around her became one with the ghostly clinking, the murmur of voices. Dolly stared before her. It was all real in her mind, but her eyes saw only empty fields fast being taken over by hardhack and brush. Her ears heard only silence. She turned Don's head and started down the long stony road to the valley, to flesh and blood people and busy farms.

Dolly went fishing with her grandfather until his years made journeying from the house impossible for him, then she went fishing in the company of a village boy who obligingly let her tag along. Aware of her privilege, she never asked any favors of him and her pride kept her silent even when it came to wading through the Battenkill. The river, knee-high for the long-legged boy was waist-high for Dolly, but what she lacked in size she learned to make up for in other ways.

There were rainy days when Don dozed in his stall and everyone kept within doors. Dolly had the attic to play in.

Hung with drying popcorn and filled with old hair trunks, dusty piles of the New York Tribune, boxes of letters, diaries, yellowed deeds, and every kind of relic, it was a world of its own harboring the past. There was nothing in it that had been broken by neglect or rough handling and everything worked as well as it always had. Using the spinning wheel in the attic, Great-aunt Mary had taught Dolly how to spin, for no matter what evidence there might be around her or what anyone said, Aunt Mary refused to believe that it was right for a girl child to grow up not knowing how to spin.

Dolly liked to read the old schoolbooks. Most of them dated from the eighteenth century, and she was as fascinated by their words and pictures as she was amazed at the knowledge which even she knew was now inaccurate. One rainy day, sitting cross-legged on the floor of the attic, she took a shabby book from a pile and started to read a story about the Indians. She had grown up on stories that told of the friendly good feeling that existed between the settlers and the Indians in Vermont, and was surprised to read the hair-raising account of an Indian raid. Thrills and chills of horror ran over her; then something began to happen inside her. A small revolution stirred in her mind. She put down the book for a moment to gather her forces for the intellectual effort that she felt challenging her, for she was doubting what was set down on the printed page and that was something she had never done before, something she had not thought was ever done.

When the inner upheaval settled down, she drew a long breath and looked again at the words. This time, as if some of them had been underlined in invisible ink which now showed clearly, she questioned them as she read. Doubt encouraged disbelief, and reason upheld her inner feeling. A little startled by her discovery, Dolly realized that truth was something to be determined by oneself when one had the facts. Icy Palmer, the Indian woman who lived in their valley, came to her mind.

Icy was so old that she seemed to have gone beyond time;
she was small and straight-backed, and her dark brown face
was calm and deeply lined. She had no home of her own but
settled in anyone's home for a few days or a season, making
herself useful in household chores or preparing the horseradish
which was her specialty. She could lend a hand with anything
from boiling down cider, drying corn and making a quilt to
tending a cosset lamb or a runt pig. Yesterday when Dolly had
been visiting at the Brick Farm House she had heard one of the
old people say, "There's Icy coming up the road. I guess she
plans to settle with us for a while." It was good to know where
Icy was. Dolly wanted to see her and talk with her. When the
rain was over she would saddle Don and ride out to Uncle
'Niram's.

"Dolly!" Great-aunt Mary was calling her.

Dolly stirred, wondering what was wanted of her.

Aunt Mary was standing at the foot of the stairs with a large
bowl and a knife. "What have you been doing, child? It's soon
time for supper and we need the butter."

Dolly went down to the cellar readily, but she took her time
when there. While the attic was a long arm reaching back to
the past, and enfolding its treasures; the cellar was an open hand
held out to the future to meet its needs. Past the shelves with
their preserves and homemade wines, past the crock holding
eggs in waterglass, Dolly went toward the great yellow mound
of butter that had been laid down in salt. From it she carved out
carefully the amount needed for the kitchen. She stopped at
the keg of maple sugar, dark brown and crystallized, and
reached in for a crumb of the "sweetnin' " to put in her mouth.
She gazed around her at the bins of potatoes and root vegetables,
the barrels of apples, the onions spread on shelves, the flitches of
bacon and hams. It gave her a good feeling, to see the things of
the earth laid up here against summer drought or winter storms.

Then she went upstairs with the butter.

"For a young one so quick to do some things, you can take a lot of time to do others," Great-aunt Mary said. "Now you'd best do your practicing before supper. I haven't heard a sound from piano or violin all day."

Practicing was one thing, so was playing pieces to grownups wanting to be entertained, but working with John Conroy was quite another. He was a house painter with a taste for classical music and he took Dolly far beyond the realm of the beginner. Evening after evening he came to the Brick House and played first violin with Dolly a wavering second, while Aunt Mattie pounded on the piano. Sometimes they could play by pages, often they could advance only by phrases.

"Oh, John, where *are* you now?" Dolly cried out again and again as she tried to follow him.

Whatever they played, whatever they sounded like to a passer-by on the street, Dolly advanced with every note into a world of pure joy. Bach's voice was heard at least once every evening, and among the other composers Dolly developed an affection for Haydn like that for a favorite fun-loving uncle. Beethoven was like another uncle, but one who commanded an awed respectful attentiveness.

Books surrounded her life. One room of the Brick House was crammed with them from floor to ceiling. Some she knew by heart, like Grimm and Anderson, Aesop and La Fontaine. She read any book she could put her hands on, racing along over the words to find out what happened next. Sometimes a character cast a three-dimensional shadow from the page and acted like a living person; then Dolly's whole being quickened.

She was twelve when she picked up *Vanity Fair* because it was lying on the table, and started to read. Before she knew what was happening, Becky Sharp leaned out of the pages, caught her by the hand, and drew her into the book. This is life, Dolly thought, breathing deeply. She did not understand it all but she had flashes of insight, so she read on. But something had taken place in her. Once she had read to find out what would happen in the story, now she was reading to find out what had happened. In that was the answer to the questions that had so often puzzled her as to why people did the things they did, said the things they said.

She remembered seeing a blank page that had been written on with lemon juice reveal its words when held before the fire. So life made its invisible marks on people that could sometimes be interpreted by an understanding heart. A notion brushed across her mind that events could shape or misshape human beings. Life was complex. Feelings were complex. And there were underlying reasons why people acted as they did. An inner time clock was striking, a clock whose hands would never be turned back.

At summer's end she returned to her parents, leaving the enfolding valleys and green-clad mountains for the wide flat reaches of the Midwest. She was brown and sturdy. She had grown perhaps a fraction of an inch taller. But something more than country air, plain food, healthy exercise had gone into her building. In Arlington she was always sure of who she was and the tradition that had made her. Time took on a unity—the past was not something to be forgotten but lived up to, the future was not something to be dreaded but prepared for, and the present was something to be enjoyed wholeheartedly.

Chapter 3

Widening Circles

"EXPECT me when you see me!" Flavia said to her husband when she went off on the first of many trips to Europe, taking Dolly with her. James, remaining at home with his son, wondered if Flavia would ever find a place that she cared to live in for long.

Flavia found rooms for her daughter and herself in a girls' boarding school on the Rue de Vaugirard, in Paris, not far from the studio where she wanted to study. Dolly attended the school, taking rapidly to the new language and the method of study which was hard and intense. She was nine years old but her mother relied on her as their interpreter.

"*Pain!*" Flavia exclaimed, not attempting to pronounce the word as the French did. "Whoever heard of such a word! If they mean bread, why don't they say bread?"

Dolly rolled her hoop down the broad paths of the Parc Monceau and played with other girls in the dingy public garden back of the Cluny Museum. Rainy days were often spent inside the Museum moving from one poorly lighted and cluttered but beautiful old room to another. She became familiar with the attendants and the visitors. The Cluny was a friendly place, rather like the attic of the Brick House, filled with valuable relics, and odds and ends that nobody had ever thought to discard.

Flavia often called Dolly from play to pose for her. Minutes went into an hour. Dolly wearied from sitting still, and her smile drooped.

"How much longer?" she asked.

"Until I get this finished."

Dolly sighed. That could mean another hour or the rest of the afternoon. Gloom settled over her face. But Flavia worked on, finding the dark expression quite as paintable.

Flavia spent hours in the great galleries, gazing at the master-pieces on their walls. Dolly, trotting along beside her, carried campstool and paintbox in readiness for the time when her mother would want to sit down to copy one of the paintings. When her duty was momentarily done, Dolly would set off on a walk around the galleries to see the pictures for herself. She was so short that often she could see only the lowest parts, unless she stood well back in the room. But there were many artists, Bosch and Breughel especially, who placed their most fascinating de-tails in the lower halves of their canvases. Dolly studied them intently, but she could not stay too long away in case her mother needed something.

Hurrying back one day, she was horrified to see that a group of sight-seers had gathered around her mother.

"Shoo them away, Dolly, shoo them away," Flavia said sharply.

Dolly, in a flood of voluble French, freed her mother, then she leaned against the picture railing, wearily wondering how long it would be before her mother's painting would be done.

There were many Americans studying art in Paris and during the evenings they met in each other's studios. Talk flowed on about their work and Dolly listened wide-eyed. Through it she began to see that in paintings there were things to be discovered that were not always visible on the surface, just as there were in books and people.

"Breughel may like his greens and blues, but that touch of red he always adds—"

"How El Greco relates light and shade! The shadow, there, brings out the purity of color here—"

Dolly's eyes opened wider. That was like Uncle 'Niram and his sick wife. In his house there was always the feeling of the glory and the shadow. Was the one more noticeable because of the other? And what did they mean about Breughel's red? There were people in whose presence one felt warm and happy. Was that what an artist was saying when he dressed a person in a red jerkin?

She spent hours wandering around the old Carlorossi Building where many of the studios were. No doors were ever locked and Dolly went casually from one studio to another. She watched classes painting from the nude and realized that the human form was often far from divine. She chatted with some of the models who were waiting to be hired—large sallow Italian women with sagging breasts and faces upon which the stories of their lives were written; young girls with white skin and fine figures who were arrogantly sure of their own value. Dolly stared at them, thinking how petulant and self-indulgent the beautiful young girls were, how filled with weary quiet were the older women.

There was a frankness about French life which might have been shocking to some but was not to Dolly. She had been gently broken in to many aspects of life by the talk she had heard in Arlington, the things she had seen. There had been nothing particularly remarkable or exciting about sex in Vermont. It was an underlying part of life. There was nothing to disturb her about sex in Paris, even though it rose more to the surface.

In fact, in many ways, Paris was not very different from Arlington. When visiting in a French home, Dolly was aware that by far the most important person in the household was the grandmother. Her word was always final. One day the young daughters of the household, together with Dolly, were dressed in their best to go out for a walk, and presented themselves to the old woman. Dolly, proud of her new shoes, elegant bonnet and dress, said, "Don't you think this costume is lovely, gran'mere?"

"*Oui, tu n'es pas ridicule.*"

Dolly chuckled. The same words could have been said by any one of the old people in the Brick House.

The wife of the little shopkeeper at the corner of the street amused Dolly. Always she apologized for her Breton cousins when they came to the city wearing peasant dress.

"Tante Marie-Jeanne is so behind the time. Why must she hang on to those stupid old-fashioned ways of doing things!"

The Breton farming folk did not care. They felt no need to keep up with changing fashion. Dolly loved them the more for clinging to their old ways. They knew what they wanted to do and they did it. Vermonters were like that.

"No credit to them," Flavia said.

Dolly did not reply. There were plenty of things on which she and her mother saw differently, but she never questioned her mother's standards. Flavia's life was dedicated to a search for the best. What she sought in art, she enjoyed in literature and music. Never would she spend five minutes of her time on anything that was of low quality. "I'll have no truckings with the second-rate," she said, and her tone was as final as gran'mere's.

Dolly became as familiar with the Quarter in which they lived as she was with the side roads and mountain trails in Arlington. There were three statues that she passed often and each one said something particular to her. One was of Danton, striding forward as if to thrust his way through any difficulties life might present. *After bread, the first need of the people is for education* said the inscription under him. Her father might have said that, Dolly thought. Many of the political beliefs which he so passionately held had already become part of her. They acted like a magnet to draw to her mind the humane and democratic elements of modern French feeling.

The statue of Bernard de Palissy was a favorite of her mother's. "He made enormous sacrifices, Dolly, so he might go on with his discoveries in the development of pottery. One night," Flavia said, "in an attempt to keep the kiln going in which some of his finest pieces were being glazed, he burned up the household furniture in spite of his wife's protest."

Dolly was silent, as she studied the statue with a sharp and anxious eye.

"One should be ready to sacrifice anything for art," Flavia added.

Trotting along the Quai Voltaire with her schoolbooks under her arm, Dolly stopped before the wizened smiling figure of Voltaire in his massive draperies. He stood for spirited resistance to the tyranny of conservatism, and Dolly had great respect for him as she was beginning to realize the vitality of new ideas when contrasted with the rigidity of outworn ones. She smiled back at Voltaire with fellow feeling, knowing that she too belonged to the revolution against injustice that was constantly going on in the world.

Another young American, who was a student of political economy at the Sorbonne, lived at the girls' boarding school. Always referred to as "the Intellectual," she made an unforgettable impression on Dolly Canfield. Emily Balch was tall and slender, with a high forehead, hair worn in classic simplicity, and eyes that were clear and calm. She scorned frills for her costume as she did the "frizzies" then in fashion for her hair. The French, respecting fashion as they did, had even greater respect for distinction of person, and the school was proud to have her. One of the teachers explaining to a class the symbolism of Greek myths could say no more about Athena than *"Elle est comme Mees Balch, elle est l'Intellectuel."*

Often at night when Flavia's nerves were on edge, Dolly had a difficult time calming her mother and getting her to bed. But Dolly felt she was not alone. If things got beyond her strength and powers she knew she had only to run down the corridor to get help from the kind, calm Miss Balch. She never had to, but the knowledge steadied her. Emily Balch became to Dolly a symbol of intelligence and goodness. Dolly missed her when Flavia packed their trunks to go to Italy in the spring, but she had the comfort of knowing that they lived in the same world.

Dolly's ready mastery of languages stood her in good stead when she was at school in America, as well as in France or Italy. When she was old enough to be a student at the Sorbonne, she began intensive work in philology and looked forward to a scholarly winter. But that was the year the Parisian art world rocked with talk of Velasquez.

"We must go to Spain, Dolly," Flavia announced. "I must see his work for myself."

Dolly sighed. It was midwinter. Spain would probably be colder than Paris. There would be all kinds of difficulties, though language would be the least of them for her. Trunks were packed and they went to Madrid. Dolly had her books along so she could keep up with the work at the Sorbonne; to them she added a Spanish grammar and dictionary.

At the Prado, Dolly learned that it would require special permission for her mother to make copies of any of the paintings, so while Flavia stood gazing at a Velasquez, Dolly hastily filled in the necessary forms.

"Mother, where were your parents born?" Dolly asked, pen poised over the long questionnaire.

"Oh, gracious, child, how should I know? Tell them anything that comes into your head."

While Flavia painted, Dolly studied, staying within call in case anything was needed. The gallery was cold. Little heat spread through it from the brazier of coals in the center of the room. Dolly sat on her hands to warm them, she tried to double her toes inside her shoes. Closing her book, she glanced toward her mother to make sure that she was all right. Unaware of anything but the glory before her that she was trying to capture on her own canvas, Flavia painted on. Dolly got up and left the room. She walked quickly to another, then to another, finding them all cold, only the paintings on the walls seemed to have any warmth. Held by the spell of rich glowing color in Velasquez' portrait of the dwarf, Sebastian de Morra, Dolly stood before it. She studied it, not as her mother would with an eye for composition and balance, but with a constant questioning of herself as she tried to penetrate to the inner meaning, the core of the artist's intention.

The same inner time clock that had struck for her when she read *Vanity Fair* was striking again as she looked into the sad eyes of the strangely misshapen human being. What had caused this condition? What causes all the tragic social conditions—poverty, disease, war? Can not the reason be found? Once found, could not the conditions be treated as medicine treats human ills? Her heart ached for Sebastian de Morra. His eyes would not let her go. Returning their gaze, she saw not only one victim of man's inability to mend flaws in the social structure, but countless victims through the years—victims of man's ignorance, greed, lack of compassion.

This was what art could do, she thought, as it made one not only aware of beauty but of tragedy, of suffering endured with dignity, of life lived valorously within limitations. There was so much to think about in connection with Velasquez' dwarf that Dolly found herself wondering if the days would ever be long enough for her to think all that she wanted to about all kinds of men and women in their ceaseless pilgrim's progress through the ages, about their grandeur or baseness, about their responsibility for each other's happiness or misery.

"Mother, Mother," Dolly said aloud as she longed to share what she was feeling.

She walked quickly back through the long galleries. When she saw her mother still busily painting, she ran toward her and placed her hand on her shoulder. Dolly wanted to put her arms around her but she restrained herself. She could not have done so without disturbing her, and Flavia did not like to be disturbed.

"She's reaching for the only stars she sees," Dolly said to herself as she went back to her chair and picked up her book. "What better can any of us try to do?"

The Canfields moved from Kansas to Lincoln, Nebraska in 1891 when Dolly's father was made Chancellor of the University. She was ready for high school, her brother was ready for college. Lincoln was a new prairie city and the University was small. Few Nebraska farmers were rich, many were very poor after that summer's devastating drought, but James Canfield took up his work with characteristic ardor and energy. "If they can't earn, they can learn," he said.

He gave many speeches during that first year as he traveled through the state, making friends for the University and trying to bring it into closer connection with the schools. Dolly often accompanied him. She liked listening to his speeches and found her mind laying hold of principles in which she believed as fully as he did. Night after night she lay awake in bed, her mind ringing with phrases of her father's. "Responsibility is the greatest educator," was one of his favorite sayings. "So far as the people of this country have felt their responsibility, they have responded well."

For some years he had been secretary of the National Education Association, now he had been made president. Flavia had not wanted him to take on one more thing, feeling that he was already living up to his capacity.

"You'll kill yourself, James."

"Worry kills quicker than work," he replied.

Dolly knew that her father's capacity was elastic and could stretch to include anything that was worthwhile, or needed.

James Canfield introduced athletics for girls at the University and the new course caused almost as much discussion as some of his speeches. Dolly had fencing lessons from a young Army man who was stationed at Lincoln, John James Pershing. Her small body was well muscled and she used it cleverly. The swift clashing of foils, the constant parrying and defense, then the sudden thrust through to her opponent's well-padded figure exhilarated her.

"You're quick as a cat, Miss Dolly," Pershing said, "and you've got a natural-born fencer's wrist."

Boxing lessons came next. Her father felt strongly that many of the troubles women experienced throughout their lives resulted from their being too protected. "Criticism, for instance," he said. "Most women take it so personally, Dolly, that they can't profit from it. Some rugged treatment now and then, even getting hit, can help."

"Criticism," Dolly repeated the word, holding it off at arm's length so she could observe it.

"I don't know what you will do with your life, but whatever it is you can't escape criticism," her father went on. "You can make it serve you if you learn how to appraise it and rebound from it."

So Dolly with a group of her friends had boxing lessons. They learned how to use their gloved fists in defense and attack; how to overcome the mistakes that took them off guard; how to keep their tempers under control.

"Don't 'urry," the wiry little Cockney instructor who taught them and fought with them would say. "There's no need to 'urry."

After boxing, the girls went for a swim in the warm-water

pool belonging to a private sanatorium which was open at times to the public. No diving board was ever too much for Dolly, and her friends watched her enviously as she stood poised on the highest board, then, with perfect control, cut through the air and into the water. On the way home, Dolly stopped suddenly and put one hand over her ear.

"What's the matter, Dolly, have you got that pain again?"
She nodded.

"Perhaps you shouldn't dive."

"It isn't that," she said crossly. "I get it when I don't dive."

"Shouldn't you tell someone about it?"

"*No*. It's all right. Just a nuisance. There, it's gone now."

"Dolly, please—"

"I don't want to fuss," she said firmly. "Canfields never do about their health."

"Or Vermonters either." Her friend laughed. "I suppose you'd only call in a doctor for a broken bone."

"Or for having a baby."

"That's just about it," Dolly agreed. "Come on, race you to the corner."

A pain in the ear, the solicitude of friends, was forgotten as the three girls raced across the campus toward the Canfield house on S Street.

Now all the talk on campus was about the prize contest that was to be held in the University magazine, *The Sombrero*. Willa Cather, a friend of Dolly's brother and in his class, was talking about it with a group of young people in the Canfield house. Dolly listened longingly, wishing she could take part.

"Why don't you?"

Willa and Dolly decided to combine their talents. They set to work and wrote a story about a captain of a football team who died before the year's final game but returned in spirit to lead his team to victory.

"It's shivery," some of their friends said.

"It's vivid enough," others remarked.

The story did not win the prize but it was published in *The Sombrero* and the two girls looked at their combined effort with pride. It was the only time Willa Cather ever collaborated. It was the first time Dorothy Canfield saw her name in print. It looked exciting to her. What would it be like to write and see your name in print often? She took a glance at her future. Music was what she wanted to do. If music failed, then she would be a teacher of languages.

After four years, James Canfield was invited to become President of Ohio State University. Dolly said good-by to Lincoln and all that it had meant to her. Peering out of the window as the train left the flat prairie country and approached the green farm land near the Mississippi River, Dolly felt excited at the prospect before her. Music was to become as much a study as her academic subjects. There were many fine musicians living in the German colony in Columbus. With one of them, Dr. Eckhardt, Dolly was to have lessons.

Dolly soon found that work with Dr. Eckhardt included playing second violin in a string quartet composed of her teacher and two other members of the German colony. Now, when she went whistling across the campus with her shock of curly brown hair tossing in the wind, her violin case was under her arm quite as often as her textbooks. There were times when her violin seemed her only sure means of communication and she played with the zest of the little girl who had tried so eagerly to keep up with John Conroy, and the fervor of the young girl who needed to find some way of expressing her thoughts. She played against the humming in her ears which was often louder than the music itself.

At times, old Dr. Eckhardt seemed to know what she was thinking. "Yes, yes, Miss Dolly, music is having something to say, but it is not to say it in words."

He placed his fingers over hers to correct their position, then he shook his head and asked Dolly to open her left hand wide. Dolly did, wondering why he studied it so intently. "What is the matter with my hand?"

"Nothing, Miss Dolly, you have good hands, but they are small. So small."

"Does that matter?"

He shrugged his shoulders. "For playing—no; for concert work—perhaps, yes." His tone changed as he motioned to her to take up her violin. "Come now, let me hear what you have done with that Beethoven concerto."

Dolly tucked her violin under her chin and drew her bow across the strings. The notes that sounded in the stillness of the room were like a voice speaking. Her bow quickened. Now, sound that was brave and living filled the room, filled her. The notes sang together in glorious friendliness.

"That's the way things ought to be, that's the way people ought to be," Dolly thought to herself.

Music lifted her into a world where the things that ought to be true could be true, Arlington brought her down to earth. But things were not always the same there as they once had been. Like a tide receding, the old people were being drawn away. It was hard to imagine what life would be like in the Brick House without Uncle Zed. It was impossible to think of it without Grandfather. Paralysis now confined him to a wheel chair and Aunt Mattie's days were taken up in caring for him.

Dolly liked to sit with her grandfather, talking together, sharing thoughts as she had for so many years. One afternoon when Aunt Mattie was away, Dolly and John Robinson, the hired man, sat with Eli Canfield. The house was quiet. Dolly was aware that her grandfather had said nothing for several moments. Now he began to breathe with difficulty. She left her chair to stand beside his bed. His hands felt moist and cool as she took them in hers. John Robinson stood on the other side of the bed.

Dolly realized that her grandfather's eyes were looking at her. His lips moved as if to speak, but there was no breath left for words. Instead, the shape of a smile came over them. Dolly was never sure how long she stood beside him, his hands in hers. Suddenly Grandfather gave a quick short gasp, then over his face came an expression of peace such as Dolly had never seen before. It was such utter beauty of peace that life was made worth living in it alone. She could not take her gaze from her grandfather, nor stir her hands.

John Robinson's low voice broke the silence. "He's gone, Miss Dolly. There's nothing anyone can do for him now. You'd best go for Fred Brownson. I'll stay here. Miss Mattie will be back soon."

Dolly walked through the early evening dusk to the end of the street where Mr. Brownson lived. She told him that her grandfather had died. Together they went back to the Brick House. Dolly went in to the kitchen to get the things Mr. Brownson needed. John Robinson went home to his supper.

Outside, under the June stars, Dolly walked up and down in front of the house. She wanted to stay near in case she was needed and to meet Aunt Mattie when she returned. Vaguely aware that something strange yet exalted had taken possession of her, she did not question it. She accepted it and felt grateful for it. She had thought death a dread experience, but now she had found that it was as natural as breathing. She had not known until that moment when she stood in the presence of death how free she was of any fear of death. It was as if Grandfather who had given her so much had given her one last gift. Reasoning to herself that every experience can either liberate or imprison, she knew that because she had met death and felt as she did, she could face life with more assurance.

Chapter 4

"To know you are needed for work that
belongs to you ———— "

At Ohio State University, James Canfield soon discovered that a large industrial community had problems different from those of an agricultural area. Speaking openly his deep convictions, he created opposition but throve on it. He took a passionate stand on free trade, believing that it was the basis of stability in the economic life of the world.

"You might as well preach free love," Flavia warned him.

James laughed. "No cannon will ever cross the barrier where trade has rolled."

"Business interests are the mainstay of a State University," his wife reminded him. "You don't want to lose your position, do you?"

Dolly did not always share her mother's apprehension. She was too proud of her father.

James Canfield liked approval, but he was not troubled if his outspoken words made enemies for him. The free spirits among the students were drawn to him and it was in their minds he kindled flames that he knew would continue to burn long after their college days.

Flavia found herself drawn into the Woman's Club movement. And she relished it. Zealous in her devotion to art, she had little interest in women's suffrage but a great feeling for what clubs could do to offset the barrenness in women's lives.

"Oh, Dolly," she exclaimed to her daughter, "I have only to look back on my own early days and the struggle I had to obtain an education in art! I have only to recall the way so many of my friends in Kansas and Nebraska lived! And still live. Humdrum, that's the only word for their lives."

"What do you mean, Mother?"

"Mean? Why, that the life of the average woman is still bound by the traditional three C's—the crib, the cookstove, and the chicken coop. Don't I know that ache to do things, see things and meet people? I'm going to establish weekly meetings for the women of Columbus if I don't do another thing."

When the student who lived at the Canfields and did the chores was not available, Flavia relied on Dolly to help her make her calls. Going out to the barn, Dolly hitched their big bay, Dan, to the family surrey, and drove up to the mounting block for her mother. Together they went up and down the streets of Columbus, stopping at one after another of the neatly painted houses, each one separated from its neighbor by a plot of carefully trimmed grass. Dolly sat in the surrey and read a book while her mother made her calls, endeavoring to interest housewives in a series of lectures on art.

"One hour," Flavia murmured as they drove home ahead of the twilight, "one hour a week is all they can set aside for art! Still, that's better than nothing."

The sound of Dan's hoofs as they clip-clopped down the quiet street mingled in Dolly's ears with the sad but determined tones of her mother's voice.

Flavia more than fulfilled her promise to the women whose lives she felt were so humdrum, and she fulfilled it not only in Columbus but later throughout the state. Speaking at her weekly lectures with a power her family scarcely knew she possessed and a vast flood of sympathy, she put her listeners in touch with beauty as she knew and revered it, satisfied that she had begun to open their hearts and eyes to a world that ranged far beyond the confines of their homes.

As her father and mother took their stands for what they believed in, so Dolly began to take hers.

One night when she was having dinner with a classmate whose parents lived in a hotel, Dolly found herself attracted more to Margaret's father, who was grave and preoccupied, than to her mother, who was dainty and soft-voiced. Margaret's mother talked throughout the meal about the dangers of life and how escape could be made from them. Dolly was fascinated. She had thought of danger as a Kansas flood or a Nebraska snowstorm, fire or a runaway horse. This was a new kind of danger and listening to it she felt oddly disturbed.

"The only way to live is in a hotel, until the servant problem is solved," Margaret's mother was saying, "for no woman can do herself justice if she is burdened with the cares of house-keeping and children. Of course, I always had a nursemaid for Margaret. A woman can't afford to use up herself and her good looks in family cares."

"But—" Dolly tried to speak as the idea rose in her mind that youth and good looks were commodities like fruit and fish which should be used while fresh or no one would get any good from them.

"I believe that it is every woman's duty to make the best of herself," the smooth voice went on. Margaret looked down at her plate. Her father seemed absorbed in his thoughts. Dolly followed the words that described the beauty treatments under-gone weekly, the frequent massage. "Wednesday afternoons I take an airing in the car, and Saturday afternoons are always kept for visits with my New Thought practitioner."

Dolly stared, then she turned her attention to her plate. She was fearful that she would laugh out loud, so comical did it seem to spend life cold-storaging qualities that would ultimately fade and wither without ever having accomplished anything real for their owner.

When the evening was over and Dolly left for home, she laughed aloud in the silent street. "I may be only eighteen," she exclaimed to herself, "but I've lived long enough to know that life is a thing that can be saved or spent, but that it has value only as it's spent! Why, Margaret's mother is hoarding fairy gold, gold that will soon turn to dry brown leaves of no use to herself or to anyone else!"

Then she saw Margaret's mother as a tragic figure, holding an empty cup in her hands, a cup that might have been brimful.

Walking through the dark streets, Dolly went on philosophizing about life. "It only has worth and dignity if we *do* something with it," she said, "and isn't the doing what makes people of more value than machines? For every person in the world there must be something he can do a little better than anyone else. If he doesn't do it it will be left undone, and that would be a pity."

Dolly saw clearly, and as if for the first time, how vitalizing was the expression of creative energy, not only in music, painting, writing, but in plain useful work. "That's what Mother does to people when she talks to them about art! That's what Father does when he encourages his students to see that education can quicken every avenue of their lives! Why—" she stopped short as a tremendous thought took possession of her mind, "—life is to know you are needed for work that belongs to you, just because you are you, work that nobody else can do."

She quickened her steps. She had made a discovery.

That summer in Arlington, she continued with John Conroy the violin concertos she had begun playing in Columbus. Music was her world. And yet, whenever she thought of it as being her work a vague doubt edged her mind. Dr. Eckhardt had never referred to her small hands again, but she had not forgotten his remark. It would not matter to her mother what she did with her life so long as it bore some dedication to art, or to her father so long as she lived up to the full use of her powers, but she felt compelled to make a decision for herself. She did, one afternoon near the end of the summer when she was standing on the railroad platform at Manchester, waiting for the train. Loving her violin as she loved her life, she felt called upon to examine two facts—rationally, like a scholar, not impulsively like an artist—two clear, hard facts that stood between her and music as a career.

No matter what people said to her in kindness, she knew in herself that she did not have enough talent to carry her the long way she would have to go; she did not have the inborn quality which was not to be acquired by years of study. Opening her two hands wide before her she looked at them, turning the palms up, stretching out her fingers. Such small hands! She sighed. They were quite in keeping with her size, but they were not adequate for the bowing and reaching required of a master violinist. She had been born with them. They would never grow any larger. They could not be changed. They had to be accepted as they were, and used.

The train whistled in the distance as it approached the Dorset station. Dolly dropped her hands to her side and looked up at Mount Equinox, heather-colored in the late afternoon light. She thought about the difference between a creative artist and a skilled violinist. The artist's conception of his undertaking would grow as fast as his ability. A skilled musician would reach a point where he would be doing something as well as it could be done and he would go no farther. That was how she would play the violin, with her talent what it was, her hands being what they were. In the true artist's life there could never be anything static. Before his vision, perfection would grow grander and more unobtainable as his means of reaching perfection improved. Creative artists could never cease from their work, but to their last breath struggle on to the goal of "better" although they might already have passed goals which at an earlier time had seemed all they could want. A long journey stood between an artist's development and his ideal. It was a journey that was always lengthening, for when the end that seemed within reach was attained, it proved to be no end at all, only another aspect of the way. Compelled to honesty, Dolly knew she did not have the necessary equipment for that journey.

The whistle of the train sounded nearer as it approached Manchester. Only a few miles, only a few minutes, divided the towns, but the space and time had been long enough for Dolly to think through to an important decision. The violin would not be her life work. Music she would always love, but she would bend her energies to something else as her livelihood. That something else was teaching. It had long been a family tradition. Her forte was in the languages that came so easily to her.

She boarded the train and sat down on the stiff plush seat, leaning her head back and closing her eyes with relief at the decision made. The train jerked itself forward, gaining speed as it left Manchester and the mountains behind. She opened the book she had with her and began to read, making her way up the steep ascent of the Inferno with a Dante who had long been her friend. When she came to the last line of Canto XXXIV she glanced out toward the countryside that was misty with coming night and said words that might have been written for her, " 'Thence we came forth to rebehold the stars.' "

She had always been moved by the ending of the divisions of the Divine Comedy, for each one had its heart-lifting look up to the stars. " '*E quindi uscimmo a riveder le stelle*,' " she said the familiar words to herself. They were like something lived rather than read. With them she looked up out of the darkness into the light. They were like the promise of something

bright to come, or rather the assurance of something bright that
was always there. She turned the pages until she came to the
ending of the Purgatorio. It was quieter and more gentle,
" *'Puro e disposto a salire ale stelle.'* " Then she turned to the
ending of the Paradiso, " *'L'Amor che mova il sole e l' altre
stelle.'* " It was all one needed for a creed to live by; it was a
living creed.

Now she knew, as Dante did, that always there were the stars.

With a sense of release, she threw herself into her college
work. She wrote themes and poems, she filled notebooks with
her observations. Her handwriting changed from the careful
penmanship of the schoolgirl to a smaller, quicker hand, neat
and efficient. People began to call her Dorothy. She put up her
hair and lengthened her skirts, wore large stylish hats and
learned to dance. Becoming as conscious of her clothes as all
her friends were, she scorned the whalebone they relied on
for their trim figures.

"Muscles serve better than manufactured stays," she said.

She read much, thought deeply, grappled with the problems
of the universe, and in endless conversations with her contemporaries rebelled against the beliefs established by the older
generation. Cultural fashions were rapidly changing. Ibsen was
a god not to be questioned; people spoke of Wagner as they had
spoken of Beethoven; Van Gogh replaced the Watts who had
been the idol of their parents. The tyranny of style, whether in
clothes or art, was no longer to be tolerated. Women's rights
were to be advocated as long as breath would hold, and demon-
strated in the determination to wear skirts as high as boot tops
on rainy days; domestic slavery was to be scorned as any
slavery; motherhood was something that spelled bondage and
was therefore to be dismissed. They did not think they were
sophisticated, they knew they were; and they were proud to
call themselves radicals. Beyond a point of thinking some would
not go, but Dolly ventured on—often alone. Measuring herself

against heights her friends had not dared to climb, she felt an inner response that was more than muscular.

The head noises that had begun to bother her at Lincoln came back repeatedly, but often she was too busy to give them any particular heed. She began to find, to her annoyance, that she was having to ask people to repeat what they had said to her. She became painfully attentive to those around her and took to sitting in the front row at classes. Her friends accused her of being unsociable when she took herself off on long solitary walks—always her father's remedy for relieving any kind of pressure, mental or physical—but from them she returned with the look of one who had met Apollyon.

The string quartet, now known as the President's Quartet, was often in demand at college functions. They met weekly at Dr. Eckhardt's house or the Canfields' and, though Dolly had ruled out music as a career, she played with even greater zest. Rehearsing a Mozart quartet one evening, she waited with bow poised, counting to herself as the first violin approached the end of a running passage. Lost in the sound of which she had now become a part, Dolly drew her bow across the strings.

"No, no, no—" Dr. Eckhardt tapped his bow on the music stand and the room became silent. "Again, please, four bars after letter 'D.' "

She waited for her entrance, her mind hearing the fullness of the sound, her curiosity aroused as to where the imperfection had been.

At the same place, Dr. Eckhardt tapped again for them to cease playing. He put down his bow. "Miss Dorothy, gentlemen, in an ensemble you must listen to the others as well as to yourself. Only so can there be the perfect balance. Some of you play too loudly, one of you was behind the beat. Those notes upon which you enter, Miss Dorothy, must not be quite so predominant. We, who are we? Four people with instruments. It is not one of us, it is all of us, the fifth voice that is to be heard. Come now, again." He turned back the page of music.

They played again as each one strained to hear the least nuance in tone, the slightest variation in pace.

"Father," Dolly asked, when returning from Dr. Eckhardt's she found James Canfield still at his desk, "what is a hunch?"

"Oh," he said, looking up from his book and at his daughter, "something that enables one to guess the best way to surmount obstacles."

"Where does it come from?"

"Probably from that vast amount of accumulated experience every one of us has. It's some kind of half-conscious co-ordination of various elements. Why?"

"I had a hunch about my music."

"Tonight?"

"No, some time ago. Last summer on the station platform in Manchester."

He smiled knowingly. She returned the smile gratefully, then went out of the room and up the stairs whistling. James Canfield picked up his book again. He was glad that Flavia was at a Woman's Club meeting. She had never understood what Dolly's whistling meant nor how important it was to her.

The head noises became more persistent and Dolly was sent to an aurist who gave her ears a careful examination and tested her hearing.

"It is an infection of the middle ear," he said. "I am afraid your hearing is already impaired. Have you ever done much swimming, Miss Canfield?"

"Yes—" Her mind went back to the warm-water pool at Lincoln.

"It could be that the infection started there. Obviously the trouble goes back some time. If it had been treated sooner—"

"You mean—" she interrupted, but did not finish her question.

"There is some treatment we can try. There are also certain aids that can be employed in time. An ear trumpet, for instance."

"But these noises inside my head, when will they cease?"

He looked at her. It was not easy to say what he had to say to an eager talented girl, but there was something about the straightforward honest glance directed at him that demanded honesty, that would settle for nothing less. "They are something that go with deafness, Miss Canfield."

Dolly was silent. Though he had not said it in so many words, she knew that the head noises were something she would have for the rest of her life—like her small hands, her unruly hair.

"Of course, it will be several years."

She thanked him and left his office. She walked briskly home, her head high and her arms swinging. Over and over she told herself that the one thing she had to remember was that this concerned her and nobody else, that what she had just been told was not of the slightest interest or importance to anyone but herself.

She worked with even more energy and ardor during her last year of college. Book information had always been easy for her to acquire, but she was aware that something far more important had been happening through the years. A small treasury of living seeds of real knowledge had been implanted in her mind. They would continue to grow as long as life lasted. She kept up her music, was active in sports, and when her mother was away from home, acted as her father's hostess. Glancing ahead at her future, she drew her gaze quickly back to the present. All that she was doing now was adding to her knowledge of human life. Such knowledge would serve her well whatever her work might be.

In the spring of that year, 1899, James Canfield was offered the post of librarian at Columbia University in New York. He accepted. When graduation time came, Dolly went up to the platform to receive her degree from Ohio State. Her father handed it to her with a smile that he saw no need to conceal. It was one of his last official functions as a college president. It was his daughter's first step toward an academic career.

Dolly did not find it easy to leave Columbus—the good friends, the quartet, particularly her brother James who had married and was remaining there. But she had been brought up to believe in the principle of growth. Her mind accepted it, though her heart might temporarily rebel. Growth meant change. Life was full of opening doors.

Unpacking her father's books and placing them on the shelves in his study at Columbia, Dolly unpacked the three framed mottoes that had gone with him from one university to another. She dusted them off and hung them up.

> *All at it and all the time at it; that is what wins.*

> *What you can do, begin it. Boldness hath genius,*
> *power and magic to it.*

> *The public business of America is the private*
> *business of every citizen.*

They were eloquent of her father's attitude toward life. Familiar as she was with them, they appealed to her anew.

She went to Europe for two years to continue her study of languages. The first winter was spent at the University of Paris; she went to London for the summer for further work at the British Museum. Willa Cather was visiting England then and the two friends of Nebraskan days spent much time together. Dolly went on to Oxford to see her father receive an honorary degree. He wore the University's flaming scarlet gown of antique cut; the academic cap rested on his thick white hair. She thrilled to the noble ceremony and the degree that praised him in sonorous Latin for his enthusiasm for "books as tools of students." As the honored men walked solemnly by in procession, she saw the twinkle in her father's eyes as he passed her.

"Dolly," he said later, "I feel with Martin Luther that the Devil shouldn't have all the good tunes. I'm going to try to persuade Columbia University to brighten up their academic marches with some lively music."

"You'd do anything to quicken the life of the intelligence, wouldn't you, Father?"

"I'm beginning to think you will, too," he answered.

In the fall, Dolly went to Hanover for a year's work in German. The discipline of scholarly studies had always been dear to her, but into her mind as well as the acquisition of knowledge went impressions of other ways of life. Images, observations, personalities, moods—all were being stored up like timber cut in a woodlot and piled for seasoning.

Walking with a group of friends through a rural district one golden September afternoon, she stopped with them in a village for a drink of water. The music of fiddles and flutes filled the air. The villagers told them the harvest dance was on and invited them to join in. Approaching the barn, the students were greeted by peasant families eating and drinking at generously spread tables. Near them, on a platform, young couples were dancing. Soon the students were whirling around in the arms of jovial partners. Dolly was delighted. She had been going to dances for years but they had been formal evening affairs. This was sheer joyous expression of being in the honest sunlight of a common day.

"Why, this is fun!" she exclaimed to her unknown partner.

It made sense to her and she wondered why in the life she knew at home people waited until near bedtime to dance, then changed into elaborate dress and their least comfortable shoes. As rhythmic activity, natural and spontaneous, caught her up, she was challenged by the thought that in the same way all tradition-ridden habits could be replaced. The experience went as deep in her questioning mind as the Goethe she was reading.

Back in New York in 1902, she launched into the work at Columbia that would merit her a Doctor's degree. With that and the four languages she had mastered, she would be ready to teach. The days were filled. She took a secretarial position at the Horace Mann School, acted as housekeeper to her parents, and collaborated with her father in writing an article that was to be published in *The Outlook* on *The Three Greatest Libraries*—the British Museum, the National Library at Paris, and the Imperial Public Library of Russia at St. Petersburg.

James Canfield, with his enthusiasm and capacity to accomplish a vast amount of work by a well-organized use of time, had poured life into Columbia's library. Many times his daughter had heard him tell his favorite story of the college librarian who looked complacently around his empty room and filled shelves, saying, "Every book is in its right place, except two, and I know where they are. I'll have them back tomorrow."

Dolly knew that her father's criterion was different: activity in service that constantly made more readers.

Chapter 5

Golden Circle

EVERY morning Dorothy and her father left the house on 116th Street to walk to their work—the University Library, the Horace Mann School. With the long swinging stride of practiced walkers, they went through the streets and across the campus. Their minds moved easily together. Intimacy flowed through their conversation and around their silences. There was always plenty to talk about—books read, theories of education, James' plans for further writing, Dorothy's work at the school. One morning Dorothy told her father about an article on pelota she had read in the *New York Times*.

"But the person who wrote that article never could have seen Spaniards playing pelota," she exclaimed hotly. "He described it all wrong."

"Why don't you write an article for the *Times* about the way pelota is played? You must have watched it often enough when you were in Spain with your mother."

"Me! Write for the *Times?*"

"Why not, if you have a story to tell?"

It was something to think about. Of course, she had been writing through the years, themes and papers; but she had never thought of writing in the way her father meant. And yet, why not, if, as he said, she had a story to tell? Her mind went back to one of her first school compositions which she had called *The Village King*. It was about Uncle Zed. Writing about him

when she was in Kansas had given her almost as much pleasure
as being with him in Vermont. Her teacher had given her a 9+
in red pencil in the top left corner, she had also written a comment, "The sketch is very true. I have seen the old man myself.
Did you get the idea in New England?"

Another theme had been called *A Fishing Excursion*. It had
merited a good mark and her teacher had called it "Cleverly
written." Dorothy remembered that in it she had said something
that her Arlington days had made her happily sure of—that old
people and young could enjoy each other as they shared their
wisdom and enthusiasm. She found she could recall some of
her words, "Grandfather gave her no instruction for he wanted
to see how she would go at it." When she drew a small fish out
of the Battenkill and he a large one it seemed completely
reasonable, for, "How could a little girl catch as big a fish as a
grown-up man?"

She had not lacked ideas for themes in her school days. There
were plenty of experiences in Arlington or Paris to recall,
there was any amount of studio talk or old people's conversation to recapture. Now her father was suggesting that she write
an article for the *Times*. Well, she would!

She did. It was accepted. When the editor sent her a check
in payment he asked for another article. So she wrote one about
the Maundy Thursday washing of the feet in the Royal Palace
at Madrid. As she wrote, the scene came as vividly to mind as
when she had been present. It was a farce of humility as King
Alphonso and the corseted ladies of the court pretended to be
something they could not be. Rebellion against pretense rose
easily within her and fired her words. Again the editor sent her
a check and asked for more.

"Why, that's easy money," she said to her father. "My
memory is filled with such things."

She wrote a short story but it was returned to her with the
suggestion that it seemed more suitable for a woman's magazine

than for a newspaper. She sent it to *Harper's Bazaar* and received a check by return mail.

But there was more serious work at hand as she prepared to write her thesis. James Canfield took her to New Haven to ask his long-time friend, William Lyon Phelps, for some advice. They made a handsome pair, the large distinguished-looking librarian of Columbia University and his pretty vivacious daughter. Dr. Canfield never wasted any time on words or preliminaries. "This is my daughter and she has got to write a thesis in Old French for her Ph.D. at Columbia," he said.

"God help her!" Dr. Phelps exclaimed.

"No, *you* help her."

"But I don't know anything whatever about Old French. The only French that interests me is modern French."

"Yes, but you once wrote a thesis in English and got a Ph.D.," James Canfield reminded his friend.

"That is quite true, and I made up my mind then that if the Lord would forgive me I would never write another."

"Well, this thesis has got to be written, and we have come to New Haven to discuss the method of its production with you."

So Dr. Phelps did his best to point out the way in which original work, if it was to be valuable and important, should be done. He told Dorothy what to include and what to emphasize, what to omit. When the librarian and his daughter returned to New York, Dorothy had a clearer idea of what her best could be.

The days were not all work. There was plenty of gaiety. Dorothy had many opportunities to be her father's hostess; she was often called on to pour tea at faculty parties. The Canfield home had always been a rendezvous for young people. Dorothy charmed young men as readily as she shocked her girl friends. Her revolutionary ideas included a firm refusal to wear the corsets girls accepted as a matter of course and propriety.

To the protest of one of her friends Dorothy shook her head

saying she had tried one on once, "For a moment or two. But the Inquisition had few things worse than those Nuremberg Virgin contraptions," she exclaimed. "I'll never wear one. Why, my breathing would be cut off to the suffocation point!"

Horrified, and standing majestically erect in her ironclad re-inforcements, the friend said, "I don't see how you *can* go without. How do you dare dance with a man?"

Dorothy looked startled, for dancing was one of her greatest pleasures. "Why— What—" Her face was blank.

With an expression of fascinated repulsion her friend ex-plained, "When you stand up with a dancing partner and he puts his arm around you, he must—" she lowered her voice and looked around to see if anyone of the opposite sex was within listening range, "—he must feel as if he were touching something alive."

Dorothy's laughter rang out. She could find no words to counter the shocked dismay on her friend's face.

"Come on," she said, slipping her arm around the girl, "let's go to the drugstore and get a maple nut sundae. We might even have two."

Life held gaiety, and yet there were times when gaiety was only a mask which Dorothy and her contemporaries held up to life. Behind it they were often uncertain, afraid to trust the future, and desperately afraid that what they did not secure im-mediately would be lost to them forever. When they could not reason things out in talk, they eased the pressures on themselves by playing tennis with enormous energy, skating with endless ardor. And they could always dance. Sometime during the hours of activity or romance it often happened that the mask fell away and gaiety became again for them the simple, natural expression of youthful exuberance.

Four times a year James Canfield went up to West Point to lecture on history to the cadets. Dorothy went with him. His trips were always made on a Saturday and after his classes he returned to New York while Dorothy stayed on for the evening Hop. But four Hops a year were not enough for the "dancing-est" of young girls and she went up often between times.

The cadets, handsome in their uniforms and all of them perfect dancers, were not Dorothy's sole interest at West Point. She liked to visit with her father's friend, the librarian. Dr. Holden was a cynic and his favorite saying was, "There's nothing new and nothing true, and it doesn't matter." Dorothy was enchanted by his wit and did not in the least mind his cynicism. She knew quite well that her discoveries of life were for him only indications of the puppy stage that all youth went through. He always had a story to prove his point.

"My brother is an industrialist. A locomotive made in his factory was sent to the Philadelphia Centennial Exposition. A group of workmen were given the day off, with pay, to go to the Exposition in the hope that they would see things that would broaden their minds and widen their horizons. What do you suppose they did?"

Dorothy shook her head. She did not have the slightest idea what the workmen did.

"Instead of looking at the wonders that filled the halls, those workmen spent most of their time leaning over the railing that fenced off the locomotive, gloating over the engine they had made! Now, do you see what I mean?"

Dr. Holden might have proved his point of man's unimaginativeness, but Dorothy saw something different. "Don't you think the men evidenced the pride they felt in their own craftsmanship?" she asked.

Dr. Holden's reply was an explosive negative.

Dorothy knew that he had once been an astronomer. "Perhaps one can look at the stars too long," she thought to herself. "The near view is needed as much as the far." Check and balance. That was what her father had been saying that afternoon in his lecture about the Constitution of the United States as he pointed out to the cadets that as citizens in a democracy they should know that their national government rested on the idea of checks and balances.

Dorothy's escort appeared at the door, tall, trim, buttons shining. She threw her feather boa over her arm and went off with him. Her head reached to his shoulder but that was high enough for her gay talk to reach him and she had learned long ago that it did not matter in the least if she did not hear all that was being said to her. It was good to be whirled off into the first dance, to feel the cadet's strong arms guiding her, lifting her from her feet. Too breathless to talk, too gay to think, remembering only that the long work on her thesis was at last over, she felt lost to anything but the music and movement of the moment.

"How I hate brainy girls!" the cadet exclaimed suddenly. "Anybody would know, just to look at you, that you didn't know anything."

Dorothy threw back her head and laughed. It was still the kind of world where a girl could only whisper the word intelligent. Perhaps this, too, was part of the checks and balances of life.

During Christmas vacation a group of faculty wives and daughters gave a tea at which Dorothy was asked to pour. She accepted readily, although she had no great liking for large rooms filled with many people all talking at once. The party seemed to be more of a shouting babel than ever and Dorothy was glad to be sitting at a table pouring tea and not having to do much talking.

A student approached her table. "Miss Canfield, I'd like to have you meet one of our football players—"

A stocky young man with bushy brown hair stepped forward.

Dorothy did not always catch everything said to her and she rarely asked people to repeat, but this time she did. "What did he say your name was?"

"John Fisher," the young man replied, speaking so clearly that Dorothy heard him without effort.

The student moved on to talk with someone else and John Fisher stepped forward to take the proffered teacup. Brown eyes looked into blue; across the world, across time, over a tea table. He was unlike anyone she had ever met; not because of the firm build and capable hands but because of the quiet expression in his face.

"I really wasn't going to come to this party," he was saying. "I was supposed to meet a friend of mine in the library but he didn't show up. Goodlatte caught me just as I was edging my way out."

Dorothy signaled to another hostess to take her place for a while. She stood up beside the football player, discovering to her joy that he was not much taller than she and conversation between them was that much easier. They talked together and the noise in the room receded.

There were other tea parties during the winter that John Fisher went to, not by mistake but in the hope of seeing the daughter of Columbia University's librarian. They met at skating parties and the dances that followed basketball games. Dorothy invited John to join the group of ten or more young people who went walking along the Palisades on Saturdays and during vacations. Of course, we enjoy each other; of course, we are interested in each other. That much they could admit to themselves while resolutely closing their minds to the possibility that the road they were traveling might lead to anything but deeper friendship.

One night Dorothy was taking part in a play that was being given by the Alliance Française. Cheerful chatter all in French, excited hubbub, was going on backstage, accompanied by the frequent opening and shutting of doors as girls in rustling taffeta dresses ran back and forth between the dressing rooms. Flowers had begun to arrive in long boxes.

"Oh, Dorothy! American beauties—oh, what monstrous ones! Why, they're as tall as you are. They must have cost a lot of money."

"Here's another box with some yellow ones!"

Dorothy picked up the huge clusters of roses and looked at them with distaste. There was something ugly about the idea of beauty being bought with money. Then another box was placed on her dressing table, a small square box. She opened it. It contained a great clump of hepaticas, frail and delicate and varicolored. She took them out of the box, shaken by all the associations they brought back to her of springtime in Vermont woods.

"Dorothy, what are those little flowers?"

"They're hepaticas, wild flowers."

"But I never saw anything like them in a florist shop."

"They can't be bought for cash."

"How does anybody get them?"

Dorothy was silent.

The dressing room door opened again. A girl, drifting yards of tulle over her bare shoulders, looked in. "My grandmother would be furious if she could see wild flowers picked that way and made into a bouquet. She's down on people who pick wild flowers. They'll kill them all off, she says."

"But these are hepaticas," Dorothy repeated. "They don't grow on a branch that you break off. They *grow up from the roots*. Even if you pick them all off, the roots are still there in the earth to send up more."

"Mesdemoiselles!" There was a loud knock on the door. "You have only ten minutes left till the curtain goes up."

There was a scurrying of slippered feet. The door opened and closed and Dorothy was alone with the hepaticas. She knew who had sent them without looking at the card; she could see the strong skillful hands that had picked them.

During the intermission there was another animated hubbub

behind the scenes, only this time the voices had a different tone. A piece of property essential for the third act was nowhere to be found. Dorothy, peering through a crack in the curtain, caught sight of her mother and father sitting in the audience. "Our apartment is close at hand," she said quickly. "Somebody go and get my father to come around to the stage door and I'll ask him to fetch a frying pan."

Within a few moments, the silvery-haired man in his black evening caped-coat was standing at the stage door. "Why, of course, Dolly, I'll bring you a frying pan for the third act."

When she went to the stage door during the second intermission she found her father having an animated discussion with a faculty colleague whom he had met on the street. "But a frying pan is a perfectly respectable object," Dr. Canfield was saying. "Why should I bother to wrap it up or hide it? And it's needed for the play these girls are doing."

"But—"

"I tell you," Dr. Canfield made an impatient gesture with the frying pan, "if conservatism could see these girls! One of them is majoring in mathematics, another in international law. The idea that having trained brains or the vote is going to make girls unfeminine!"

"Dr. Canfield, I can see that you are a feminist."

"Father, please—"

"Oh, Dolly, here it is." Dr. Canfield turned quickly to face his daughter and hand her the frying pan.

She watched the two men walk away, thinking how like the Raeburn portrait of "The Old Academician" her father looked. Later, peeking through the crack in the curtain, she saw her father sit down beside her mother, and she smiled at them with approval. Flavia's Vermont ancestry would have made her as unperturbed as her father had been by the idea of carrying a frying pan through the streets of New York.

She went back to her dressing room and sat down before her

mirror. Had she put on enough eye-shadow to cope with the glare of the footlights? Looking harder at her face it seemed to be an object quite remote from her personality. A knock sounded at the door and the French coach in charge of stage direction came in.

"Will this do?" she asked, turning her powdered and painted face toward him.

He studied her face, then deepened a shadow under the eyes and put a highlight on the cheeks. Standing back to see the effect from a distance, he gazed at her upturned face with an utter absence of any human or personal interest in it. His scrutiny was familiar to Dorothy from the long hours in the past when she had posed for a circle of painters, each one focussing on her a gaze devoid of all concern with her as a human being.

"That will do," said the coach, shutting down the cover of the make-up case. Like those artists before their easels, he spoke as if he had put the last touches on a door panel he had been painting. "Five minutes, mademoiselle." He turned and left the room. The door closed behind him.

Dorothy went to the corner where the florists' boxes were heaped and opened the longest one. "It's as big as a child's coffin, and it looks like one. The more cash, the more beauty," she thought, as she looked at the huge showy flowers. "Zut!" she exclaimed angrily, and thrust the cover over the box.

Then she took the dawn-colored hepaticas from their box and pinned them on the bosom of her tulle dress. Was it possible, could it be possible that John Fisher felt what hepaticas meant?

"Mademoiselle!" There was a knock on the door.

"I'm coming—"

That night she put the hepaticas carefully in a vase, wondering where John had ever been able to find so many. William Blake might have seen a heaven in a wild flower. Here was a whole handful of wild flowers: stuff of heaven, stuff of dreams, stuff of solid warm reality.

Dorothy's thesis had been satisfactorily completed and merited for her the degree of Doctor of Philology. *Corneille and Racine in England* was dedicated to James and Flavia Canfield and published by the Columbia University Press. At the Commencement Exercises in June 1904, when John Fisher received his B.A., Dorothy received her Doctor's degree from the hands of President Nicholas Murray Butler. James Canfield looked as proudly at his daughter as she had at him two years before in England. As she stepped down from the platform his black eyes caught hers, both were shining with pride and delight. Then the brass bands started playing and the candidates marched with quick steps in time to the music. The breeze billowed at Dorothy's gown and pulled wisps of her hair from under her academic cap.

"What will Dorothy Canfield do with a doctorate but hang it around the neck of her first baby?" was what was being asked around the University.

She was not there to answer. She had gone to Arlington for the summer and did not return to New York until early September.

John was in law school and captain of the football team. They saw each other often for walks along the Palisades, and at dances after games, but they began to move away from their friendly group to do things by themselves. By June they knew they wanted to get married, though when was in a very indefinite future. Dorothy had been hearing within her an echo from her childhood, an old rule as believed in by country folk as the earth's turning, "Never marry a man just because you think you could manage to live with him. Don't do it unless you are dead sure you couldn't live without him." That was how she felt about John. The way was far from clear for them both. He had, as yet, no definite leaning toward a life occupation; she was beginning to put more and more time into writing, since during the past year there had been enough sales of stories and articles to warrant her thinking of writing as a career.

That summer John took a job at a Lake George hotel and Dorothy went to Europe, first to Germany, then to visit Norwegian friends. There was time to read, to think, to write, and something of all three were expressed in a letter to her family—

Vik, Norway
July 30, 1905

Dear Family . . . . I can't remember that I have ever spent 4 happier weeks—Father sends a warning note in his last letter "Not to keep too much company with yourself. It is dangerous." Well, it must be dangerous on the Puritan principle that whatever you enjoy you shouldn't have too much of—for I've enjoyed my own company immensely. Don't laugh—too hard, that is, I expect you to laugh some—I honestly have. I never knew there were so many lovely things to think about if one only had time. I take long walks, or I clamber over the mountains, towering above the fjord, as I lie on a peak of rock in the sun and I think such interesting and lovely things and imagine such moving scenes that I am never ready to stop. I haven't written much . . . but I've thought a lot more about my Norwegian story. If I could write that as I now conceive it, it would be something I'd not be ashamed of. But of course, I can't. I expect a fearful set-back, when I begin work on it—the method will have to be so different from any written-at-one-spurt short stories. I have it pretty well planned—fourteen chapters, scene here and in Christiania, but oh, my hero is so frightfully complicated a person. It wears me out to follow him in and out of the labyrinth of motives he gets himself tied up in. The old aunt is Aunt Phebe with a sense of humor added. She's the only one from life—every scrap of the rest is pure make-up—"made out of my own head" as the young wife told the old professor of the pudding. I'm afraid I've set myself too hard a task in managing so many people; but it won't do any harm to be thinking about it. Did I tell you I had a long letter from Mr. Sedgwick (*Leslie's* Editor, you know) very warm and friendly and unexpectedly serious. He says that my "talent, heaven be praised, lies outside the ordinary channels of magazine literature. Don't try to make it run in those shallow ways. You can write stories with big ideas and true ones, back of them. *Do* it! Don't be willing to be amusing when you can do more." etc., etc. He winds up by saying he doesn't want to spoil my holiday with over-earnest exhortation but I am to bear in mind that "we in the office are following your work with the greatest interest and belief" —something like, I've mislaid the letter somewhere or I'd send it to you. I wrote Mr. Sedgwick that his letter came most opportunely when I was just getting up the nerve to take my writing more seriously. I said "big ideas" as he put it weren't exactly in my line but I did mean to try honestly to have the ideas I was trying to express true ones, and to try and move people to more than a passing interest in a certain verbal dexterity. I was ashamed to send the letter for a while after I'd written it. It's all very well to say to my family whatever "biggety" idea is in my head but I was afraid to him it might sound pretentious. I sent it all the same. I'm getting up a fine strong variety of "literary nerve" if you know what I mean by that.

One afternoon when Dorothy was sitting in the grape arbor looking across the Sagenfjord, she began to turn over in her mind the story Dr. Holden had told her of the locomotive that was sent to the exposition. What did the workmen think as they leaned over the railing and looked at what they had helped make? How were they affected by the remarks of other sightseers? The idea took hold of her imagination. Looking below the surface of the anecdote she saw that its essence was in what craftsmanship could do to the individual. If she lifted it out of a machine shop about which she knew nothing, and set it in

Vermont about which she had deep and comfortable knowledge, she might have a story to tell. She began to think of her characters, especially Aunt Mehetabel who pieced her quilt together and took it to the County Fair. She knew Aunt Mehetabel's kind well, and she had been to at least one County Fair a year for as long as she could remember.

What is "to make up"? she thought.

She answered her own question as she wrote her story and called it *The Bedquilt*.

On the way home from Norway she stopped in Belgium, then went to France to spend some time with old family friends. The letters home rang with good fortune. "Am I not the luckiest person—" she wrote after witnessing a festival procession, or when finding the perfect hat to go with her costume. Telling of adventures she had and the kindnesses shown her, she said, "What do you think of my luck? Is there anybody in the world but me who could have such. . . . I am already quite French again, thinking and dreaming in the language. It is like running a train of cars over a switch to another track. . . . No more at present from your wandering and very gay daughter! Except love!"

The frank approach to life that she had always found in France made her do some realistic thinking on her own account. In her advance toward adult life, she had become aware of the part sex played. She had no expectation that it would give more than it could; she had no impulse to blame or repudiate it for not giving more than it could. Because she was in love, and had been for more than a year, she could see clearly that unlike sex with its physical limitations, love had no limitations. It had an endless capacity to grow as the human being in whom love lived grew.

When Dorothy returned to New York, she and John told their families that they were engaged. John took Dorothy to Swiftwater, Pennsylvania to meet his family. At the station, his father, a practicing physician, greeted her warmly; at the house, his mother and sisters, Elizabeth and Esther, waited to welcome her.

"It seems impossible that I haven't been borned one of you!" Dorothy exclaimed.

But whatever plans they had were still far in the future.

Dorothy wrote stories and articles, worked on her novel *Gunhild,* and did editorial work at home. When Ellery Sedgwick and William Morrow started the *American Magazine,* she accepted the position they offered her as final reader. Manuscripts over which the editors had a difference of opinion and those that required rewriting were sent to her. Often she was asked to work with the writer of some particular piece to help bring it into acceptable form.

John decided that he did not want to be a lawyer and dropped out of law school to take whatever literary jobs he could find—criticism, reading for publishers, writing occasional sketches. He was as eager as Dorothy to prove that it was possible to make a living out of writing, though the living might be lean.

The editor of *Everybody's Magazine* offered Dorothy a regular salary—larger than anything she was making with her sales of short stories—to read and edit manuscripts. It was a tempting offer. Dorothy left the office considering it seriously. As she was walking down the street, Virginia Roderick, one of the staff, caught up with her and walked along with her.

"Miss Canfield, you have a gift for writing—creative writing. Editorial work will not help that gift to come to its fullness. I beg of you not to decide hastily. Think what your decision may mean—how far it may reach."

Dorothy did think seriously. She decided against editorial work and for putting all her time and energy into writing; nothing but writing.

On Palm Sunday in that never-more-beautiful spring than the year of 1906, John and Dorothy announced their engagement. They talked endlessly about how they could afford to get married, where they might live. They considered the Pocono Mountains. They thought of one of the New York suburbs so John could go into the city every day; but something within them recoiled from such living, though it was becoming an accepted pattern for young people. There was always Arlington, and in their close-to-earth budgeting they began to feel that Arlington was the place where they could live on the smallest possible cash outlay.

"We want to live plain." After all their talking, they came back invariably to that.

Two small book jobs came to Dorothy. Neither one was particularly creative but she knew that if she was to be a writer she would have to be ready at times to turn her ability to literary chores. One was a textbook written with Columbia's Professor R. G. Carpenter, *English Rhetoric and Composition;* the other was a book of games and activities, *What Shall We Do Now?* She knew they were good for what they were, though not important.

"All bridges can't be Brooklyn Bridges, Dolly," John reminded her. "There have to be plank spans for streams. The important thing is that they be built sound so they can serve in their way."

The following spring Dorothy and John saw clearly that what might seem to be obstacles to their marriage were actually challenges to the strongest and best within each one. They were determined not to conform to any pattern, nor bow to any pressure. They would be themselves. They would live in Arlington, and write for a living. Dorothy was twenty-eight; John was a year younger.

As a wedding present Great-aunt Mary gave them a small old house and a quarter acre lot that bordered the Canfield land. She had bought it for $250 and the house was badly in need of repair, but at least it was a place to live in. A pine tree was planted to mark a corner. It seemed quite near the house and when Dorothy asked if they could have a little land, Aunt Mattie replied, "Oh, goodness, child, take all the land you want."

There was some money in the bank—bequests Dorothy had had, earnings from her work, about $7000. It seemed like a fortune. They knew that it was a nest egg and must serve as such against sickness or any catastrophe. Their combined writing income was small by metropolitan standards, but it was ample by the standards of Vermont. Living simply as they wanted to do, they knew they would waste no money in keeping up with any social set. With land that was their own they would always have something to fall back on; and John had clever hands. He could build things; he could make things grow.

On May 9, 1907 they were married from the Canfield home in Pleasantville, New York. Into the envelopes announcing the marriage of Dorothea Frances Canfield to John Redwood Fisher was slipped a small engraved card which said,

AFTER JUNE 15

AT HOME

ARLINGTON, VERMONT

They went off to live the life they were confident they were meant to live, and only a few people knew that they went directly to the old farm on the slope of Red Mountain in Arlington.

Spring had been late that year. Now, in the second week of May, it was fairly tumbling over itself as it ran into the arms of summer. The hepaticas were still in bloom along the brook beds while the azalea was bursting into pink flame. The elm twigs were shouting their delight. The sun sent down a warmth which the earth returned with the added fragrance of sweet pine and fern.

Dorothy and John stopped at the Brick Farm House long enough to see that fat buds were already forming on the old peony bush that great-great-grandmother had brought with her in the 1760's when she had first come to Arlington. Then they walked across the fields to the little house that was to be their home.

"We're going to have a home of our own," Dolly said over and over again, while with her inner ear she seemed to hear the same words as they were said by others back through the centuries.

They crossed the threshold of the house and walked through the small plain rooms.

"It's so simple, and dear," she breathed ecstatically.

"It's good to know that it's always been lived in by working people," John said.

"We're working people, though pens and typewriter will be our tools, not plow and ax."

The house was exactly right for the kind of life they wanted to live. It would be a background, not an occupation as a spacious handsome house could become. From it a feeling of home already poured, a feeling that came not from the low-ceilinged rooms alone but from the fields that embraced the house, the pines that shadowed it, the brook that ran near, and the mountain that bulwarked it—the whole rugged, timbered bulk of Red Mountain that was Canfield land, up to the "height o' land" that ran along the ridge.

The small front room, nearest to the best company room they ever wanted to have, was already furnished with things that had been brought up from Connecticut in the eighteenth century by Canfields and Hawleys and Hards. There were no chairs for the kitchen table but the carpenters had left some nail kegs which they could use. A woodshed led off from the front room. John, looking around him, saw in his mind's eye the paneled dining room he wanted to make some day, the upstairs study.

"We'll have plenty of need for desks and files and straight chairs and good lights for long working hours in the winter."

"We'll need another shed to hold our tools in the summer, our snowshoes in the winter."

"Oh, there's a lot to do."

"And a lifetime to do it in!"

All that was prose, Dorothy told herself as she gazed around. Written small on the margin, like a footnote, lay the miracle poetry. It was to a human life what the sun was to the earthen ball on which it shone.

They packed provisions and blankets, closed the door of the house behind them, and followed one of the trails that led up Red Mountain to a familiar clearing. There, where a brook came down the slope, and the wind blew fresh and the birds sang and the wild flowers grew, they camped for the first weeks of their marriage. Happy, at last, to have escaped from friends and relations and to be alone with each other.

They sat on the moss and leaned back against a sun-warmed granite boulder. John took a small book from his pocket and began to read aloud. Dorothy listened and gazed down into the valley. Below the sunny pastures, the fern-feathered brook ravines, the dark pine woods and groves of stately maples, the Battenkill followed its swift winding way.

The sun's last light on the wall of mountains rising eastward of the valley dazzled her and she closed her eyes, but she could still go on seeing the wall, knowing well how its timeworn line-of-beauty flowed harmoniously from north to south. She could feel the past flowing into the future as harmoniously as the mountains flowed through the landscape. Where Canfields had lived for a century and a half, Canfields would live for a long time to come. She opened her eyes and let her gaze follow the line of the mountain down to the white house that was their home. She could see the sparkle of the brook where her father and his father and grandfather had made dams and caught trout. She could see the curve of the road as it wound through the valley, turning like the river, linking houses and school and distant village together. It was the same road over which the first settlers had come with their ox-carts, along which droves of sheep and cattle had been driven, and boys had marched to join the Union Army in the War Between the States; farm wagons and buggies now went over it and an occasional automobile, noisily chugging. As her eyes followed the course of the road, she sensed the continuity of life, while feeling as grounded as one of the pine trees whose roots went deep into the soil. Like the tree, something of themselves would always be there—part of mountain and valley—even long after they had left the white house for the old burying ground in the village.

All that was what it meant to feel at home. That was what marriage was: a condition in which one came to trust life and love and nature in its serene progression of birth and growth and death.

John was reading from Meredith's *Love in the Valley*. Dorothy leaned closer so she would not miss a word. How she loved the sound of John's voice, deep, slow, clear, uttering words with the affection he felt for them—

> "Could I find a place to be alone with heaven,
> I would speak my heart out: heaven is my need.
> Every woodland tree is flashing like the dogwood,
> Flashing like the whitebeam, swaying like the reed.
> Flashing like the dogwood crimson in October;
> Streaming like the flag-reed South-west blown;
> Flashing as in gusts the sudden-lighted whitebeam
> All seem to know what is for heaven alone."

Chapter 6

"We who now live are parts of a humanity that extends
into the remote past, a humanity that has interacted
with nature."   JOHN DEWEY.

SUMMER was a supremely happy, gloriously busy time. There
was the house to be settled and made into a home, the garden
to be planted, old friends to be seen, neighbors to be called on,
letters to be written. Every day, Dr. Canfield wrote to his
daughter, a cheerful affectionate letter though it was sometimes only a line or two. Flavia made flying visits, often leaving
again before she had unpacked her bags. She loved the beauty
of the Vermont country, but with a world to live in she could
not understand how John and Dorothy could settle on a mountainside. Many of their New York friends tried to tell them
that they were cut off from everything, but the young Fishers
knew that what they had done was to make their own declaration of independence. It was the key chord from which the
harmony of their life together would develop.

Dorothy looked up from a letter she was reading. "This is
a warning that if we intend to be writers we should be seen
at literary gatherings. We should be able to drop in occasionally at editors' offices. If we don't, we'll soon be forgotten.
What do you think of that, John?"

"Maybe there's some truth in it, Dolly, if what we want is
routine work, but that's not what we want."

"No, indeed it is not."

Dorothy had not been built to conform, and just as she had resisted steel and whalebone around her body so she refused to accept any corset of conventionality around her thinking. She felt certain that for creative writing, nothing counted except the editor's judgment on the manuscript that reached his desk. The stories she had already sold had interested a number of editors and a wide group of readers. She intended to continue along the same lines, trusting skill and perception to grow with time and practice. Now it was difficult to remember that she had once seriously considered another career for herself, so easily had the transition been made from the trained teacher-of-languages to the writer.

John picked up a letter from a college classmate. "This is full of hints at the risk we're taking in incurring intellectual and spiritual dry rot by giving up the stimulation of the city. Sooner or later, we're being told, we'll find life very drab."

Dorothy shrugged her shoulders, content to ignore the mournful prediction. She knew there would be dull spots in country life, but no village gathering would ever be as unrewarding as the bridge and golf they had escaped from, the crowded parties with their ceaseless chatter. The neighborhood activities that she had known since she was a small child had always made her feel closer to people. Not the sort of people who had a protective surface of polite manners and whose conversation revolved around the latest clichés, but deep-hearted people seasoned by living who met life on its own terms. Country living was full of drama. Now that it was to be her life, she began to see more clearly the drama below the surface of ordinary events.

"Living in the country is like being married to humanity for better or worse," she said, "not just being on speaking terms with it, as one is in the city."

By midsummer their New York friends were saying in their letters that the country must be a good place in which to spend the summer, "But wait until your first winter."

"All right, let them wait!" Dorothy laughed and got a book from the library on figure skating. She wanted to be ready for the Cut-off when it froze.

John made repairs and small additions to the house, and kept to his hours as a writer. Dorothy added Spanish, Portuguese and Italian translations of foreign events to her magazine work. It was arduous and when the check of eleven or twelve dollars for a month's assignment arrived it seemed out of proportion to the time and energy she had spent. She did not mind hard work that kept her at her desk, for it was as much a writer's lot as spading the soil was a gardener's lot; and she had no patience with people who could not endure necessary routine, but she soon felt that her knowledge of languages was worth more than she was being paid. She asked for more; not given it, she turned entirely to the writing of fiction.

She had been at work on her novel *Gunhild* since the summer in Norway. At times she had doubted whether she should venture away from the short story to the novel's more complicated structure, but good or bad, when her work was finished it was finished and *Gunhild* had been sent to the publisher. It came out that October. Reviewers agreed that it was a promising first novel, notable more for its poetic descriptions of the Norwegian countryside than for plot development or character delineation. Dorothy's contract called for a royalty of ten percent after fifteen hundred copies. The book sold six hundred copies and then was forgotten.

With the short stories it was different. *Munsey's, McClure's, Everybody's, Ladies Home Journal, Good Housekeeping,* the *American Magazine,* backed by income from newly developed mass advertising, were bidding for talent, forcing the older magazines, *Scribner's, Harper's, Atlantic,* to pay better prices. Sentimental escape reading was what the women's magazines preferred, but the editors were also publishing some serious fiction, and one or another bought everything Dorothy wrote. Her mind was a storehouse of things seen, heard, felt, long thought about. From it she could draw what she needed at the time. Examining an idea for its basic truth and using it in her own way, she discovered that adaptation was nine-tenths of art. There were any number of problems around her to observe and ponder; she worked out solutions to them as she reduced each one to its human common denominator.

John came upon her one day with her finger in a book of John Dewey's. She pointed to the sentence she had been meditating on, "New vision does not arise out of nothing—old things in new relations serve a new end."

She settled down to an undeviating morning routine in the study they made of the warmest room in the house. One after another stories, fashioned from life and fused by the heat of sympathy, were written. When she put a long thick envelope in the mailbox she did not promise herself anything. All too well she remembered John Robinson's inevitable answer to Aunt Mattie's morning question, "What will the weather be like today?" "I'll tell you tonight, Miss Mattie." If the stories came back they were sent out again. Checks began to come in return. They were marveled at and thriftily put in the bank. Into the ledger that summarized monthly expenses and income, John entered the amounts. Pennies were counted carefully but comfortably; even during the first months of their experiment in living, no wolf was heard scratching at the door. There were times when one of the magazines wanted to use another story of Dorothy's in the same issue. If one was ready she sent it under the nom de plume Stanley Cranshaw.

"Am I just lucky?" Dorothy asked John. The question launched them into one of their continuing discussions.

"What is luck anyway and why do some things fall together rightly for some people and not for others?"

John reminded her of the saying in the business world that the man who starts on his own has to be able and bold, but that he needs a little luck too. "It's a propitious moment for stories," he went on. "Women are reaching out, they're reading more, buying more, doing more. The ten-cent magazines are smart enough to know what this means to them in terms of circulation and advertising."

Dorothy never lacked ideas, but an urgent request from a publisher for a particular story by a particular date met only with amused scorn. "Why, I couldn't write a story to order! An article yes, but not a story. It would be like being asked to fall in love next Friday."

Dorothy might think she was lucky, John knew that she possessed the one ingredient without which skill in words, brimming mind, responsive heart would have lacked motive power, and that was discipline. Dorothy wrote. She rewrote. And, if it was necessary, she did not hesitate to rewrite again. She worked until the words carried her intention, until their sound rang true in her inner ear; until their sense met the demands of her exacting mind. Hard work was something she had learned through other disciplines—games as a child, and as a student, languages and music. She remembered the evenings with Dr. Eckhardt when the string quartet might repeat a passage ten times before it was right.

Some days words came easily and her hand, quick to convey something that had come alive to mind and heart, raced over the page; other days the words came more slowly, but she was never tempted to leave her desk. Her hand moved over the paper. When the work was finished, she tapped out what she had written on the typewriter. Often, when she was reaching for the right word, a memory from the past streamed across her mind. She remembered hearing Grandfather Eli talking to the hired man one morning and telling him that it was time to exhume the potatoes.

John Robinson's face had become, if anything, a trifle more impassive, then he had turned and left the room.

"Grandfather, why didn't you use the right word?" she had asked, looking up from the game she was playing on the floor.

"My dear," he had said humbly, "I couldn't think of dig."

As a writer, she had to think until the right word was achieved. In school in France she had learned to keep at whatever she was doing until she got it right. She had learned to work. Now she put that ability to good use. It was rigorous, this discipline of the creative impulse, more so than any bodily or intellectual discipline ever employed before. It was aided, not by the English composition of her school days, of which she had had little, but by French composition of which she had had a gread deal. Standards of style had been set for her then and had become her own, as were ideals from the great liberal thought of the eighteenth century. Discipline was a word she respected, a process she enjoyed, and the discipline for writing was in writing. Its essence was the honesty that compelled her to see a given situation as it looked to her after long thought on it, with as much depth of divination as she could possibly bring to bear. Honesty was like fresh air to her. She knew she would suffocate without it.

To Dorothy there was no so-called technique in writing which would be of any value in or of itself; nor did she study the use of any special style because she thought style in itself had merit. She used what came to her from the whole body of her observations, as others had before her in the long line of literary tradition. If as a teller of stories, a writer of fiction, she had any secret it was the possession of an inner alchemy. Brooding over a chance event, something within caused it to emerge slowly as the possible raw material of creation. A human happening, meaning little or nothing to most people, became the base for a development of ideas. Much of the long work of thinking out a story was done away from her desk. Dorothy had never been a good sleeper. Waking up in the middle of the night, her mind filled with absorbing reflections, she was not able to go to sleep again until she had followed them through. Often the line of thought was the development of a story. Contemplation, reflection, meditation were mental and spiritual occupations of the dark which prepared the way for her work when she sat down at her desk in the morning.

Dorothy began to read some of her stories to John in their first draft. He was as quick as old Dr. Eckhardt had been to catch shading and nuance. Often he would raise a debatable point and a stop would be made in the forward process. A question of John's could go quickly to the heart of a situation. There were times when his phrasing and rhythm were better than hers. In their supple collaboration it was often not her thought nor his that resulted, but something new to them both. Dorothy, quick to take up the thread, wove it neatly into her fabric.

"Yes, that's good. Yes, that's *much* better!"

After a few of Dorothy's stories had appeared in magazines, Paul Revere Reynolds wrote to her to say that he had just opened a literary agency in New York, and wanted to suggest that he take over the marketing of her writing. Dorothy did not know there was such a thing as a literary agent, but as she had never had time or inclination "to study the market" she thought she would try Mr. Reynolds for six months and see how it went. At least postage would be saved and rejection slips

taken care of. With letters from editors that required attention
being answered by Mr. Reynolds she would have that much
more time for actual writing. Long before the end of the six
months Dorothy was so impressed by his skill in marketing,
and by the prices secured, that she continued to send her stories
to him. When one arrived at his office, he wrote a two-line
note to say it had been safely received. If he could, he sold it,
sending her the check with his ten percent commission de-
ducted. If he couldn't sell a story after submitting it a number
of times, he sent it back telling her what seemed to be the
reason, though he never offered her any literary advice.

"How you write your stories is a matter for you to decide,
not for me," he had said to her. He told her occasionally when
the editor of a certain magazine had said they were looking for
specific material, but it never did Dorothy any good as she was
not able to write fiction "to order."

Material was all around her in the interplay of human lives,
the interweaving action of events. A New England setting was
always convenient for her to use for her ideas as it required
no research to get location and atmosphere right, but she gave
many of her stories cosmopolitan backgrounds. She had always
been interested in people. Growing in years, she had grown in
the capacity to look more deeply into others' lives, to feel more
as others felt. Now, writing what she had long been thinking
about, she set it down with such realism that readers who were
blind to the drama in their neighbors' lives were moved by the
same drama when they read it in her stories.

Arlington was no model village, but it was the world in
miniature: a place where William Blake's "minute particulars"
could be clearly seen and compassionately observed. Under its
elms, over its marble sidewalks, moved people who were part
of that ceaseless pilgrims' progress through the ages which the
eyes of a dwarf in a Velasquez painting had once made her see

so startlingly. They were all a symbol of the great world—
toiling, achieving, doing little or nothing. In them she had her
answer to city people who wondered what country people
did when they were so far from everything: "We just live."
That was it, that was all. "We just find our way through life,
as anybody does."

Many of the stories were rooted in the soil in which she was
rooted. They were stories of courage and starkness, of people
not afraid of sickness or poverty or hard work, people who
accepted life as they accepted the weather. And the weather
meant something to them all. Not a wind that blew but was
particular. It foretold snow or clearing, it could sweep fire
before it or bring rain. The country people she knew might
live embattled lives on a rocky soil but they could hold their
own when city people came to live among them with their
standards of wealth and sophistication. They knew what happiness there was in work well done, what misery in bad temper.
Living close enough to reality to feel its savor, their lives of
steady effort and quiet endurance were full of epic significance.
From one generation to the next they passed on their hard-
learned wisdom.

Words of Uncle Zed's or Grandfather's, or others Dorothy
had listened to years ago, filtered through her storytelling
sieve. She could put into a professor's mouth for her story's
purpose something that had echoed in her mind since childhood.
"Live while you live, and then die and be done with it." She
could make an old soldier sum up a lifelong philosophy to a
young boy, while in her mind she saw a small tousle-haired
girl looking up into the lined face of an old man. "Ay lad . . .
there is no hell but in our own hearts when we do evil; and we
can escape a way out of that by repenting and doing good.
There is no devil but our evil desires, and God gives to every
man strength to fight with those. No man but only your own

heart can tell you what is wrong and what is right. Only *do not fear*, for all is well."

She was tongue for people who said little, whose emotions ran too deep for the surface to reveal; even more than with people her concern was with elementals, with the things that do not change but that affect individual lives. She loved the people she wrote about, as they were; and they liked what she said about them. So did a growing body of readers who saw, in the mirror held up to them and often called Vermont, the vast landscape more aptly named human nature.

Winter came to the mountain world. The Fishers spent regular hours at their desks, made regular trips to the Post Office. Off went the fat envelopes to New York—Dorothy's with her stories, John's with articles and reviews. After work there was skating on the black ice of the old ice-pond, locally known as the Cut-off, skiing when snow covered hills and fields, endless tramps together through the woods, and the same Wordsworthian delight in the frozen countryside which they had felt in the green season. In the evenings, they had music from the pianola, and they read enormously, often aloud; poetry, history, translations from the Greek, solid Victorian novels. They talked. They never tired of exploring each other's minds, delighting to find new areas where they thought alike, or challenged by areas of different approach. Spring came and summer, and Dorothy and John took their first trip away from Arlington when they went by train to Burlington to visit Henry Holt at his home on Lake Champlain.

Doubt and despair about human life in general, her own life in particular, had often assailed Dorothy during the years of her growing up. Now that she felt herself grounded in the shared companionship of married life, the old doubts had begun to dissolve. The good life she had once dreamed of was rapidly becoming the reality. She was happy. She knew that she was happy, from the depths of her being, from the sun's rising to its setting, and through the night. A faith she had once questioned came back to quicken her. She savored, as she had for years, the wisdom to be found in Montaigne. She read Pascal with new understanding, realizing that if he had only been able to feel comradeship with his fellow humans, even a comradeship of misery, his view of life would not have been so black.

"Even if life isn't all good," Dorothy exclaimed to John, "it isn't all bad either. And it's worthwhile to try to make it better."

Come to nearby Manchester for the summer was one of Dorothy's dearest friends, Sally Cleghorn. They had met years ago when Dorothy was sixteen, Sally a few years older, and Sally had said then that from the first moment she met Dorothy she could not take her eyes off her. "No wonder people talk about Dorothy Canfield. I soon began to talk about her myself." During the years, meeting often in Vermont or New York, sharing like thoughts and an interest in writing, they had grown to be sister-close friends. Sally, writing her biography *Threescore*, said of Dorothy—

When I'd begun genuinely to know Dorothy I made the fundamental discovery that she really meant it. All those gracious welcoming ways, that lighted-up look when you came in, weren't forms of politeness at all. They were Vermontishly honest and real. . . . I saw her meet other people, welcome them, and when they had gone retain the same kind of look for them, as she told me about them in the same cordial voice. Then I saw that these were fast colors. . . . She felt that way. . . . She felt that way about old and new friends, bashful strangers, Arlington neighbors, children in the elevator, old gentlemen who had known her great-grandfather. It was as straight from nature as the rich sweetness of maple sugar. . . .

Her cleverness and learning were only the spices that enriched the sweet juices of her nature.

During the summer they met often to read aloud together, Sally her poems, Dorothy the rough draft of a story. "She reads aloud in a clear light voice, in a matter-of-fact manner, never stressing a point, never putting in a footnote, always leaving her narrative to stand alone," Sally wrote. "In the evening, her husband would read aloud—George Meredith's poems, or Dorothy would read Blake's. The attraction I felt in Dorothy was only an intenser degree of what everybody seemed to feel. . . . She fulfilled my two great hungers—my passion for inclusiveness, and my intense desire to see life lived with amenity, with grace, in every direction. To her, every creature seemed an object of respect, of concern, and of a pleasure to behold."

Sally Cleghorn was only one of many good friends in their widening circle. Contrary to what their New York friends had said, Dorothy and John were never isolated from the only social life they thought worthwhile. Now that the year was rounded and work was going well, they made an occasional visit to New York to see Dr. and Mrs. Canfield, hear a concert, attend a theater. Sometimes there was time for a visit to a gallery or museum before the train took them back to Arlington. The first sight of their Green Mountain ridges was always a heart-lifting moment. There was nothing about those tree-clad walls that hedged them in; but there was everything to give a sense of being greatly protected.

By the end of the year, there was enough margin on the ledger, enough work accomplished, to allow them a visit to France.

Chapter 7

Family Circle

It was John's first trip abroad. European civilization with its reminders of great past ages—cathedrals, monuments, ruins, galleries that had long been familiar to Dorothy—now enriched their life in common. Dorothy's Parisian friends welcomed John warmly. Listening to their conversation, and trying to make sense out of their volubility that was so different from the slow puzzling out of three or four pages of Racine or Victor Hugo done for a college course, John learned to speak French as a puppy thrown into a millpond learns to swim.

On March 30th a cable came to tell them that Dr. Canfield had died. Numbed by the news, Dorothy accepted the fact of his death though she did not fully grasp it until the day came when the morning mail brought no letter from him. In a custom begun years ago, he had never failed to write her every day when she was away from home.

Dr. Canfield had often said that the noblest epitaph that could be written for a man was, "He loved the State and was loved by its children." A nation-wide press carried tributes to him; friends across the country wrote letters about him. William Allen White, an old friend and former student, when describing his funeral said—

The last hands to minister to him were those of youth: the boys—the last generation of the long line of boys, a line going back for thirty years—to whom always he was 'Jimmy.' They kept him young and he made them wise.

Dorothy and John returned to Arlington in May to await the birth of their first child. One evening, late in July, after they had been picking wild raspberries, Dorothy was aware of a peculiar pain and thought she had probably eaten too many raspberries. She telephoned the doctor, answering his queries with mild surprise.

"You get right to bed as quick as you can, and I'll come as quick as I can," he said.

Dorothy did as he had told her. Shortly after the doctor arrived, Sally was born. Dorothy and John looked with joy at the small heir of humanity who was now a part of their family circle. Dorothy felt the present moment deepened with overtones of past and future as she gazed at the mountains that framed her immediate world. She felt as peaceably one with the old woman she would grow to be as with the young girl she had outgrown; she felt as much a part of her husband and child as she did of the dearly cherished landscape. The willow that leaned over the brook and was almost a hundred and fifty years old had never grown indifferent to the new leaves it put forth every spring. In a way of wonder that stirred her to endless contemplation, the miracle of birth seemed to have forged even stronger links for her with the life around her.

Sally Cleghorn, for whom the baby was named, was delighted when she was asked to be little Sally Fisher's godmother. She wrote a long poem about Dorothy which was published under the title *Dorothea* in the *American Magazine*—

> Young she is, and slight to view
> In her homemade cambric dresses;
> Are her sweet eyes gray or blue?

Shade of twilight are her tresses.
Fairy-fine at first she seems;
But a longer look confesses
She's more wholesome stuff than dreams.

*   *   *   *

O but in her maiden days
How she led the children trooping
Through the old familiar plays!
Up her sash and flounces looping,
If the tiniest lost his cue,
To his side she ran, and stooping,
Caught his hand and danced him through.

Met you her in Hemlock Wood
In the white midwinter weather,
When the pine's a tufted hood
And the fern's a crystal feather?
Heard you then her yodel sweet
And a far reply, together
Float in echo where they meet?

Ariel voice, from range to range
Lightly tossed and sweetly flying!
All her notes to murmurs change
When the winter light is dying.
All in magic murmurs she
Laps and lulls the wee one lying,
Pearl of twilight, on her knee.

The year 1909 had been a memorable one for them. When John added up the ledger before turning the page to the new year he was pleased at the healthy state of their finances.

Some stories had sold as high as $350, some brought $20. The trip abroad had cost little more than life at home. Second-class return steamship tickets for them both had come to $210. Dorothy's ability to find livable quarters and produce good food for a very few francs kept down the cost of their stay in France. Most of the time between January and May had been spent in Paris, but there had been a few trips to northern France and Belgium. The smallest items were meticulously entered and the total cost of their first trip abroad came to $1000.10. There had been some other expenses, the most important one being Sally's birth. That, including delivery and after care, had come to $45. The year was finished with a working cash balance of $111.88.

A baby in the house was a wonder and joy to them both, and a care in which they both shared; but the baby did not interfere with the schedule of work that had been established. When they had first planned their expenditures, they had set aside money to hire local help for some of the routine housework, but not the cooking. That was something Dorothy delighted in too much to turn over to anyone else. Years of living thriftily in France had given her the knack of running a household economically and she felt about cooking as the French did.

"It's a tool of living," she would say to her American friends, "and excellent results can be obtained with so little money if you care enough."

"You just have a flair for cooking, Dorothy, the way you have for clothes."

She shook her head. "Cooking is far more important than clothes. It's a life element. Dressing only feeds vanity, cooking feeds life. Isn't the well-being of your family a major concern to you? It is to me!"

John replaced the kerosene lamps with a 32-volt electric system which was too small for power but gave each room one hanging bulb. He installed a wood-burning hot-air furnace in the cellar, and rebuilt the sleeping porch so it would take Sally's crib as well as their bed. His vegetable garden flourished. The flock of hens gave all the eggs they needed and a bird now and then for the table. Dorothy finished writing her novel and sent it to *Everybody's* for serialization before publication.

A week later, when Dorothy went to the mailbox, she found in it a long envelope from the editor of *Everybody's*. It contained the biggest check she had ever seen—$3000.

"John! John!" she called, waving the envelope to him as he worked in the garden.

He threw down his hoe and taking the wheelbarrow trundled it to where Dorothy stood, then he picked her up in his arms, put her in the wheelbarrow and pushed her in triumph up the road to the house.

"They've changed the title from *A Suitable Marriage* to *The Squirrel Cage*," Dorothy said after their first ecstasy had passed.

"Well, editors have a way of doing that," John commented. "I'm not sure, Dolly, but that *The Squirrel Cage* doesn't better express your real intent."

"It's what the suitable marriage became."

In the different titles was all that stood between a seed and a full flower. The book had been growing in Dorothy's mind ever since she had been an undergraduate at Ohio State. One evening in her mother's absence, she had been helping out at a faculty party, running between kitchen and parlor with extra cups and plates, passing cakes, helping to dig out ice cream from the freezer. In the midst of all the hubbub, the faculty wives exchanged some kindly gossip. "Such a suitable marriage," Dorothy caught the phrase, but bent on her errand did not catch the names. She would not have known them in any case for people of marriageable years were far removed from a girl of seventeen. The next time she passed she heard her mother's friends discussing what they considered a suitable marriage to be . . . a whisper of wealth . . . a murmur of prestige. Dorothy was shocked. It sounded appallingly vacuous to her, and not at all what she thought real suitability in marriage to be. The phrase lodged in her mind, nudging her gently now and then.

When the book was written it told a contemporary story of a wealthy American family living in Ohio. It was a protest against conformity with the materialistic standards that were then accepted as the only standards. To question them was radical, but Dorothy had been questioning them for a good many years.

When *The Squirrel Cage* was published as a book, *Current Literature*, commenting on it, said that Dorothy Canfield's first novel came as a surprise since she had achieved her success hitherto as a writer of entertaining and salable short stories, but that the book placed her in the vanguard of young novelists who were writing from a full social consciousness, employing vital values versus the whirl of society and the American process of "getting on." The Springfield *Republican* said: "The significance of the book was that the agent of destruction is not a criminal mind but the excess of the very idea which seems to be at the root of our present society." The New York *Evening Post* wrote: "We recall no recent interpretation of American life which has possessed more of dignity and less of shrillness than this—uncompromising as it is."

A copy was sent in a parcel of books for review to a man vacationing in Michigan whose influence in the literary world was far-reaching. He read it first of all the books in the parcel because the name of the author was unknown to him. The title had beguiled him and the first paragraph caught his interest. He read the book with steadily increasing admiration, feeling that it contained unmistakable evidence that its author was a genuine, realistic—without being sensational—writer. Somewhere during its perusal, he caught the sound of the voice of a thesis-haunted girl in his study in New Haven. He wrote a letter to her in care of the publisher asking if it were really she. He received a letter in reply, confirming his suspicion.

"What a development!" William Lyon Phelps wrote. "The girl had become a Ph.D., a wife, and a novelist! As I considered *The Squirrel Cage* I thought how strange it was that this author had ever supposed her 'vocation' lay in Old French or in any-thing other than creative work. . . . I dare say that her labor in old French was not fruitless; the painstaking accuracy of that thesis was transferred to a wider and more interesting domain. Her education in France, where precision of language is thought to be important, was as valuable for her as for her older contemporaries, Anne Sedgwick and Edith Wharton."

With such a windfall as the check from *Everybody's*, John and Dorothy decided that there was no reason at all why they should not go to Europe again. Few countries required pass-ports or any lengthy formalities; the baby was healthy and adaptable. In October they went to Rome to spend the winter, accompanied by Flavia, Sally Cleghorn and her aunt, and joined later by another friend. Dorothy spoke Italian well and was constantly called on to translate for everything that pertained to the business of living as well as trips to the dentist, encounters with lawyers, and all kinds of extras incurred by a group of active people.

Before leaving New York, William Morrow, who was soon to publish a book by Madame Montessori on her pedagogical system, had asked Dorothy to call at the school in Rome and talk with Madame Montessori regarding one of the chapters in the book. Dorothy's call at the Casa di Bambini lengthened into several visits so interested did she become in the work being done and so fully did it complement many of her own educational ideas, giving them practical working support.

Watching the children at the Casa di Bambini, she wondered at first why one of the teachers did not help a little girl's fumbling fingers on a button as she herself had so often helped Sally. "No, dear, Mother can do that so much better. Let Mother do it." But she realized, when the child finally accomplished the near-miracle, that had a teacher or parent, no matter how well-intentioned, intervened it would have been as if a professional had seized the cue from John's hands in the midst of a fascinating game of billiards and said, "You just stand and watch me do this. I can do it much better than you."

There was something so restful and unhurried at the school that it made Dorothy wonder about the need for haste in the American way of life. What was it hurrying so to accomplish? She had always felt scorn for the parties of Cook's tourists, clattering into the Sistine Chapel for a momentary glance at the achievement of a lifetime of genius, then hurrying on down through the *Stanze of Raphael.* Instead of really training children, perhaps some educational methods were dragging them on a Cook's Tour through life.

The Casa di Bambini children were to all appearances given freedom, but that freedom was contingent on their not hurting or annoying another. Wasn't it through just such freedom that the principle of democracy developed? Dorothy asked herself. She had long been convinced that totalitarian authority was wrong, in teaching or governing, as it strangled the natural growth of the individual. Step by step these children were being led from self-control, through self-discipline, to self-government. Learning to help themselves and consider others was growth away from the imprisonment of selfish interests which had always been the age-old enemy of humanity.

Hadn't the great Pestalozzi said, "I have found that no man

in God's wide earth is able to help any other man. Help must come from the bosom alone." And there was a saying in Vermont, "Every child has got to do his own growing." Every bean placed in the ground had to grow because it was governed from within by the mysterious element of life. Dorothy saw clearly that any help not positively necessary was a hindrance to any growing organism: the gardener's part, or the teacher's, was to enrich the soil.

On their return to Arlington in the spring, Dorothy noticed that people greeted them with more interest than was usually given home-coming travelers and with eager demands to hear all she had done. Often the questions were so similar that she grew tired of answering them. "You've seen the Montessori schools, you've met Dr. Montessori, tell us all about it. Is it really so wonderful or is it just a fad?"

"Is it true that the children are allowed to do exactly as they please? Doesn't it spoil them beyond endurance?"

"Do they really learn to read and write so young? Isn't it bad to stimulate them so unnaturally?"

"What is there in it for *our* children?"

"There've been any number of articles in the magazines," Dorothy replied. "Madame Montessori's book has been published. You'll find your answers in them."

"But you've been an eyewitness. There are all sorts of practical questions you can answer for us."

"You are a parent like us. Will the new system really work?"

Clearly there was nothing for Dorothy to do but write a book herself. She had been greatly impressed by the Montessori system and she had thought deeply on its value in teaching the rudiments of learning as well as the fundamental matters of the conduct of life. Its usefulness depended on its comprehension by the greatest possible number. To remain not a theory but become a practice, everyone would have to collaborate. She could aid that by putting her impressions into book form, writing as an American parent who desired the best possible chance for her child and addressing herself to the innumerable legion of her companions in that desire.

She wrote the book *The Montessori Mother*. It was not a translation but a simplification and adaptation in an easy, half-humorous style of the Montessori system for American mothers. The questions people had asked her were answered in the book which Dorothy signed for the first time with her full name, Dorothy Canfield Fisher. She had written it as a married woman, as a mother, and as an impassioned educator. Some part of her that linked her back to a long line of educators rejoiced when the book was published. It was one of the first books to mark a progressive trend in education. Publication in Canada, England and India soon followed, as well as translation into several foreign languages. The book was disapproved of in Germany and attacked as "anarchic subversion." It was years before a German edition was published.

Many of the magazines were now beginning to carry articles on the rearing of children. Dorothy wrote a series which incorporated what she had absorbed in Rome as well as what she was putting into practice in her own household. The sensitive, high-spirited Sally was fast moving out of babyhood and Dorothy found that it was not only the new principles that were needed but the old theories that had proved worth preserving. Letters in response to the articles encouraged her to develop them into a book.

Mothers and Children was published. Her words challenged current custom. There were some readers who said, "This can't be done. It's against human nature."

Remarks such as that were like a roll of drums to Dorothy and she welcomed any opportunity to explain further and defend her views. Often asked to speak before groups interested in progressive education, she accepted willingly. It added to their income and gave her contact with large numbers of people. Conscious that some of her listeners were shocked, she knew that there were many who agreed with her. Questions bristled. She had never liked formulas, but she found that she had to fall back on one for a particular question that was voiced by someone in almost every audience.

"Tell me, Mrs. Fisher, would you or would you not spank a child who refused to obey?"

"I'll answer your question if you'll answer one of mine first."

"All right. Ask it."

"How big is a house?"

The questioner looked puzzled. "Which house?"

Like a tennis player deftly placing a ball, Dorothy replied, "Well then, which child?"

In the Fisher house there were many mementoes of travel. Some, that had no immediate use, were put in the attic. With them, Dorothy now placed her violin. Life was rich and full, so much so that she could bring herself to part with this old responsive friend. She hoped that she would always be able to listen to music, but to make it was no longer possible for her. The infrequent examination of her ears had confirmed her own suspicion that they registered differently. She could never be entirely sure when playing that she was sounding the right note; but when writing she could be sure of the right word on a page.

The more she wrote, the more there was to say, and though she felt that writing on educational matters was distinctly worthwhile she was far more interested in the attempt to convey her ideas through fiction. She felt that one of her early observations was constantly being confirmed: fewer converts were made by straight exhortation than by apt parables. She knew that she could best express abstract truths in the form of human drama. Her love of liberty and fair play, her hatred for cruelty and the tyranny of caste, her contempt for the spirit of competition that carried one to the top by pushing another down, made their way through her writing to a widening and increasingly articulate circle of readers. The spring from which she drew was replenished in the events of life around her. A tragedy happened at one of the neighbors'. She wrote her mother a long description of it and concluded, "I must try to forget it since I can't do anybody any good by thinking of it." But it lodged in her mind. Worked upon by her imagination, the tragedy took its own dramatic form until from it a story grew.

"Did it happen just like that?" a friend asked.

Dorothy closed her eyes a little, a habit of hers as she saw beyond the particular to the general. "Not just like that," she answered.

Those near her knew, sometimes only John knew, what the ingredients for a story had been—a chance happening, a turn of phrase, sometimes no more than a revealing look in the eyes of an acquaintance; but each one had a living element. With her perception and constantly developing skill, she could recreate a scene or an event so vividly that her readers thought it must be a factual replica of something that had actually happened to her.

"Not at all, not at all," she would say, and then smile disarmingly.

Often, during the mild weather, John and Dorothy sat on the porch after sunset talking with friends or neighbors, watching the twilight slide down the mountain to meet the mist rising from the Battenkill. Scent of lilacs might be on the air, flowering wild grape, or the strong clean breath from newly plowed fields. Unconsciously people would begin to drop their voices as if to harmonize with the dimming light. Dorothy would get up and change to another chair to bring the better of her two ears close to the visitor whose talk interested her; sometimes, with an impulsive gesture, she would suggest that they all move into the lamp-lit room. Surprised at her request, for the evening might be mild and the slow appearing of stars in the sky that roofed the valley something lovely to see, they would comply. John, knowing that Dorothy had begun to rely on lip reading to aid her hearing, realized acutely that she was helpless in the twilight. He knew that she would carry on in her lone struggle as long as possible, for she was as stoic about her own troubles as she was compassionate in the troubles of others. But he knew, as she did, that her struggle was hopeless.

On a mountain's flank two miles from the village, their living was self-contained and self-reliant. John cut and stacked cords of firewood for the furnace to consume during the winter months; he harvested ice and packed it in sawdust for the summer months. His vegetable garden grew with the years, producing most of the food the family ate during the summer and a great deal that was stored for the winter. Carpentering and plumbing made demands on him; but he found time to help Dorothy with typing and proofreading, and he had, all along, rare delight in the companionship of their growing daughter.

The small old barn north of the house that broke the force of winter winds sheltered their chickens, the brown mare who was their link with the world in good weather or poor, and the sleek cat who could be counted on for recurrent families of kittens. Now, in this year of 1913, it welcomed a new occupant—their first Ford. It became their occupation, transporting them back to the joys of childhood and forward into unexplored emotions of the future. To whirl over their familiar country roads at four times the speed of a trotting horse was a thrilling experience. John was in his element. As there was no garage near, he was constantly having to tinker with the car. Dorothy was enchanted with it. Coming back from a drive of forty miles around their green countryside at a reckless pace of twenty miles an hour, she felt that the world rather than a throttle was at her hand.

Gradually all of the Canfield land came into the possession of Dorothy and her brother James. The open pastures in the valley were let out to farmer-neighbors, but there were several hundred acres on the rising slope of Red Mountain that were too poor for any use. There was only one answer: reforestation. Dorothy and John investigated the possibilities of land improvement by planting pine trees.

Ten thousand white pines, costing five dollars a thousand, were ordered from the State Forestry Department. Plans were made to set them out as soon as the frost was out of the ground. John and Dorothy, James and his wife Stella, and six neighbors worked at planting the three-inch trees as the forester had showed them. There was nothing to be seen in the rock-strewn old pasture even after two days' work, fifty dollars paid to the State Forestry Department and two days' wages at two dollars a day to six men.

"John, can anything come of such an effort?"

His guess was as good as hers.

"Just look over there and see the Fishers' pine forest," Arlington folk remarked humorously as they pointed to a bare dry hillside with nothing green visible.

Dorothy and John often felt dubious, for the minute specks of trees seemed to stand still though all through the first summer weeds and grass and brambles grew around them.

One day, when Dorothy was coming home from berrying, Sally ran ahead of her. Dorothy watched the plump little girl jumping up and down in the field and wondered which of her many games she was playing. "Whatever are you doing, Sally?" she called.

"Jumping over the pine trees, Mummy, so when I am big and they are big, I can tell my little girl I once jumped over their tops."

A few months later the little pines were blanketed by an early snowfall.

When Christmas week came it was a very special time to the Fishers, for their son James, named after Dorothy's father, was born.

Chapter 8

Demanding Days and the Heart's Response

DOROTHY's morning hours were dedicated to work; the rest of the day belonged to family and household. As the children emerged from the golden age of cocoon-like babyhood, she found that teaching them the complex rules of the human game was an engrossing procedure. In one of her published articles Dorothy made a confession of faith, feeling that all women who filled two roles as she did were honor-bound to give themselves some such test in their daily lives. "I owe a *debt to my children*," she wrote. "Having brought them into the world, their father and I owe it to them to furnish them a happy, free life of physical health, cheerful industry, intellectual growth, and moral dignity and sanity. To pay my part of this debt I have at my command a certain amount of money, physical strength, intellectual vigor, nervous energy and spiritual force. If I am to keep my honor untarnished I must, as every honest debtor does, use my resources *first of all* to keep up the payments on my debt."

During the early summer of 1914, a shadow began to fall over Europe which the Fishers' French friends found hard to admit and their American neighbors harder to believe. The letters from France ceased, and newspapers told of the armed might of Germany rolling across Belgium, crushing people as if they were cobblestones; rolling on until stopped by the reckless, determined valor of the French army. Dorothy felt as if she herself had been stabbed by a bayonet. When the letters began to come again they were far more grim and sad than any account the newspapers carried. Dorothy and John talked endlessly of what they could do, must do, for a country and people they loved deeply.

One evening during the summer as they sat on the porch and watched the sunset light fade, Dorothy read aloud from Robert Frost's newly published *North of Boston.*

"What cool, heart-refreshing naturalness," Sally Cleghorn commented.

In the silence following Dorothy's reading, each one felt an affirmation of the spirit, desperately needed at a time when war thundered at the edges of their world.

Until the way became clear to help in the war effort, they did the work at hand, planting another ten acres of pines, continuing their writing. Baby James was growing sturdily. Sally had started school in the little schoolhouse where Dorothy's great-grandfather had said his A—B's. Four generations had passed and almost nothing had been done in all those years for the stony playground and small frame building that had always been thought sound enough. Dorothy wrote an account which was published in the *Delineator* about the way in which the people of the North District raised funds to improve their school—

. . . we are a slow-living, slow-changing set, we Vermont mountaineers. . . . Perhaps that is why, when the project of 'doing something for the schoolhouse' gradually began to grow . . . our thoughts turned naturally to the old times . . . and there came the idea of being our great-grandparents. It was not to be a play—no, for it was to be real. We were not to act a part—no, for it is not acting to be your own great-grandfather. We 'North District people' of 1915 would simply bring to life the North District people of 1791 and show them to the rest of the town. . . .

If we were all to have a part in the play (and we all wanted to be in the fun), it must represent some old-time occasion when people would naturally gather together. . . . So an eighteenth-century Thanksgiving party it was. Yes, so simple as that is the creation of drama when you plant it and let it grow. . . .

Then . . . up comes the audience swarming on the stage: 'There're some folks here from Manchester, and they want you should give it there.' 'A couple of teams came up from South Shaftesbury, and they're asking if you won't give it in their Town Hall.'

Some one else says, dubiously, 'Of course you took in a lot of money, but your expenses must have been enormous.'

We look at each other calculatingly. 'Let's see, what *are* our expenses? Why—' we are astonished, ourselves—'our expenses are just exactly nothing at all!' Yes, all that we made can go to the transformation of the dreary little schoolhouse and grounds into the natural, cheerful, attractive children's school home, which we long to see it. . . .

What we can't understand is why all these people, who ask to see our play, don't grow one of their own, with their own traditions and jokes and ancestors. . . .

Rejoicing in the fun we have had out of our own plunge, we call out to similar communities, north, south, east and west, 'Dramatize your own past. Be your own great-grandfathers.'

Hillsboro People, a collection of short stories that included several of Sally Cleghorn's poems, was published, soon to be followed by Dorothy's novel *The Bent Twig*. She had begun the novel shortly after finishing *The Squirrel Cage* while her mind was still filled with thoughts of her heroine whose sensitive spirit had been almost broken by her upbringing at the hands of well-meaning but materialistic parents. "Can I honestly pretend," Dorothy asked herself, "that a different home atmosphere would have solved her problems? What about a daughter with a forceful personality of her own? Won't she feel that she is being starved on a diet of bread and cheese and Emerson? Won't she rebel as soon as she gets the chance and go after *paté de fois gras*, champagne and pseudo-sophistication?" Dorothy thought she would.

But, as such a daughter became mature, might she not have character enough before it was too late to swing back to a way of life that was free and her own? Yes, Dorothy decided, if the simplicity of her parents' life rested on conviction, and if she had intelligence and depth of feeling enough to distinguish finally between reality and sham.

With the basis for a novel of character conflict, the only kind she ever wanted to write, Dorothy then asked herself, "What is the deepest thing I want to say? Is it the color line that is the rotten spot in American democracy? Is it the exploitation of workers? Is it the relationship between parents and children?" She said them all, and more, while expressing her firm conviction that, though young people must be exposed to many experiences, they will make their own decisions well if their parents have built strength into them.

Some critics felt she was too violent. John did not.

"You can't make much of a symphony if you use only the flutes and oboes," he said. "What are the drums and trumpets for? What indeed but to blare out that some themes are not for hair-splitting intelligence but, addressed to the primitive, the fundamental, they go straight to the heart!"

Dorothy wrote an educational book, *Self-Reliance*, for the Childhood and Youth Series. It said what she had been saying in her talks to New England audiences and it stirred up the same kind of lively interest and controversy.

The movement for Women's Suffrage was being taken up by many people, both men and women. Dorothy considered the vote a logical advance but was never able to get particularly excited about it. Her faith was in the working of events and she felt that suffrage would come as a natural outgrowth of women interested in life beyond their homes. However, when Henry Holt asked her to write one of the chapters in a composite novel, *The Sturdy Oak*, Dorothy agreed. Fourteen American authors developed the story progressively and all profits from the book went to the Women's Suffrage Movement.

By 1916, when the war news was grimmest, the Fishers came to a decision. John sailed for France in April to enter the American Field Service. Dorothy and the children planned to join him as soon as necessary arrangements could be made and work already started brought to completion. She had learned long ago, she was saying it with everything she wrote, that anything was better than to let a barrier grow up between parents, or between parents and children. Advantages beyond reckoning would belong to all of them as they shared in generous-hearted action.

Visits were made to the family in Pleasantville, the family in Swiftwater. The house was rented. Sally went to camp. Dorothy and Jimmy stayed in a nearby village, and she devoted time and energy to the work that must be finished before she could leave for France. Long, swiftly written letters went to the family circle. She poured out in them her love and her heartache, related stories of the children's doings and sayings, relayed John's news and copied excerpts from his letters. It made her want to cry with happiness when she thought of the affection she had for them all and their affection for her. "Oh dear, what a heavy heart I have about leaving so many people, to balance up the redeemed-out-of-captivity feeling I have about seeing John again! . . . I just don't dare let myself think about leaving you all whom I do love so dearly. . . . What a fearfully distracting, perplexing and heart-searching business it is to live."

Sometimes the letters could not be long: "This isn't a letter—only a kiss thrown to you, over all these weary miles between us!" Heart-close they were to her and she would always keep them so, "dear faithful people on the very thought of whom I rest myself."

One of the tasks she had to finish was a book for children which Alfred Harcourt had persuaded her to write, *Understood Betsy*. Drawing on memories of her own little girlhood, using the countryside she knew well and placing her story on a farm which provided plenty of material for self-reliance, Dorothy said in narrative form what she had said in her three educational books.

Early every evening, taking Jimmy along, Dorothy drove over to Sally's camp and read the story aloud, chapter by finished chapter. The little girls enjoyed the story and their comments and questions heartened Dorothy for the next day's work.

"Where does Cousin Ann really live?" was a question often asked.

How to answer—for Cousin Ann, real as she had come to be on the pages of a book, was Dorothy's feeling for all that was best in the older generation.

Writing *Understood Betsy* in the mornings left Dorothy free to work with Sally Cleghorn in the afternoons on a book they were writing together.

"Just one of Dolly's combinations," Dorothy's brother James had commented when told of the project.

Sitting on the grass in the orchard, the two friends took out their manuscripts from baskets more accustomed to hold sewing. Weighting loose pages down with apples, they read their dialogues aloud, for *Fellow-Captains* was to be a series of conversations among a group of five women.

Dorothy, in a rapid easy manner, read through a first draft. If it seemed a trifle angular they worked over it until it satisfied them. Sally wrote later that it was

always illuminating to see Dorothy in process of stabilizing all she writes by her constant re-pinning of it fast to the common lot, to generic human experience. Her greatest achievement lies in her power to stand firmly on this realistic ground while at the same time she pulls a possible future right through the present. . . . Teachers do it for individual children, whom they know fairly well; Dorothy does it for an unknown multitude. In her public speaking there's the same double reflection of the audience—a picture soberly true, yet expanding under its own eyes, in full daylight, into a whole category of its possibilities.

In developing the dialogues, Sally's cloud-high idealism was often brought down to earth by her friend's robust common sense. "Let's dig down together, to all our respective foundations, right now," Dorothy said. "Come on, everybody. What are yours. . . ."

So they discussed God. To most of them he seemed like a glorified human father, but not to Dorothy. "I never had much of that feeling about my father, for all I loved him so dearly. Even as a very little girl, I knew perfectly well that I was the one who had to stand the pain of the tooth-pulling, no matter who held my hand. And I feel that way now a good deal; that I must stand on my own feet and bear my own burdens and have plain, sheer endurance for a daily ingredient in my life; and mustn't try to throw the responsibility upon anybody else —not even on God—even if I had that personal idea of God, which I haven't at all. . . .

"I haven't a bit of the mystic in me, you know, and I get dizzy at the very idea of contemplation. . . . I used to depend entirely on what the Quakers call 'the inner light' (what the rest of us call conscience) and just try to do the best I could from day to day. . . . But a question of little Sally's brought home to me what that inner light really means to me. Haven't you noticed how the children are always making you go to the heart of things? Sally came to me one day when she was about four years old, with her great friend and playmate, Lillian. She said, 'Mother, what is God? Lillian says he's an old man with a white beard who lives up on top of Red Mountain and looks down on us.'

"Well, there I was, face to face with the question I'd been dodging all my life. Sally looked up at me confidently and I had to answer. And in trying to make it simple enough for a four-year-old child to understand, I made it, for the first time, simple enough so that I could understand. I said right away, as though I'd had that answer ready for years, 'Why, little daughter, I think that God is the feeling in our hearts that makes us want to do what's right. . . . '

"And ever since then I've realized that I trust the inner light because I really believe, even in my blackest moments, that there is something immortal and eternal in it."

Essentials came up for discussion. Dorothy was all for a balanced ration in life with plenty of earthiness, humor, homely pleasures, plain tonic roughness and activity that harked back to the days when physical necessities made up a large share of life. "What *does* seem essential to me," Dorothy continued, "is a clear diagnosis of what's wrong with me, before I undertake to set it right. I don't really see how anybody can call up his best strength and send it out to do battle unless he knows what he's fighting against."

Dorothy told of a device she had made use of from something learned years ago when one of her aunts had started her off with a little savings-bank account. She banked in her mind the fine, beautiful, joyful things that happened to her or of which she became aware, and drew on them when distressing things hap-

pened. Often there were times when she had need to draw on
her account of beauty, strength, success to offset the drain made
on vitality by ugliness and failure. "Many's and many's the
time, when my job has been to keep something back—a rising
flood of exasperation, the slow advance of disheartenment, or
tears, perhaps—I've put the strength of the Kensico dam at my
back and braced myself against it."

Some of Sally Cleghorn's poems and selections from Dorothy's notebook of quotations completed what the two friends
referred to as their "Home Grown Secrets of Serenity." At a
time when the world was being greatly shaken, *Fellow Captains*
spoke out confidently for the things that remained.

Dorothy finished reading proof on a second collection of her
short stories which would shortly appear in book form as *The
Real Motive*. The date of her sailing for France, August 5th,
was drawing near. One of the final tasks she gave herself was
to answer the many letters that were piled on her desk. The
fundamental truth in her stories made a bridge between herself
and her readers. It was no one-way passage over the bridge, for
back to her came letters from people who read the stories. Then
back to them went her own appreciation of their words. Master
of her time as her father had always been of his, Dorothy was
able to write one last long letter before the Rochambeau sailed.

Grand Central Station
New York City
August 3, 1916

Dear Professor Phelps:

I've been trying desperately to find a moment in which I might
write you, but packing and children, and getting our house ready
to leave for the winter and saying good-byes have so more than
filled every moment that it's only now, at five in the morning, as I
arrive from Vermont on an early train, that I see a breathing-space,

and feel I can write you the "report" I've been wanting so much to make to you. For, do you know, I feel that I owe you an accounting for what I do. That's one of the penalties you pay for your generous interest and sympathy! I really want you to know what I'm up to, for I'm counting on your help to make the most I can out of my life.

. . . I am going to France, . . . for the very simple, elemental reason that my husband is there, and that we are the kind of husband-and-wife who find it almost intolerable to be separated. Life's too short to miss any of that perfect companionship! . . . I'm going to establish a quiet little French home in a suburb of Paris, near the American Ambulance in Neuilly where my husband will be, for the most part, in service, and just live there through the winter to come, instead of on our Vermont mountain side. I'm not going to write, because I've written a great deal this last year, and I want to give myself time to do a lot of thinking and living before undertaking anything new. And I hope our two children will enjoy their French winter as much as a Vermont one. . . . It all seems quite simple and natural to me, my husband giving up a year of his life to France, and I going to live near my dear French friends in this very dark moment of their lives—like going to help out one's cousins in need. I think we'll both be happier all our lives to have done this. I hate war . . . but like nearly all of my generation I'm terribly, tragically bewildered by the complexity of the situation. And it will ease an aching heart to do the simple, obvious, human thing, even if it is not very deep or far-reaching, establish a home near my husband who is alleviating pain, and fill my house, small though it will be, with a succession of homeless Belgian and French children who can share in the mothering I give to my own. . . .

Chapter 9

War Years in France

DOROTHY did exactly as she had said. A month later she wrote to her family, "I'm sitting in a charming little garden, which is ours for the next two months, and the children, rosy and happy, are playing on the grass." Around her were heartbreaking evidences of a war-weary world but what mattered most during those first weeks was the safe acclimatization of her children. When they later moved to an apartment in Paris, her passion for homemaking soon turned it into a world of their own as the boxes from Arlington arrived and familiar articles took their places among the French furnishings. The rooms rang out with a clear brave note of friendly things chosen because they gave pleasure and comfort and spelled home.

During one of John's leaves, they packed a luncheon basket and took the children to Chartres to see the cathedral. The heavyheartedness of wartime did its best to make people forget that beautiful things still existed. Fighting, disaster, suffering, death filled minds, dominated conversations. Dorothy had not felt in a mood to be impressed by the cathedral but she wrote to her family, "I hadn't more than stepped in before the unearthly beauty and impressiveness of that nave swept my mind clear of everything but the thought, *'Men* did this! The same men who are making the war. They did this and they will do it again, when this war is a forgotten bad dream.' After a while Sally whispered, 'Why Mother, what is that on your cheek?' and I saw I was crying . . . very happy tears."

John felt that they were all responsible for the war.

Dorothy wondered if the suffering the world was going through might not be comparable to human birth. "Perhaps the world is trying to give birth to a new idea," she said. "People have talked about it for ages, but never really felt it before—the idea that all of us, each of us just as you said, is responsible for what happens to all, to each. It's like a new baby—it costs agony, it needs protection, but it's alive, it will grow."

"Discussions in this world of 1916 are not apt to be very cheerful," she wrote home, "especially if one member of the party is John, who is not very cheerful about the war and its meaning. Well, I'm not myself, but I have more of a willful determination to see the hopeful side of things. John calls it just bull-headed on my part, but I have a feeling, deep-rooted as the necessity to breathe, that if we just hold on hard now, through this time, the eternal elements will come into view again. John says sceptically, maybe they aren't so durned eternal as we have been thinking."

Music was one of her compensations and there were frequent concerts. No one dressed for them and a ticket could be bought for a few *sous*. Across the anguish of the time, the assured dignity and worth of old friends spoke clearly—Beethoven, Bach. Who would say the human race was ignoble who knew those voices, thought Dorothy, as listening to them she felt new life flow into her.

Distant gunfire punctuated the days and life in Paris was full of privations and grim reminders, but Dorothy had many sources of strength. One was in a snapshot pinned over her desk. It was of John's tennis partner in undergraduate days playing monkey-on-a-stick on the tennis court to express his delight at having won a match over John. In July, when she had been packing, she had looked for some cheerful object that would be a bright spot in the dark days, and she had chosen that picture. It was so full of life, good humor, zest that it made her laugh just to look at it; and if she was too tired to laugh, it never failed to make her smile.

A letter from home brought a newspaper clipping telling of the woman at a fashionable Rangeley Lakes hotel who had posed as Dorothy Canfield, the successful author of *The Bent Twig*. "Just what action the real Dorothy Canfield will take when she learns of the use of her name is not known." Dorothy wrote her family that she was too busy to enter into any controversy. "I don't see what harm it could do but a lie is always a good thing to step on on general principles, because you never know how far it may go." She had begun to wonder if she had left her writing self, and the recognition that had been coming to her, back in America. Here she was known as Lieutenant Fisher's wife, and he was known far beyond his own Ambulance Section as a superb mechanic, a man who could get anything to run. Now, as head of his section, he had a double row of braid across his uniform. "Honorary nothing-in-particular," he announced to Dorothy.

Alfred Harcourt wrote that *St. Nicholas* had accepted *Understood Betsy* for serial publication. "I'm ever so much pleased," Dorothy replied, "both financially (though of course a children's magazine isn't such a tremendous prize financially as a grown-up) and because I like to appear in *St. Nicholas*, childish associations, I suppose."

Sally started school at the Lycée Lamartine. Dorothy found a peasant woman and her daughter to help in the house, as well as a young girl who was a physical education student to stay with the children when she was out. "They are allowed to do anything they want so long as it's not wrong," Dorothy told the student.

Then she began to devote her free time to relief work at the

Phare. Because of the lack of helmets during the early days
of the war, many soldiers had been blinded by bursting shrap-
nel. Provisions for their care had been made, but there were
few provisions for their re-education and reading matter was
greatly needed. Henry Holt's daughter, Winifred, who had
worked with the Lighthouse in New York, had arrived in Paris
with willingness to help, a good deal of money, and no knowledge of French. Dorothy, acting as translator and organizer,
began writing simple stories to be published in Braille and distributed to all institutions for the blind in France. With homemade presses and against many odds they worked until more
efficient Braille printing presses could be imported from
America.

Dorothy had never felt more conscious of her small size than
she did during the hours spent in long lines waiting for ration
cards; but her body that had been toughened and strengthened
in play long ago served her without complaint. Everyday sanity
came to her aid and when her work was over at the Phare she
hurried back to the children. In the park, watching them as
they rolled their hoops and shouted gleefully, she felt herself
responding to their marvelous quickening, thrusting her heavi-
ness aside as the elm in the pasture at home had split the granite
at its base. Holding her head high, she forced herself to draw
one long regular breath after another. Even in the midst of
the tragedy and suffering of that spring of 1917, something
came to her mind to persuade her that the anguish was not
eternal. It was a line from a history book that she had studied
when she was not much older than Sally: "The ancient Gauls
said they feared nothing; not enemies, not tempest, not
death. Until the skies fell upon their heads, they would never
submit."

Letters to and from the family circle in America were a line
of life. "I live on letters!" Dorothy said as she poured out her
heart in them. At home, a friend reading her letters suggested

they be sent to the *Atlantic*. Dorothy did not want that, insisting that her letters were only of "entirely domestic, common, material episodes." "John thinks of the apple trees and little pines and how he could improve the garden. I think of the peace and quiet of the 'Little House,' strewn with papers, and with the sun coming in on my desk." Achingly in her heart was a homesickness to be in a country not darkened by the night of war. She longed to be once again among people who were living their daily lives in peace. Sally Cleghorn sensed the strain her friend was under. "Dorothy's letters were rather panting, as if with carrying a huge load of vicarious sorrow."

Dorothy sent home a picture of herself on the steps of the Phare, along with some photographs of the children, and of John. Few of her friends realized that she weighed less than ninety pounds.

From Arlington came a letter saying that some of the century-old pines on the northern edge of their land should be cut. "Be sure you leave some seed trees!" Dorothy and John replied. Instructions were followed and a check amounting to $890 for the lumber was sent to them. Checks began to come in from Dorothy's books. Letters from friends contained money orders for relief work. Dorothy established a Fund to Aid French Children, telling her friends what she had done.

"Two or three days ago came a notice, saying that Mrs. Thomas had sent me frs. 233," she wrote. "The size of this sum quite staggered me, as I had not begun to hope for any such big contributions and had only thought of small sums from a number of people. This morning's mail brought a letter from Betty Fisher, enclosing a thumping big money order . . . and yesterday's mail brought a notice from a Paris Bank, saying that Mrs. Emery, of Cincinnati, had sent, by telegraph, 500 francs to be paid to me. . . . You can think how immensely relieved I feel to know that that plan is going on so well, and how very proud I am of my American circle."

Dorothy with Sally and Jimmy.
1915.

With Jimmy and "Prince."
1923.

Dorothy on the steps of the Phare, Paris, 1917.
She wrote a message to her family on the photograph.

In March her letters to the Fisher family told of a throat infection she had been nursing without success. "My throat and ear don't get better as they ought to and, against all my principles, I'm going to see a specialist this afternoon to see if he can suggest something. If it weren't for my fear of deafness I think I'd worry along without specialists. . . ." A letter followed her visit to the specialist: "He sees no reason to think my deafness will greatly increase, *if* I keep my general health good. Same old story, you see. As to the intense pain in my throat and ears, that is due, he thinks, to pressure from the nerve on the enlarged gland on my neck, which has become considerably larger in the last few months. He thinks that must be treated at once, and sends me to another doctor whom I am to see on Monday. . . . No more time, dear, *dear* folks! John is fearfully homesick and awfully tired of his devouring job. But *very* proud of the number of volunteers who make it devouring, and both of us very happy to be here—'happy'? That's too big a word for 1917—you know what I mean."

Soon she wrote to the Canfield family, "I have been to see two specialists since I last wrote you, and have come away considerably lighter in purse and not very much wiser than I was before, because they told me nothing new. . . . I remember . . . when Sally was a little thing . . . Dr. Cochrane's giving me some advice and saying that what I needed more than anything else was to say about other people's affairs and things: 'I don't give a damn about that.' The French specialist put in very elegant French precisely the same advice, so that, even as he talked, I burst out into a fit of laughter, remembering the homely Anglo-Saxon vigor of Cochrane's previous counsel! The upshot of it is that they neither of them will undertake to do anything for me, that I have got to take charge of myself. . . . I now promise solemnly to follow all the good advice that has been given me at such a high price, until I am quite restored. Well, that is enough of a not very important topic. . . . John foams and frets about the Ford chassis that won't come up from Bordeaux when they are promised and about the impossibility of getting men out to the Front as fast as they ought to go. . . . I spend so much time compressing articles for Braille publication and figuring out with Cohn exactly how many lines to put on a page, and how many words to a line, in order to fit the matter neatly on to the brass plaques, that, as so often happens in real life, I quite lose myself in the mass of details and it comes to me once in a while, with a start and with such a sense of sudden happiness as you can imagine, that, after all, I am really doing something useful for the war blind!"

When the Braille printing press was running competently, the work was turned over to Marguerite Fischbacher, the daughter of the French publisher of Dorothy's books. The Conseil d'Administration du Phare presented Dorothy with a silver medal for her "great service rendered the war blind." She accepted it with appreciation of its significance.

"But whatever can anybody *do* with a medal!" she exclaimed to John.

They were at Versailles for the day and the children were scampering ahead of them over grass white with petals from blossoming trees. Dorothy found herself looking through the loveliness around her back to the hospital where men had almost lost desire to live, back to the Paris streets with their many thin black-veiled women. "I had almost the illusion that all that beauty about me was like transparent stained glass through which I saw the rest of France."

Then the United States entered the war.

"Now we can hang out *our* flag from *our* balcony!" Sally said.

Dorothy unpacked from the trunk, where she had placed it the summer before, the flag which had fluttered from the small pine staff at the Arlington house to celebrate famous birthdays. The children waved to the soldiers as they marched by. John saluted soberly. Dorothy felt her eyes fill with sudden tears of pride and love and homesickness as the French breeze fluttered the silk folds of the stars and stripes. "What birthday is it celebrating now?" she asked herself.

"Oh, Mother, why do you look so sad?" Sally asked, as she took her mother's hand. "You and Father work all the time to help in the war, aren't you glad our country is coming in to help, too?"

In June, Dorothy and the children joined John at Crouy where he was running a training camp for American ambulance drivers. It was near Soissons, in the war zone, but Dorothy was able to find a small house and garden. Her knack for making any place into a home soon had it livable "with my Norwegian rugs and some pretty pieces of embroidery and some books and a lot of wild flowers in vases" she wrote, " . . . but let your last pictures be of a little rosy, fat, round-faced boy, trotting all over an old house and garden singing to himself, 'We've got to the country.' "

Dorothy took over the direction of getting and preparing food for the camp, with five French women working under her as cooks. She found rooms suitable for the men to read or write in so they might have some quiet for their leisure time. She hoped to have time herself to do a little writing and told her family that she was beginning to feel "like a bottle of cider that has 'worked' and is all ready to explode if somebody doesn't pull the cork and pour it out in a glass!"

An admirer of *The Bent Twig* sent Dorothy a new typewriter that aided letter writing. Friends from America who had not been seen for years began to arrive in Paris. Seeing them did much to revive war-tired and gloomy spirits. Dorothy called on her former fencing-master one day. Waiting for him at his hotel, she did not hear him coming up behind her, then "somebody took me in his arms and gave me a great kiss . . . imagine, that plain soldier from the Middle West and plain me sitting down to breakfast!"

"You always were a natural-born fencer," said General John J. Pershing as he smiled at her across the table.

William Allen White sent a message to Dorothy asking if she would act as his interpreter for a few days. She was delighted to accept. Kansas newspaperman that he was, he was so used to being at home in life that he was wholly at home in the Hotel Crillon on the Place de la Concorde, and with the French men of affairs with whom he was dealing.

"John, today I heard an admiring American ask Will White why he and his family didn't settle down to live in some great center. 'Center of what?' he replied."

John chuckled, "He long ago found in Emporia what we're finding in Arlington—more than enough human nature for a lifetime's study."

President Wilson's speeches during the presidential campaign began to hint at the formation of a group of nations that would work together for the common interest.

His words stirred Dorothy. "If this is to be, and it must be," she said, "then there is hope that the men who have died in this war have not died in vain."

That winter, back in Paris, Sally came down with typhoid fever. It was a long and anxious siege, but the little girl held to life until the crisis passed. "I had the distinct feeling that the world stood still and waited," Dorothy wrote. Sally's illness and slow climb back to health had been a heavy strain. "My head is ringing like mad with those head-noises which always fill my ears when I get nervously tired," Dorothy said in a letter home. There were zeppelin raids over Paris. The end of the war was not in sight. The vigor of the American army had not broken the massive force of the German armies. In December Dorothy left Paris with the children for Guethary in the Pyrenees, where the Villa Désirée became their much-loved home. With a Basque woman to help in the house, Dorothy had a little of the longed-for time for writing.

Paris was now filled with refugee children and the Germans had begun shelling the city with their Big Bertha gun. Dorothy, at the request of the Red Cross, opened a home in a large house near her small villa, where she and Marguerite Fischbacher could take care of forty rickety, fear-ridden children from the war zone. There was not much time left for writing, but Dorothy was determined to accomplish a thousand words a day, taking advantage of whatever quiet there might be around her to write a first draft of the most urgent things in her mind, setting it aside and endeavoring to use the scraps of time that appeared for revising, polishing, cutting, typing. Her old desire to collect languages came forward and she learned a little Basque.

Flavia wrote, warning Dorothy that she was using up her youth. Dorothy replied, "I am—what is left of it—but haven't a regret. Youth is money that you can't keep in your purse—it goes, one way or another, and I am grateful I have had such things to do with what there was left of mine."

At Guethary, Sally grew strong again, and the thin little refugee children grew sturdy. John came on leave. Some of the stories Dorothy had sent to America were published as a book, *Home Fires in France*. Alfred Harcourt prefaced the collection with a note—

This book is fiction written in France out of a life-long familiarity with the French and two years' intense experience in war work in France. It is a true setting-forth of personalities and experiences, French and American, under the influence of war. It tells what the war has done to the French people at home. In a recent letter, the author said, 'What I write is about such very well-known conditions to us that it is hard to remember it may be fresh to you, but it is so far short of the actual conditions that it seems pretty pale, after all.'

"But John, look, this is what means so much to me!" Dorothy held out to him a new book by Edith Wharton. On the flyleaf the author had written "To Dorothy Canfield Fisher with an appreciation of the complete honesty of her stories about war time France."

Honesty! John knew what the word meant to Dorothy. It was her breath of life.

Home Fires in France did what Dorothy's letters had done—touched hearts, stirred consciences. Letters began to arrive with money orders for her fund. People told of sitting in groups sewing or rolling bandages. Listening as the book was read aloud to them, new skill came into clumsy fingers, new life into dismal hearts. There were letters intimate and eager, though the names were unknown, asking if the things Dorothy wrote about had really happened to her.

"I'm not a reporter of facts you know," she replied, "but a real sure-enough fiction writer. It is all fact, but not literal fact. There is a difference."

One letter, coming from a young reader, asked for advice on what she should do with her life. The earnestness of the plea prompted Dorothy to reach across the Atlantic with a friendly handshake, and her reply later grew into a magazine article. "Don't feel you can teach or give to others everything," Dorothy wrote, "and guard yourself from the Prussian idea that Providence has given your country any monopoly of what is desirable or virtuous. If you look down, even in your heart of hearts, on people, no amount of technical doing them good will prevent your doing them harm."

The Refugee Children's Home was running smoothly and could be turned over to a French organization for its continuance. With Sally and Jimmy, Dorothy returned to Paris shortly before the Armistice.

"When can we go home?" Dorothy asked John.

John had applied for his discharge immediately after the

Armistice, but he knew that official wheels moved slowly. "Getting out of an army is as slow and deliberate as making peace," he said.

So, Dorothy started a nursery school for children. She sent another collection of sketches off to her publisher, *The Day of Glory*. William Allen White returned to Paris to report on the Peace Conference. The Fishers had dinner with him a few hours after the announcement was made that, contrary to all promises, some of the meetings were to be closed to reporters. Everyone was enraged, but Will White ate well of the excellent food and kept up his usual flow of witty talk. Dorothy and John went with him to the door of the room where an indignation meeting of newspapermen was being held. He waved cheerfully, "Well, here we go, boys," he said and marched into the room.

The protest meeting was successful. Dorothy was certain that it was Will White's presence that had cleared the air.

John was demobilized in April. They returned home in May. Mélanie and her daughter who had kept house for them in Paris went with them, and Kiki, the fiercely independent little terrier who loved them on terms of absolute equality and who had become a part of their family. Jimmy's English had not survived the French-speaking life and Sally was constantly having to translate for him.

The little house in Arlington was waiting for them, as they had known it would be. "We're home," John said, and one after another echoed the magic words.

No one was there to welcome them, but there were flowers in vases. The table was set for supper. There was a fire burning in the stove. A slip of paper on the table caught Dorothy's eye. She picked it up and read, "Creamed potatoes on the stove. Baked beans and brown bread in the oven."

John picked up another slip and read, "Cocoa for the children on the stove. Gingerbread in the cake tin. Applesauce in the ice-box."

"John, that's always been our favorite supper, what we've had so often, sitting around this table!"

"The neighbors have been in."

"Just like Vermonters—not many words."

Dorothy stood in the doorway to look out over the valley she had seen so often in her dreams. Breathing deeply, she was aware of a delicious smell—rich, damp, the smell of the earth at its first turning in the spring. The moon had risen from behind the mountains and in its light she could see a dark square on the edge of the pasture.

"John, John," she cried out. "They've even plowed and harrowed our garden for us!"

After the children had been tucked into bed, Dorothy left the house and ran across the grass, over the brook bridge to the rising land where the little pines had been planted. Astonished, delighted, she stood in the midst of a tide of living green. Some of the trees must have grown six feet, others even more. They were doing what the forester and the forestry books had said they would do. It would be hard for Sally now, even though her legs were lengthening, to jump over some of these upward-thrusting pines.

Here, in this place where roots went deep, was the only answer Dorothy knew to the questions she and John had puzzled over during the war years. Human beings had died tragically, but the race went on. If there was despair, it was in thinking a single life was all, instead of seeing the pattern of which it was a part. There was no small or great. What they had done in France, what they would do in Arlington, was all there was for them to do; it was enough.

When Dorothy went back to the house, she saw John sitting at the old pianola, his feet moving slowly on the treadles. She stood still to listen. Happiness flowed over her. Happiness, she thought, the greatest of creative artists because it could catch up the most ordinary moment, making it sing like a seraph or glow like a lighted window.

"It's Bach!" she exclaimed, realizing that he was reminding them, as only he could, that in the end all became parts of one harmonious whole.

Chapter 10

Dear Light of Everyday

DOROTHY was at her desk. John was in the garden. The children were playing by the brook. Mélanie was busy in the kitchen. They had been home a month and none of them seemed any the worse for the years away. That morning, at breakfast, John had made some remark about the war. "War?" Sally asked. "I don't remember anything about France except school and playmates and reading. Was there a war going on, too?"

Dorothy looked out the window, realizing that she did not hear the children's voices; but she could still see them. Sally had taken Jimmy's hand in hers, careful big-sister that she always was, and they were walking toward the pine plantation.

It seemed almost in another life that she had written books on what was best for children. Who could say in this year of 1919 what that best was? Taking down one of her books from a shelf, Dorothy read at random, shocked by the easy-going confidence, the casual managing of young lives. "This is verandah-talk!" she exclaimed. "Pre-war." She wondered if other mothers felt as she did, now that so many eyes had been opened to social inequalities and desperate needs. If there was one absolute essential in education, it was to learn how to live with others. "But *can* humans live on the globe without hurting each other?"

Certainly the challenge before present-day parents was to learn themselves, and to teach their children, in small matters as well as big, how to be neighbors and brothers.

That afternoon Dorothy and John drove in to collect a package at the railroad station in Arlington. The stationmaster told them of a young artist who had been in town looking for a place to live but not finding one had just gone on to Manchester.

"Telephone to the station and tell him to come back," Dorothy said, "we'll find him a place. What was his name?"

The stationmaster did not know, but the telephone call reached Manchester before the train and the message was delivered.

An hour or two later, Rockwell Kent, his wife and five children arrived at the Fishers'. In a few days a house was found on the southern spur of Equinox that exactly suited the Kents, but they despaired of buying it.

"Why?" Dorothy asked.

"The price is three thousand dollars. I have exactly two thousand in the bank, and no more until some work gets done," Kent said.

"We'll let you have the thousand dollars," Dorothy quickly replied. "Now buy the place."

Without losing any more time, Rockwell Kent bought house and land.

The Fishers were able to do things like that now. *The Bent Twig* and *Understood Betsy* were selling well. The short stories written about France were being bought by magazines. The famous nest egg had doubled. And, best of all, Dorothy was being taken seriously by editors and critics.

Asked to write an account of how her stories came into being, Dorothy replied that no two stories were ever constructed in the same way. She did not believe in rules or recipes

for writing. Creative fiction for her began with a generally in-
tensified emotional sensibility.

I have no idea whence this tide comes, or where it goes, but
when it begins to rise in my heart, I know that a story is hovering
in the offing. It does not always come safely to port. The daily
routine of ordinary life kills off many a vagrant emotion. Or if
daily humdrum occupation does not stifle it, perhaps this saturated
solution of feeling does not happen to crystallize about any concrete
fact, episode, word or phrase. It seldom crystallizes from an actual
happening offered by friends who are sure that such an interesting
event 'ought to go in a story.'

The beginning of a story is then for me in more than usual
sensitiveness to emotion. If this encounters the right focus . . . I
get simultaneously a strong thrill of intense feeling, and an intense desire to pass it on. . . . *Flint and Fire* thus hovered vaguely
in a shimmer of general emotional tensity, and thus abruptly crystallized itself about a chance phrase and the cadence of the voice
which pronounced it. For several days I had been almost painfully
alive to the beauty of an especially lovely spring, always so lovely
after the long winter in the mountains. One evening going on a
very prosaic errand to a farmhouse of our region, I walked along a
narrow path through dark pines, beside a brook swollen with
melting snow, and found the old man I came to see, sitting silent
and alone before his blackened small old house. . . . The old man
said quietly, 'Seems to me I never heard the brook sound so loud
as it has this spring.'

Walking home again, Dorothy remembered that his grandfather had drowned himself in the brook. Her mind began to
work on a story.

I said to one of the children, 'Yes, dear, wasn't it fun!' and to
myself, 'To be typical of our tradition-ridden valley-people, the

opposition ought to come from the dead hand of the past.' I asked a caller, 'One lump or two?' and thought as I poured the tea, 'And if the character of that opposition could be made to indicate a fierce capacity for passionate feeling in the older generation, that would make it doubly useful in the story, not only as part of the machinery of the plot, but as indicating an inheritance of passionate feeling in the younger generation, with whom the story is concerned.' I dozed off at night, and woke up to find myself saying, 'It could come from the jealousy of two sisters, now old women.' I darned a sock and thought out the relationship in the story.

My daily routine continued as usual, gardening, telling stories, music, sewing, dusting, motoring, callers, . . . and as usual with my story-making, this plot was sprouting out in a dozen places, expanding, opening up, till I perceived that I had enough material for a novel. In fact, a novel was seriously thought of but for a number of considerations was discarded. As it was, the material had to be compressed drastically.

An important detail finally decided the form of the story, and Dorothy felt ready to write. One morning, with a feeling of mingled anticipation and apprehension, like that of a skier, she sat down at her desk.

I 'went' almost as precipitately as skis go down a long white slope, scribbling as rapidly as my pencil would go, indicating whole words with a dash and a jiggle, filling page after page with scrawls.

After what seemed a half-hour she was called to lunch.

The next morning, back at the desk, I looked over what I had written, conquered the usual sick qualms of discouragement at finding it so infinitely flat and insipid compared to what I had wished to make it, and with a very clear idea of what remained to be done, plodded ahead doggedly, and finished the first draught before noon. It was almost twice too long.

After this came a period of steady deskwork, every morning, of re-writing, compression, more compression, and the more or less mechanical work of technical revision. . . . The first thing to do each morning was to read a part of it over aloud, sentence by sentence, to try to catch clumsy, ungraceful phrases, overweights at one end or the other. . . . When I begin to suspect that my ear is dulling, I turn to other varieties of revision, of which there are plenty to keep anybody busy . . . revision to explain facts . . . revision for suggestiveness . . . for ordinary sense . . . for movement . . . for sound, sense proportion, even grammar . . . and always interwoven with these mechanical revisions recurrent intense visualizations of the scenes. This is the mental trick which can be learned, I think, by practice and effort. Personally, although I never used as material any events in my own intimate life, I can write nothing if I cannot achieve these very definite, very complete visualizations of the scenes. . . . I can write nothing at all about places, people or phases of life which I do not intimately know. . . .

Now the story was what one calls 'finished,' and I made a clear copy, picking my way with difficulty among the alterations, the scratched-out passages, and the cued-in paragraphs, the inserted pages, the rearranged phrases.

Her interest and pleasure lasted through the process, but on reading the typed copy she wondered why she—

. . . had the presumption to try to translate into words, and make others feel a thrill of sacred living human feeling. . . . I heard again the incommunicable note of profound emotion in the old man's voice, suffered again with his sufferings; and those little black marks on white paper lay dead, dead in my hands. . . . I would never write again. All that effort, enough to have achieved a masterpiece it seemed at the time . . . and this, *this* for a result!

From the subconscious depths of long experience came up the cynical, slightly contemptuous consolation, 'You know this never lasts. You always have this same fit, and get over it.' So, suffering from really acute humiliation and unhappiness, I went out hastily to weed a flower-bed.

And sure enough, the next morning, after a long night's sleep, I felt quite rested, calm, and blessedly matter-of-fact. *Flint and Fire* seemed already very far away and vague, and the question of whether it was good or bad, not very important or interesting, like the chart of your temperature in a fever now gone by.

Jimmy went down the road to call on a neighbor, Kiki running beside him. Dorothy watched him go, then turned to her work. She was alone in the house when the telephone rang. Picking it up, she heard Jimmy's anguished voice at the other end, "Oh, Mother, Mother—come quick! A car has killed Kiki, come *quick!*"

Dorothy went as quickly as a foot jammed on an accelerator could take her. She found Kiki's tough little body—all bone, muscle, sinew and courage—only stunned. He soon recovered consciousness and they drove home with Kiki sitting on the front seat of the Ford. Jimmy, six years old and still numbed by the thunderclap of shock, was convinced that his mother, by coming quickly, had saved Kiki.

It was different when Sally Cleghorn phoned to tell Dorothy of the death of a dear friend.

"I must see you," Dorothy said. "I'll drive up for you at once."

She brought Sally back with her to sit in the sunny garden. There was nothing Dorothy could say and for a while she could only trust to the comfort of physical nearness; then Sally began to talk and gradually she poured out her heart to Dorothy.

The Fisher children went to school in the North District Schoolhouse; Dorothy and John took their places in village activities. Dorothy's neighbors knew her as a devoted mother, a fine housekeeper, a keen gardener. Many were scarcely aware that writing was a serious and absorbing task for her.

"Dolly hasn't more time than I," John often said, "but she is more master of her time."

Master in many ways: she was adept at securing helpers for detail work, whether in the house or with her research, and so she was able to do with hours what many people could only do with days.

Before going to France, they had divided their desk time. Dorothy took morning hours on Monday, Wednesday, Friday; John the same hours on alternate days. Now the whole allotment of morning time was passed over to Dorothy, and John's work began to shift from the creative to the consultant. Blue-pencilling one of Dorothy's manuscripts, he might find it returned to him with a playful scribble along a margin, "Oh, John, *please* let me keep this in!"

John had the skill of the real critic who sees what is good in a piece of work and how a little change can make it better. The builder's instinct was strong in him. Back of the builder was the architect, and it was as a consulting architect that he discussed Dorothy's stories with her. Before the edifice of the story was inevitably set in the bricks and mortar of printed words, he pored over her blueprints—noting, considering, commenting on every detail of structure, of total effect.

"Don't you perhaps need a column under that girder?" he would ask. "There's just a chance that without stiffening it won't quite carry the load of superstructure. And how about a foot or two more width to the main portal? Maybe some low-relief carving at the roof line will bring the façade into better proportion."

During the long months that a book was being written John constantly assured Dorothy that she would be able to do what she had done before: reduce to the halting medium of words the vision held in her heart. When the pages reached their final form and John read the finished book, he told her how it appealed to him. She had long ago learned to value his honesty. If the story got across to him, she knew that it would to others.

Flavia now made her home with the Fishers, though she was still an inveterate traveler. At eighty she was preparing to leave on a voyage around the world. "Quite alone," she said, in answer to solicitous enquiries, "except for the five hundred other people on the ship." Against the protests of friends at her doing such a thing at her age, she had one retort, "I don't think I would be any deader if I died in the Indian Ocean than in Arlington, Vermont." She wrote to a friend,

Dorothy has two children, Sally and Jimmy, both dark-eyed like their father. Dorothy is 41 and looks about 30, very happy in her mountain home. All are in robust health, the children going to an excellent country school, Dorothy busy from morning till night with housekeeping, gardening, public work, writing and answering letters. She has an enormous correspondence. Sally is eleven and much larger than the average child of that age. She is taller and heavier than her mother and can't wear her clothes. Jimmy is like his mother somewhat but he too is like Sally, a Fisher. They are both bright and active and Dorothy thinks there never were such wonderful children in the world.

Now that Dorothy had, with the women of the nation, cast her first ballot in State and Federal elections, she felt more interested than ever in the Arlington Town Meeting on the first Tuesday in March. She had been saying in words, demonstrating in her own life, that women could serve the modern world as contributors to society, while filling their roles as wives and mothers. She was soon appointed a member of the State Board of Education for two years; as such, she made an instant and direct appeal to the citizens of Vermont to do something about their rural schools. She wrote publicity, addressed local women's groups and the State Federation of Women's Clubs. She offered prizes to promote improvement in schools by installing better lighting and running water, encouraging people to see that much could be done with little money as the North District people had done with their school.

When her desk work was over for the day, she often went out among the pines that were growing sturdily. Always, it had been her self-appointed task to keep the trails that led up the mountain open and free. Now, with ax and brush cutter familiar to her hands, she found plenty of work to do among the trees they had planted.

Robert Frost, a neighbor of theirs, came to call with a bag of delphinium roots in his hands. Looking over at the pines, he said, "If you want to enjoy your old age, plant trees."

Dorothy felt a long way from old age with all the stories she wanted to write. She spoke of the novel she was working on. Beginning in Europe, it came back to Vermont, and much of its real meaning was linked to the life around her.

Robert Frost, sprawling his big frame in his easy farmer's clothes on the grass, laughed at her. "You're just like a person walking through a field of burdocks—when you want a story you reach down to your skirt and pick off a burdock. There are always plenty of them."

A car came up the road. Frost squinted at it. Getting up slowly he went across the grass to the garden, and with his back carefully turned to the visitors started setting the delphinium roots into the soil. John began edging away, walking more quickly as he approached the house. Dorothy looked around her—one man working in the garden, another making a hasty departure. "Oh, my recluse, unsociable John," she murmured.

Dorothy turned and went toward the visitors who were getting out of the car, strangers to her though apparently she was not to them. She greeted them as if she had been waiting for them, with a firm clasping of hands and words that were quick to bridge shyness. They spoke enthusiastically of their enjoyment of her books, but they told her that they felt there was something wrong with authors.

"Really?" she asked eagerly. "Tell me what you think it is."

"Most authors, not you Mrs. Fisher, but most authors keep themselves apart from the world. They don't seem to know what's going on. They don't seem to care."

Dorothy called to the man planting roots in her garden. "Robert, come and join us, this conversation concerns you as much as me."

He joined them, shaking the dirt from his hands and sitting down on the grass. For an hour talk flowed around the group, talk that embraced the land and the world. Yankee-fashion, it ranged from local gossip zestfully passed along to pungent comments on international news.

Frost, murmuring something about time to do his chores, got up and left. The visitors watched him walk toward his battered old car.

"Your Vermont farmers are certainly intelligent," one of them remarked.

Later that afternoon, after the callers had gone, Dorothy told John about them. "Wouldn't you think they would know that any author who lives in ordinary honest human relationships with other people and the earth would have plenty to talk about besides himself!"

"I don't suppose you told them who your garden-hand was—"

Dorothy laughed her ringing boisterous laugh. "Why should I?"

Then another car could be seen coming up the road. Dorothy looked from it to the mountains, alive with the flushing and paling of rose and gold that shadowed the sunset. She turned quickly to John. "John, there's just time to catch the sun's last light on Equinox if we go now."

They spun on their heels and were off. Kiki, dozing with one eye open by the doorstone, saw them, rose, shook himself and followed in joyous pursuit.

When Dorothy's novel was finished and John read the first draft, he felt as moved as by a sunrise seen from Mount Mansfield. She had chosen as her title *Some Quiet Weeks* and they had both liked it. It seemed to announce a pace for the story: something quiet and without incident as it would have looked to the average visitor from the city. The publishers felt the title would be taken too literally. *The Brimming Cup* was a reluctant second choice.

Reading the manuscript, John saw how poignantly and legitimately Dorothy had used the triangle plot, though it had not been her main preoccupation. Her stage was small. There were only a few characters whose motives and actions were closely interwoven. Like a well-constructed play, she gave the center of the stage to one after another of her actors, for a chapter letting each one be the star. Most of the book's holding power came from its sustained atmosphere of suspense, but in the last section another holding power was employed and that was in the feeling developed for Marise. Dorothy made her reader, at least she made her first reader, John, fall so passionately in love with Marise that nothing else mattered. Dinner could get cold, a train could be missed, much John cared! He couldn't be bothered with such trifles. He had to find out how Marise came through her ordeal.

John wondered if discerning readers would be able to tell where the conscientious novelist was reporting processes natural to one of her characters and where, in moments of climax, one of the actors became the author's mouthpiece. He read on quickly, and then more slowly, for step by step and with all the powers of counterplot, Dorothy was convincing the reader that brute force, driven by possessive jealousy, could not revive a waning love; could only destroy all that was worth having in love, and with that, life itself. Not to win the war, and so lose the peace: that conception raised earthly love to the pitch of religious ecstasy. But, oh, the strain of it!

The succession of vignettes in the last pages seemed to John like the coda of a Beethoven sonata. The music appeared to end. Then pure adagio melody broke out, lovely as a little meadow brook in springtime. Another pause. Again the adagio, almost the same but adding something more. And so, on and on, till the last page was turned.

John laid the finished pages on the table, saying below his breath, *"Uber allen Gipfel . . . ist Ruh,"* forgetting everything except the conviction that "all's right with the world." He did not say the first half of Pippa's song. If he had learned anything from *The Brimming Cup* it was that God could not help you, unless you looked for and found Him in your own human heart.

After *The Brimming Cup* was published, serialized first in *McCall's*, then appearing in book form, it was apparent that many people shared in John's love affair with Marise, for the book went through eight printings its first year.

Dorothy's old friend and admirer, William Lyon Phelps, called it a truly American novel, written with beauty and dignity, and founded on the unshakable truth of experience.

The Bookman, feeling that Dorothy had sounded a deeper note than any she had yet struck, spoke of her "firm handling of the intimate details of neighborhood life, a joyful under-standing of the burdens, trials and experiences of the American family. . . . She gives comfort to many persons disturbed by the radical outbursts of 1920."

Halford Luccock commented, "If Lewis and Dreiser and Masters may be said to have led the revolt against the village, Dorothy Canfield may be regarded as probably the most effective attorney for the defense. . . . She has that considerable fund of peculiar knowledge which only love can give."

Sinclair Lewis' *Main Street* had appeared a few months before *The Brimming Cup*. When Dorothy's novel was published it was known as "The other side of Main Street," and it profited by the excitement and enthusiasm that the Lewis book had stirred up among booksellers. The two were alternately first and second on the best-seller lists for months.

This contrast was sharply accented one afternoon when Alfred Harcourt called at the Fishers' with Sinclair Lewis. Dorothy and John had just returned from a climb up Mount Equinox. They were tanned by the sun, glowing from the exertion, Dorothy's unruly hair was flying; she had torn her skirt on the rocks.

Sinclair Lewis gazed at her shrewdly, "You're the biggest kind of liar."

"You must remember, Mr. Lewis," Dorothy replied, "that I see things in quite a different light than you do."

Later, after the callers had gone, Sally said, "Oh, Mother, why didn't you take me up Equinox with you?"

"We wanted you to come. Remember? But you said you'd rather stay home and play with your friend."

Sally was silent, compelled to remember her own decision. "Mother, next time *make* me come."

There was nothing for Dorothy to say. Her thoughts went back to something in *The Brimming Cup*, ". . . he did not want Marise for himself; he did not even want her to be happy; he wanted her to be herself, to be all that Marise could ever grow to be, he wanted her to attain her full stature so far as any human being could do this in this life.

"And to do that she must be free."

With her own children, as with the people in her books, Dorothy knew that she would go as far as she could, but before the questions whose answers each must find for himself she could only be silent.

Letters came from readers all over the country, assuring her that there were a good many of her sort in the world. "What you've done for us is to give us a habitation on the literary map . . . you make us articulate." Often they spoke of Dorothy as a New England writer. "But I don't want to be limited to being a New England writer," she exclaimed. "Me, born in Kansas!" Reporters came for interviews. Visitors came for autographs and with the conviction that someone who knew so much about human problems and could find a solution in the lives of the people she wrote about would be able to help them in their lives. Many refused to believe that the book was not autobiographical. Dorothy had become used to that charge. Her knowledge of and deep identification with her characters made them sound like her. Some criticized her for glorifying the commonplace. "And so I do," she replied, "but it's all a question of terms."

A moving-picture producer offered a large sum for the script of *The Brimming Cup*. Dorothy, on one of her rare trips to New York, went with Alfred Harcourt to see the producer and discuss terms. She was frankly puzzled as to how a film could be made of a story whose action, for the most part, took place beneath the surface. "*The Brimming Cup* hardly seems fitted to the screen," she said.

"Ah, Mrs. Fisher, you can trust us to insert suitable action to bring out all that."

Dorothy looked at him horrified; visions of how a Hollywood director might distort her characters raced through her mind. "I see," she said briefly, "and I am not interested." Picking up her coat, she walked out of the office.

Alfred Harcourt followed her. He knew her well enough not to protest, but he was bitterly disappointed.

John was proud of Dorothy.

The long struggle with her hearing came to a climax when she realized that it was becoming almost impossible to hear the children's voices. John's voice, pitched low, always carried to her; but she did not want to miss a single one of the children's words. She sent for a hearing aid and when it came wore it proudly. It was not the perfect solution, but even the static it created was nothing compared to the head noises she had known for so many years. And with time she became expert in using it, turning it up for what she wanted to hear, turning it off altogether for sounds in which she had no interest.

"Oh, yes, I get on very well with my hearing aid," she replied to kindly enquiries. "It's like having a good wooden leg."

Often it served her in unexpected ways.

When asked to speak at a college, Dorothy generally spent the night at the Kappa Kappa Gamma House, the society to which she had been initiated at Ohio State. When the evening festivities were over, there was always a group of girls who wanted to go on talking so Dorothy would invite them to her room. They sat on her bed, listening to her, asking her questions.

One night Dorothy had a special word of approval for the senior who had introduced her so gracefully and fluently.

"Oh, Mrs. Fisher, if you knew—"

"Tell me."

"Well, when I was first told that I'd been chosen to give the speech of introduction, I nearly said no. I've always been scared to death to get up on my feet before a lot of people. But there was plenty of time so I signed up for a one-hour course in public speaking."

The girl's roommate joined in, "Then I told her that the guest of honor was to be Dorothy Canfield Fisher."

"And I said that I couldn't speak before anyone so illustrious, that I'd just die."

"Sure you can, I told her," the roommate went on. "I said I'd be Mrs. Fisher and she could practice on me, and we did—for weeks!"

"But, oh Mrs. Fisher," wailed the senior, "when it came time for the dinner and I found myself sitting next to you at that long table I felt positively sick with stage fright, all the words I'd memorized vanished from my mind, my hands were cold, and I couldn't eat a thing."

Dorothy nodded and said, "I remember feeling a little sad when I saw that nice dinner on your plate uneaten."

"Do you remember what you did, Mrs. Fisher? You began talking to me about your hearing aid, said that you were deaf as a post and without it you often didn't hear what was being said. You told me about a banquet you had attended where a great many important people were present, the Governor of the State, church dignitaries, oh, ever so many. Then a toast was proposed and you got up and drank it, not knowing it was in your honor!"

"Yes, I do remember."

"Just the way you told that story made me begin to feel at ease. When the time came for me to give my speech, I wasn't nervous at all."

Questions tumbled from the other girls, but most of them revolved around what she thought they could do to make their lives happy and meaningful.

"College girls are always asking me that," Dorothy replied, "and I know quite well that you expect me to say marriage—"

There was a perceptible nodding of the heads.

"—and so I do, for it is deeply satisfying. But, your husband may die, hard times may come, and you must have something else to be sure that the whole succession of your days will be happy and meaningful."

There was a pause. The girls were waiting to hear what that something else could be.

"Get interested now in some work that you know is worthwhile and worth doing," Dorothy said quietly, "that will last as long as you do."

Since it had been possible to do something about her hearing, Dorothy's friends pressed her to do something about the enlarged gland on her neck. But she would not. She assured them that it gave her no trouble. Whenever she had a basal metabolism test it showed that everything was quite normal. There was no reason, except looks, why she should undergo an operation. A soft scarf thrown over shoulders, a collar on her dress, and it was out of sight. Dorothy had never been in the least self-conscious about her appearance.

She wrote to a friend—

This period of life is absorbingly filled with the small domestic cares of running a large and various family, with young and very old people in it, who all have perfectly good claims on my thought and vitality . . . they get sick and have to be nursed; they aren't able to plan for their own lives yet and have to have plannings made for them . . . and then patiently carried out through an infinity of details; they must be thought about and cared for, in the tiny unimportant always recurring ways which make up home-life. . . . I don't pretend to know whether it is a good thing or not, whether home-life ought to be something different, but this is the way mine seems to be in these years. In the summer, when the children are home from school and a house has to be run, it does not leave me breathing space. . . . I'm the most *terre-a-terre* housekeeper these days you can imagine, good for nothing but to plan for the next dinner, to read aloud to grandmothers and nurse little boys through the mumps. . . . I don't deserve the name of a woman of letters, but then there are innumerable people who were always quite sure I never did. . . .

"John," Dorothy looked up from a letter she had just opened, "here's a request from a Negro group in New York for me to make the presentation of an award tonight to an outstanding art student. I'd really like to go. It's a chance to do something, to show that I'm a dependable friend."

"Why don't you go?"

"The measles."

"Well, Dolly, Sally and Jimmy haven't shown a sign of them yet, even though all the other children in Arlington have them. I'll call Dr. Russell if there's any need."

Thus assured, Dorothy took the afternoon express from Arlington. Soon after eight o'clock she was changing into her best clothes in a little dressing room at Keith's 125th Street Vaudeville Theater. She went out on the stage accompanied by the elderly members of the Negro committee. There was not another white person in the theater. The auditorium, the boxes, and up to the topmost gallery were packed with eager faces. Formal speeches were made, explaining that the award, which represented a year's study in Paris, had been financed by contributions from Negroes all over the United States. Then a young woman came forward, very pretty, very shy.

"Not long ago," Dorothy said, "when I was in France, I saw the Croix de Guerre given to a brave soldier. This is how it was done: first, the officer pins the medal over the heart which has beaten so faithfully, which deserves so well of the Republic." Dorothy pinned a medal on the girl's dress. "Then," she continued, "in token of a welcome deeper than words can express, the officer gives the accolade, like this." Dorothy put her arm around the girl's shoulder and kissed her on both cheeks.

A happy gasp ran through the audience, then a roar of applause as the members of the committee shook hands with Dorothy and the winner of the award.

There was a midnight train out of Grand Central which Dorothy was able to catch and John met her at Arlington early in the morning. She looked tired but happy, and he had news that he knew would make her even happier.

"The children haven't broken out with a single red spot, Dolly. In fact, I'm not even sure that they knew you were away from home last night."

While spending a few months in Rome, Dorothy and John began to plan a book together. They called it *Converging Paths* as it went back into the lives of the main characters in *The Brimming Cup*, exploring the factors that had brought them together. The publishers changed the title to *Rough-Hewn*. Dorothy was reading galleys of it in Arlington when a writer from the *Bookman* called for an interview. Fifteen-year-old Sally, taller now than Dorothy, sat with them in the sunny garden; Jimmy brought a pitcher of cider he had made in his own press; John could be heard hammering in the barn. Dorothy raised her cider glass in the direction of the sound and spoke of her luck in husbands. "You see, I wanted to draw a picture of the athletic young American in *Rough Hewn*, and it was most convenient to have a football player in the house."

The mail arrived and in it was a bulky package. Dorothy glanced at the publisher's label. "That's a translation from the Italian John and I have agreed to do for Alfred Harcourt." She put it aside. "Tomorrow will be soon enough to open it."

Rough-Hewn widened Dorothy's circle of readers and recognition. The *Bookman* called it "... thoroughly American, readable, and a blessed relief from the welter of current novels where the satirist, sexologist, psychoanalyst and orientalist bash the Ten Commandments with a fool's bladder and hide behind the skirts of possible genius." The *Boston Transcript*, in a full-page story about Dorothy, concluded: "It would be sheer inadequacy to characterize Mrs. Fisher—now in the full maturity of her powers—as a novelist. She is that rare creature, a woman of letters. Whatever her hand finds to do for the printed page will be well done. . . . In an age when confusion and suspicion and even hatred abound, she reveals to us a thousand points of loving contact between us and the world as it is." Dorothy's books were now being published in France, Holland, Germany, the Scandinavian countries, and England. The *Manchester Guardian* spoke warmly of their impact: "Dorothy Canfield Fisher is one of the few American authors who, while profoundly influenced by her European experiences, and her appreciation of many things in Europe, retains a full-blooded Americanism of the best kind."

Increasing popularity brought demands for personal appearances. Dorothy could no more fulfill them than she could answer the number of letters requesting them. Unwillingly but of necessity she had a card printed saying—

Arlington, Vermont
Mrs. Fisher regrets very much that, for the present, it is impossible for her to make any more engagements for public speaking. She is at present absorbed in a long piece of work, which, added to the usual demands of housekeeping, and the care of children, leaves no margin of time or strength for public speaking.

She thanks you for your letter, regrets her inability to write a personal answer, and sends her best greetings.

With her next book, *Raw Material*, Dorothy did something

quite different. She spoke directly to her reader as she showed the raw material of human lives which her story-telling instinct had shaped, the instances which had served her as pegs on which meditations had been hung, the facts from which characters and episodes had arisen. "The writer is not born (as is his boast) with more capacity than other people for seeing color and interest and meaning in life," she said, "he is born merely with an irrepressible desire to tell everybody what he sees and feels." The book that was not short story nor reminiscence but something of both came as near as Dorothy probably would ever come to writing about writing.

Papini's *Life of Christ* which Dorothy and John had been working on was one of the conspicuous successes of the new firm of Harcourt, Brace. Alfred Harcourt, long Dorothy's editor with the firm of Henry Holt, was now at the head of his own house, with Donald Brace who had been a classmate of John's at Columbia. In his book *Some Experiences* Alfred Harcourt says—

We thought for a long time about the best person to translate the book (Papini's Life of Christ)—someone who would make it mean to American readers what it did to Italians. We finally persuaded Dorothy Canfield Fisher to translate it, for she knew Italian as well as she knew English; she had lived in Italy so much that she understood the Italian temperament, and she was a first-rate writer herself. The job was a much bigger one than any of us had anticipated, for there were references to obscure Biblical figures which Mrs. Fisher, with her scholar's conscience, insisted on verifying or changing for the English equivalents of their names. She exhausted the resources of the Manchester and Bennington, Vermont, libraries, and almost stumped the New York Public Library trying to find out the maiden name of Herod's sister-in-law. . . .

In the religious revival that always follows a war or a worldwide disaster, the book made a great stir. Even before publication, the *Pictorial Review* printed three installments—for a fee of $12,500. Protestant ministers all over the country preached sermons on it, and it became *the* Easter gift of the year. Mrs. Fisher's translation gave the real spirit of the book; her distinguished literary style took away all sense of a 'translation.' It sold about 350,000 copies.

Dorothy had agreed to the work on two conditions, that her translation be a free one and that the chapter on the wandering Jew, which struck her as being shockingly anti-Semitic, be eliminated. A thousand dollars had been the fee proposed, but at the book's enormous popularity it had been raised by a delighted publisher launching a new firm.

Reading the enthusiastic reviews as they came in, John said, "It makes it sound so easy."

"And it was so hard," Dorothy reflected, "so desperately hard—not only to find the thought back of the theology but the words to convey the thought."

She had earned her right to do something more after her heart. That was another novel called *The Home-Maker*. It was based on a long-remembered story of human life that had belonged to her father's generation. Department store background new to her was needed so she went to Boston to attend a series of lectures at the Boston School for Store Service. She was a reformer as well as a writer and her words were often the waving banners of a crusade against some of the things she felt were wrong. In *The Home-Maker* she attacked the rigid social convention that considered it degrading for a man to do woman's work. "What is home-making?" she asked. "Good housekeeping or a capacity to understand children and their needs."

After publication, Dorothy began to receive reviews from a clipping bureau. She wrote to say there must be some mistake as she had never subscribed. In reply a letter came from Dr. Funk, the dictionary publisher, saying that all through his successful life he had been saddened by the tragic waste resulting from a tradition-bound public's crazy efforts to pound round pegs into square holes. Now that an author had devoted a moving novel to exposing that folly he thought the least he could do was to make her a present of the clipped reviews of her book as an expression of gratitude.

When *The Home-Maker* was made into a film, Dorothy and John were delighted at the good taste with which it was done, and by the fact that not for a moment did it miss the point that the book had made.

Sally and Jimmy had through the years been challenging Dorothy's story-telling ability. Now Sally was at boarding school near Philadelphia, but Jimmy continued to put his mother to the test.

"I do hate fairies in stories," he would say, "they're so foolish. And I hate things that couldn't possibly have happened. And I despise a story that tries to teach you something without your knowing it. That's why I like your stories. But the thing I like best about them is that there isn't any moral in them."

"Nor any sense."

"Yes, that's another nice thing about them."

It didn't matter whether Dorothy was in the kitchen, or weeding onions in the garden, if Jimmy felt like a story he would remind her that he hadn't had a made-to-order one for quite a while. "And I'm sort of hungry for one."

"All right, have you settled what you want to have in it?" Dorothy looked at him with one corner of her mouth tucked in a little.

And then Jimmy was off, telling her exactly what he wanted in it.

One rainy day she was taking advantage of the weather to transplant some phlox when Jimmy found her. "You don't mean you'd expect me to stop in all this work and tell you a made-to-order story?"

Dorothy Canfield Fisher at work, 1943.

"These years are almost too happy, too fulfilled."
1954.

"You don't have to stop your work. You can tell as you plant. And I can listen. I could help you, too. I could tear those roots apart as well as anybody." He began to work on the roots, as Dorothy began to tell the story. Soon he stopped work to give himself to listening.

So the book *Made-to-Order Stories* grew as a boy challenged his mother's quick thinking. Sometimes the stories reached back into the Canfield past; sometimes they were about the Canfield present; sometimes John was approached for a story. His were good, but different. One of his best times for telling was when he was working on the car, greasing it, tinkering with it.

"Sure, I'll tell you a story. Keep away from that grease-gun or I'll catch it when Mother sees your clothes."

Jimmy listened, so eagerly that at times he almost forgot to breathe. At the end he said, "Do you really think it's a true story?"

"I surely do," John answered. "I know it must be true because it was told to me on the road from Soissons to Laon by a sergeant motor-mechanic, and before the war he'd been a garage hand in Kenosha, and all garage hands are notoriously truthful."

Jimmy began to think out stories for himself, sometimes enlarging on one of his mother's.

"It's almost too good to be true to have that story turn out so well, after all our worrying about it."

"Yes, I was glad, too."

"Look here, Jimmy; if you can do made-to-order stories like that, you won't need me any more. You can tell them for yourself now."

He looked surprised, "Why, that's so. I suppose I can."

Dorothy realized a moment later what it meant. He was growing up, taking first steps into independent thinking. Childhood years were drawing to a close. She wondered if she would ever again receive such Christmas presents as she had last year from Sally and Jimmy. Jimmy's had been the promise to wash his hands before he came to the table; Sally's had been the promise to look up from the book she was reading when visitors came into the room. Well, Dorothy thought, she had made a promise to herself about the children years ago. It had been kept.

Chapter 11

Her Father's Daughter

JOHN, elected to the State Legislature in 1925, was required to be in Montpelier for three months. Dorothy, at work on a novel, could carry on in a rented house in Montpelier as well as at Arlington. She had long felt deeply for an old French friend of theirs who had been left a widow with an only son. Events in the lives of mother and son from the war years to the present had given Dorothy situations needed for a story. She had thought of telling it as it happened in France; but, reflecting on it constantly as she invariably did when a novel took over her mind, she saw that it was a universal subject and might happen anywhere. She transposed the story to an American background, with American characters, then commenced to write.

When *Her Son's Wife* was published, the *Herald Tribune* called Dorothy's Mrs. Bascomb "one of the few real characters who has entered our imaginative home in many years." Halford Luccock spoke of it as "a memorable story of growth in personality, of the development of character under the challenge of what seems to be disaster." Translated into several languages, the book was even more popular in Europe and brought Dorothy a tidal wave of letters.

"I once heard Robert Frost say that good books helped 'extend our tolerance of the crude,' " one of the letters said, "but *Her Son's Wife* suggests something infinitely greater than tolerance—the possibility that our understanding of the reasons for the crudeness could make it possible to love."

Dorothy put the letter down to ponder its last words. "Could make—it possible—to love," she repeated to herself.

Her goal in fiction writing was to try to understand for herself, then explain to others, the reasons for human behavior. If, within those reasons, was the possibility for love—as the letter from an unknown reader had said—Dorothy felt that she had succeeded beyond her hope.

That summer John and Dorothy took the children on a visit to the Canadian Rockies. When they returned to Vermont, Rockwell Kent was waiting with a request. He had long ago repaid his loan from the Fishers, now he wanted Dorothy to write an introduction for his book *Wilderness*. She did.

Kent read her first draft and told her that it sounded as if it were written for the tired businessman. "And I don't care a rap for him."

Dorothy rewrote her introduction:

Had jesting Pilate asked "What is Art?" he would have waited quite as many centuries for an answer as he has for the answer to his question about Truth. For art to the artist, and art to the rest of us, are two very different things. Art to the artist is quite simply Life, his life, of which he has an amplitude and intensity unknown to us. What he does for us is to thrill us awake to the amplitude and intensity of all life, our own included. And this is a miracle for which we can never be thankful enough. . . .

Rockwell Kent's Alaska drawings . . . take me away from that tired absorption in things of little import which makes up most of our human life and make me see . . . the real wonder-world in which I live and have always lived. They make me see suddenly there is a vast deal more in the world than embittering and anxious preoccupations, that much of it is fine, much is comforting, much awe-inspiring, much profoundly tragic, and all of it makes up a whole so vast that no living organism need feel cramped. . . .

The Arlington house, comfortable as an old shoe as a family friend liked to say, was closed in September. An apartment was taken in Poughkeepsie to be near Jimmy who was now going to boarding school; nearer to Sally who was now a freshman at Swarthmore; and as a convenience for Dorothy's mother. Flavia had never liked Vermont winters and she liked them less as she grew older.

Frederick Keppel, President of the Carnegie Corporation, had been an ardent admirer of Dorothy's father and an older-generation friend of the Fishers. He suggested to Dorothy that she write a book on adult education.

She was horrified. "Stop writing fiction and return to the academic world of learning, statistics, interpretation of accumulated-by-research facts? No, indeed!"

He explained his idea more fully.

"No, Fred," she said, "nothing could induce me to take on such a task."

He let her give all her reasons, then he asked, "Don't you think your father's daughter ought to do it?"

Dorothy made no immediate reply; but, after a struggle with herself, consented to take on the task. She knew what was before her: hours of reading endless reports, days of trying to think her way through facts to significance.

"It will probably be the death of me," she announced grimly to John.

A year was a long time for any piece of work, long enough for the frequent recurrence of the question, "*What* are you writing now?'

"A book about voluntary self-education in this country."

"What's that?"

"Adult education."

"Oh—you mean the campaign against illiteracy? Oh yes, I know all about that sort of thing."

The remark infuriated Dorothy but there was no easy explanation for what she was doing. With the publication of the book, people would see for themselves.

Why Stop Learning? when it appeared was in the nature of a continuation of Dorothy's earlier *Self-Reliance*. In the first book it was children who were to be given the right tools and taught how to use them, now it was older people who were to be encouraged to continue using them. Confirmed educator that she was, *Why Stop Learning?* enabled her to express a conviction that had been intensifying through the years—that learning could not be confined to any one period of life, that real education was a process which, once started, went on. In the vast amount of material that Dorothy had studied for the book, she had constantly come upon statistics that showed how sadly the United States compared with other countries in the reading of books; and she thought of how her father would invariably conclude his speeches with some reference to the importance of libraries in a democracy.

When Frederick Keppel read the finished book he was delighted. "You *are* like your father," he said.

"I try to take his spirit forward into life," Dorothy replied.

A great number of educators and an even greater number of plain people appreciated what Dorothy had done. With characteristic vigor and the radiation of her own vitality, she had showed how within-reach were the tools of learning and, when employed, how far-reaching would be the results.

On a sunny Saturday in April, Dorothy went from Poughkeepsie to New York to do some shopping. While on the train she turned over in her mind an invitation that had come to her signed by two men whose names she had never seen before—

Harry Scherman and Robert Haas. They asked her to become a member of the first Committee of Selection of the Book-of-the-Month Club. She had plenty of reasons not to accept. She had never heard of such a thing and she didn't like the name. It sounded as if a committee were setting itself up to choose books for other people to read.

She went to Macy's to make some household purchases. The store was crowded with Saturday afternoon shoppers. Dorothy tried to edge herself through the crowds but, without success, finally backed away and went out to the street again. The sidewalks too were packed with people. When Dorothy reached the corner of 34th Street and Fifth Avenue and saw a double-decker bus come along, it looked as welcome as a floating hen-house to a person swept away in a flood. She climbed to the top and sank down in a seat.

"I'll stop at Brentano's," she thought, "and get that Spanish Dictionary Sally asked me to send her."

The atmosphere in the bookstore was slumberously peaceful, almost like that in a remote country churchyard. Dorothy was startled by the fact that she seemed to be the only person who wanted to buy a book, that the bookstore was the only place in New York which had not gone mad with buying and selling.

When she returned from her shopping expedition she decided that there was something the matter with relying entirely upon bookstores as a method of getting books into the hands of the reading public. She wrote to the Book-of-the-Month Club and accepted their invitation for a year. It would be worthwhile to try their method of distribution.

At the first meeting she found others as uncertain as she was as to what the Book-of-the-Month Club could do with its five thousand subscribers and five members on the Selection Committee. William Allen White was one of the five, and Henry Seidel Canby whom Dorothy knew slightly. Christopher Morley was there, and Heywood Broun, looking just as he had as a high school boy at the Horace Mann School even to untied shoelaces. It was a friendly get-together of people who knew each other because they inhabited the same sort of world. Wondering what it would be possible for them to accomplish, they felt like Columbus' sailors not knowing what they were approaching.

Henry Seidel Canby wrote in his *American Memoir*—

We judges were on salary, and had no ownership in the business as such, and from the beginning were never subjected to an ounce of pressure from the management in making our decisions, so that our devotion to our work was no more sullied by commercialism than a professor's in a good university. . . . Intensive reading such as we had to do was an ideal job for a writer or an editor, since the reading could be fitted into any time or place, from trains to backwood cabins, leaving the time for routine executive work or creative writing free of interruption. . . . Whoever thinks that reading new books under pressure is a brief and easy way to earn a living, must think again. In a fine book every sentence becomes a responsibility. In a just-maybe book, an intensity of concentration is necessary unless one is to waste hours of time or judge erroneously. In an indifferent book, especially a novel, equal concentration is required, for at any moment it may turn upward.

It took us a long while to learn a very simple truth. We could not choose a book on the basis of what we thought the public liked and wanted. We did not know. . . . We began to see that there was only one safe procedure, which was to choose what we ourselves liked. If we liked a book well enough, the public, whose taste was perhaps less discriminating but at least as sound and healthy as ours, seemed to like it also. The only qualification was common sense. . . .

Constant discussion attended their first meeting. "What is it you don't like in the book?" "What is the point?" No one tried to convince another against his will; each one tried to find out what was in the other's mind and then discuss it. Dorothy felt exhilarated by the atmosphere of peaceable decision that had been established. When she got home she outlined the work to John.

"But not all the new books will be sent us, John. There is a large corps of readers who read the galleys first. Their function is to keep the Selection Committee from having to read too many books, as well as to guard against our overlooking any we ought to see."

"How is that done?" John asked.

"If any one person, judging by the readers' reports, thinks that a book should go to the Committee of Selection, the book will be marked Class A and sent to all the judges. A borderline book will be put into Class B and sent to two, sometimes three, of the judges. Most books of decent quality will be read by nine readers. An "A" book will be read, as well, by the five judges, and either, or sometimes both, Harry Scherman and Robert Haas."

"How many books will come to you to read every month?"

"Perhaps six to ten," Dorothy said, "with a view to their being chosen as Book-of-the-Month. Perhaps five or six others of good quality but with special interest which might make them unsuitable for the larger reading public. Perhaps a sprinkling of five or six more."

"Say fifteen," John suggested. "The book-of-the-monthly grind!"

"Yes, but it's no more than we would read anyway. I'll need your help, John." She looked at him. He was as patient and calm in this as in everything. He would keep his head, no matter how many books came in with this new tide of work, and help her keep hers, too.

"People will ask us if we read all the books through all the time," John was saying.

"That will be a stock question and the answer will be yes to every book in Class A."

By the end of its first year the Book-of-the-Month Club had forty thousand members and showed every evidence of growing.

On one of the rare occasions when Dorothy could get John to go with her to New York, she took him to one of the meetings of the Selection Committee. The discussion took place while they ate luncheon in a room of the Club office.

"As far as I could make out," John said to Dorothy on the way home, "everyone was talking at once."

"That's because we all feel perfectly free to rush in. When there are only a few in a group, you can do that. You don't have to wait for a point of order, you just wait for a chance. It's like a conversation between friends."

"The decision you came to between one and four o'clock today," John commented, "seemed to be molded by what everyone had to say."

"Yes, we keep discussing until we agree. Almost from the very first that seemed to all of us a better way than voting."

Dorothy's salary, modest at first, grew as the Club membership grew, and each trip to New York was covered by a check for thirty dollars. The reading she and John both had to do was exacting. It was the first time in her life she had ever read more English than French; but it kept her in touch with the best that was being written in the English language and it brought her into closer touch with John in the field of literary judgment than she had been before.

In the lengthy letters that went off to Sally at college, Jimmy at boarding school, there was plenty of talk about books, but the days were filled with other things—

Saturday was brilliant with sun and a high wind, and the thermometer here at the house about ten above. On the principle of *de l'audace, de l'audace et toujours de l'audace,* we thought we would risk it, that there might be snow enough up Peru way for skiing and set off. At the top, you know where the view off south is so wide, we saw fields that looked white. Ye Gods! was it cold! I don't know what the thermometer was, but it was lots lots lots colder than down in the Battenkill Valley, and such a wind. . . . We pushed ahead, went through a gap in the fence, and found ourselves in a glorious free field, partly frozen, partly soft, and long! It was really grand ski-running. And snow about two feet thick everywhere. We kept at it till we were glowing and forgot how cold it was, and then stopped in a sheltered place in the woods for lunch and a cigaret and found it was still so cold that when you took your cigaret out of your mouth for a breath or to say something, the wet end froze before you could get it back. Then we made some turns on the lower slopes and played around generally till we were hungry and drove home with grand appetites. What air it was! So light and moving and cold and sunny you drank it in—well, you know what a joy I get in breathing anyhow. . . . The Book-of-the-Month Club of course had to choose this exact time to ask for a lot of extra work all in a hurry—books to be read and reviews to be written more than expected, so we did considerable work in the cracks of these days.

Dorothy went on to describe in detail the historical tableaux she had directed and which were given at the Town Hall two nights running—

Justes cieux! Never have I seen such a crowd in the Town Hall. . . . It was thrilling, let me tell you, to have them care so much about it, and when they began applauding as I made my curtsey, I thought "It may be idiotic to give any time and vitality to this sort of thing as everybody tells me it is, but gracious how can you help it!" . . .

This morning, here at the house, such a "clarin'-up time!" Father is doing over our bathroom so it is full of plumber's tools

and what-not, so we have been giving rather an imitation of a pair
of old bears living in a lair in the rocks. No harm done except that
I could *not* find my garters! I know, I should have lots of pairs,
and I usually do, but the supply was low and you know there is
no ten-cent store or other short of Bennington where you can buy
such. I intermittently looked for those garters all through the
vacation, and in between times pulled up my stockings. . . . Abso-
lutely not to be found. And this morning where were they—on *top*,
plain sight, in the first drawer I opened.

Well dears, this is all for now, can you read it. I've been clicking
away at my fastest speed . . . goodbye and love from

                                                    Mother

During their second winter in Poughkeepsie Dorothy was at
work on *The Deepening Stream*. It could have been her story;
in places it was, as it showed the growth of character during
and because of a shared, happy marriage. Among its wealth of
people one bore no disguise. Adrian's father was the elderly Dr.
Fisher in Swiftwater, Pennsylvania, who had recently died.
Dorothy, in her warm love and deep respect for him, put him
into her book—"the only character really drawn from someone
whom I had known, which I ever have put into a book . . . it
is more literally the portrait of a personality. I have never known
anyone so deeply Friendly to the core as he."

The similarities and differences between the slow Quaker-
Dutch blend of people in the Hudson River valley and the
incisive New England type, which Dorothy had always known,
interested her. And Quakerism interested her. She read all she
could find about it in the libraries. She went regularly to Sunday morning Meeting for Worship. Accustomed to the Episcopal ritual of St. James' in Arlington and formal church-going
when abroad, she found the exercise in contemplative silence

an exacting, rewarding discipline. The empty quiet had seemed at first like that of a waking sleep, then slowly up through the space cleared from the clutter of surface things had come the deep lifting of something more, like a slow tide rising. Always an admirer of the Friends' way of doing things, she found herself impressed by the Quaker spirit with its high value on self-direction, its low value on authority; their belief in the strength and integrity of individual life seemed closely related to the creed that the new progressive education was formulating and which she believed in so heartily. She had many friends among the Friends and she liked the way they saw things in proportion, leaving room in the spacious center of their souls for the great effort to live—not only to talk and pray about—the good life.

As John read *The Deepening Stream*, he felt that Dorothy had put more of her spirit into it than into any other book. It was her seventh full-length novel. She was nearly fifty and in the strong flood-tide of mental maturity. Experience had made her master of her craft. "Dolly never writes anything that does not leave her reader with a warning and a hope," John reflected. He saw her as one who, after long effort, had reached the sanctuary of faith in life. "Now that she is there, she feels an obligation to keep a candle burning in the chapel window as a guide for other travelers."

The Deepening Stream was hailed as a warm-hearted love story as well as a powerful anti-war tract, driving home the truth that war was terrible. The *Herald Tribune* said, "Dorothy Canfield's novels have always been forthright and courageous, but in no other has she achieved the sustained intensity she has poured into this story."

Letters from the book's readers were brought to Dorothy in baskets-full. "I am no longer stunned or puzzled or despairing because of Adrian's father—through you," one said. Dorothy felt that no labor of writing could be too great when there was response such as that.

Years later when the editors of the Modern Library asked Dorothy to select for inclusion her favorite novel, she unhesitatingly named *The Deepening Stream.*

The Fisher family went abroad for the summer—to Spain and France, then Dorothy went to England to attend the first convention of the International Association for Adult Education.

On the ship, she had a brief exchange of words which called forth anger, and later deep reflection.

"Why, nobody would ever think you were an American!" a fellow-passenger said.

She detested the provincialism that lumped all people together because of the unfavorable characteristics of a few. She took out her feelings in walking briskly around the deck.

"John," she asked, "doesn't much of our human misery come because we fail to realize that there really isn't any plural to 'child' or 'man' or 'woman'? We can't pass judgment on 'French men' or 'American women.' The way we are constituted we really can only love individuals of our 'own kind.' Internationalism would be more solidly based if we were to realize that nations are made up of a jumbled lot and that 'our kind' are scattered far and wide."

"The other kind is scattered pretty widely too, Dolly."

"Well, we must look for them where we can find them, instead of attributing them to any one nation or race," she said. She took a deep breath, "What every home needs is for the mother to fling open its windows to the positive sunshine of joy in the marvelous diversity of human character and gifts— so poorly labeled by that tepid word 'tolerance.' "

The summer following Sally's graduation, with High Honors, from Swarthmore, they all went abroad again—Sally on to Oxford, Jimmy to the Odenwald-shule near Heidelberg. French had been a dominant influence in Jimmy's life for seventeen years, now he felt that he wanted to balance it with some German. Dorothy and John, with one of their French friends, settled at Kirchzarten in southern Germany for several weeks while Dorothy worked on her translation from the Italian of Adriano Tilgher's book *Work, What It Has Meant to Men through the Ages*. Languages flowed like the air around them for even in their own small group French, German, Italian, English were being spoken interchangeably.

With Flavia's death at eighty-six, in that year of 1930, Dorothy and John realized that they were now the older generation. Dorothy at fifty-one, knew she was no exception to the laws that made women her age very different from women of twenty. The smooth-skinned, bright-eyed radiance of youth had gone, but it didn't trouble her. Her hair was gray but not yet white. She enjoyed physical activity even more than she had in her youth, since she did not embark on it so ferociously. Years had their rewards: among them was the ability to make choices, to throw away excess baggage, and—oh, best of all—to trust the future.

In Vermont again, sitting at her desk in the small shack John had made for her in the pines to use as an outdoor workroom, she reflected on the march of the years. She knew plenty of people who were obviously afraid of old age, but she found it impossible to share their fears. Having arrived at an age which, at twenty, would have seemed as forlorn to her as eighty did now, she realized that a change of tastes and desires had gone along with the years. She was willing to guess that if she continued to yield herself naturally to the rhythm of the years she would find the inner timetable making as close and accurate connection for her in the future as it was now.

She had been asked to become editor of a national magazine devoted to work with parents and children, but she had declined. Time did not have endless elasticity, nor did energy. There was so much she wanted to do and she found it common sense to save herself for what meant most. Turning the pages of a current magazine and skimming the ads gave all too clear an impression of how numbers of people spent the riches of their thinking—

"Does outdoor exercise destroy feminine charm?" (cold cream)

"Does your husband tell you all he thinks?" (booklet on slimming)

"Do you want to search for the inner meaning of love and find a way out of life's confusion?" (forthcoming novel)

There were subjects on which she thought the public should be informed, and these were often best treated in magazine articles. To bring an idea under the lens of her intelligence, then focus her full attention on it was to make it yield to analysis. The only formula she knew was to take a look all around a situation before making a decision on any of its parts. The treatment and development of the idea came often by a process of logic, sometimes by intuition. When she had thought a thing through, the words flowed as readily as a conversation with a group of neighbors. It was as if her readers were never beyond the range of her voice. Her purpose with them was the same as it had been in her recently given Kappa Delta Pi lecture to teachers, *Learn or Perish*: improvement in individual thinking on worthwhile matters. That was the first step to improvement in the whole area of national thinking.

Looking up from her desk Dorothy saw that John was supervising the moving of a large blanket chest from the house to the barn. She watched as the two boys who were helping him tried one way then another to handle the bulky object.

"I'll heave it up on my back," she heard John say, "and you two walk along with me, one on each side. Keep your eyes on the box and if it starts to tip too much toward your side, just give it a little push till it balances again."

Off they went, the two boys watching the unwieldy box,

and from time to time, as it slid to one side or the other, putting up a hand lightly to push it back toward the center.

"But that's just the illustration I need!" Dorothy exclaimed inwardly as the procedure brought home to her a truth about human affairs. What everyone was really after was a nicely-kept balance between two forces, not the victory of one and collapse of the other. She took up her pen and started to write.

When the Shepherd-Towner Act to give aid to mothers and babies was being voted in Congress, Dorothy wrote an article upholding it—

I believe in economy, but there are other lines of activity on which I should prefer to employ it. . . . I have no patience with those who ask 'But have the results accomplished been enough to justify the expense?' 'Enough' to justify an appropriation of a million and a quarter by the richest government in the world? . . . What is the cash equivalent for a lacerated mother, for a blind baby? If it has done anything, if after years it might hope to do anything to lighten the burden of those mothers and babies, would any price be too much?

When an editor of a woman's magazine asked for an article on "What Mrs. Fisher Thinks of Pets," Dorothy did not particularly want to write it, then she saw that by expressing her feeling about cats and dogs she could say what she felt about unquestioning obedience contrasted with sovereign independence. She wrote an article "Why I Like Cats Better Than Dogs" as part of her constant effort to find new ways in which to express, in living everyday terms, great principles. She had had a lifelong revulsion from the glorification of obedience-for-its-own-sake, which the Prussian army had exemplified. In her reading as a child, in her history lessons as a schoolgirl, she had flamed with detestation at conquerors who made themselves masters of men. Now, in the world of the early 1930's, a grim menace was reappearing and the same flame of anger burned within Dorothy. Wherever, however, she could raise her voice against that menace she would.

"Do you know how the future looks to us Germans?" a Berliner asked her one day. "It looks like a huge, angry wave, towering high above our little ship, and traveling down on us with terrific speed. All we can do is to stand shoulder-to-shoulder on the deck, and hold hard to the tiller and the ropes."

"You are waiting for that wave to break," she answered her friend. "If a child were there you would want to be sure he knew how to swim. The rules for that art do not alter."

Often, by choice or request, she wrote about Vermont. In a series of articles on the different states running in the *Nation*, Dorothy likened her state to—

. . . a tall powerful man with thick gray hair, rough out-door clothes, a sinewy ax-man's hand and arm, a humorous, candid, shrewd mouth and a weather-beaten face from which look out the most quietly fearless eyes ever set in any man's head . . . little money in the pockets of that woodman's coat, but there is strength in the long, corded arm, an unhurried sense of fun lies behind the ironic glint in the eyes. . . . He has no fear of being poor because he has been poor for 150 years and it hasn't hurt him; nor has he any fear of getting up the social ladder. Independent, self-governing—he can look the world in the eye and ask no odds on it. . . .

And she was always ready to write an answer to the query of why she didn't live some place else when life in Vermont had so many hardships—

But life everywhere is full of hardships and discomforts. In the country I can get more of what I like and dodge more of what I don't like. I like to fuss with an open fire. And I can't be bothered waiting in restaurants for expensive food when there's so much else I'd rather do. Plain food is always more enjoyable to me than a stalled ox eaten against a background of steam-heated air, too little sleep, and no physical activity. Elegance is something I don't want; or fashion as fashion; or Bohemia—I saw too much of it in my childhood around Latin Quarter studios.

Country life is crammed for me with physical delights. Take clothes: there's joy in wearing clothes constructed to fit the body instead of trying to remake the body to fit the latest style. I like to wear clothes I can forget once I've put them on, that bother me as little as my skin, that give me bodily ease and freedom. Shoes that are loose, flexible and heelless, leaving my feet as alive and muscular as my hands, making walking or running as brisk a pleasure as dancing. Lyric foot comfort for me in the summer is in Basque canvas sandals with twine soles; or in the winter in those felt socks and moccasins worn by lumbermen.

I detest mild wishy-washy air and delight in keen mountain air —just to smell ploughed land, wild grapes, wet forests, wood fires— is keen enjoyment. Too many people take too little bodily enjoyment and that 'little brother the body' takes it out of them in the end for not giving him his fair share of the fun.

I've always been keenly sensitive to the joy of bodily rhythm and equilibrium—dancing, skating. Living in the country I can stand up from my desk, strap on my skis, and from my very door go skimming down a snow slope. Every nerve tingling in the excitement of flight, or in a few moments walk I can be at the Cut-off and there leave the laborious stub-stub of one foot after another for the long effortless suavity of skating . . . in the summer I can lay down my pen whenever tired of sitting still, struggling with my brains, and in three minutes step out on to a tennis court for an exhilarating struggle with mind and nerve. And all year round I walk on living feet not over flat monotonous sidewalks but over interesting mountain paths, varying between rocks which make every step an enchanting problem in balance, and mossy leaf mold which springs under the foot like velvet.

I like to sit down with a book in a quiet room, sure of uninterrupted time in which to savor its wisdom, beauty, gaiety, sadness. . . . Music I love, but we can go to the city for a concert or two when we feel the hunger, and now the radio is bringing music into our homes. As for the theater, I'm deaf enough to find it a vexation rather than a pleasure. In the country I am unharried by unimportance. There are no calls to make or receive with their exchange of straw-like conversation, or gossip which is only fiction produced by non-professionals: but there are hours of leisure and the heart's wide welcome in which to enjoy real visits from real friends and conversation that is the ripe expression of mature and interesting minds.

It's all a matter of personal taste, but country life leaves me more time and strength for my work, and I like to like my fellow man. I can like him better if I don't constantly have too large a dose of him. I can stand a week in New York, survive a fortnight, but longer, I'm dazed, deafened, beaten down by the terrific concentration on material possessions, I run back to Vermont. . . . I don't like to live in New York because I can't 'live' there. It doesn't feel like life to me. It feels like being trampled under foot by the herd.

The Vermont code in accordance with which she had grown up was based on overcoming obstacles, rather than in contriving to find a way of life without difficulty. Dorothy valued that code more as the years went on.

Chapter 12

R. F. D.

THE days had their pattern. Dorothy breakfasted with the family at eight, though she had often been at her desk for two hours or more fortified by an early cup of coffee. At breakfast they listened to a broadcast of news and weather, and played one of their favorite records—a Bach saraband with its lively joy, or something of Beethoven's to send them into the day with a sense of triumphant exaltation. Then Dorothy went to the kitchen to discuss meals and housework, to the downstairs study to talk briefly with her secretary or chat with a neighbor coming in to do some mending. Domesticity dispatched, she turned to her desk.

During the winter she worked in the small upstairs room that was just big enough for her desk and reference books. It had one window from which she could see only sky. Moods of the weather and the passage of clouds accompanied her working hours, undisturbed except for the rare intrusion of a long-distance telephone call. A thumping on the floor below announced the time for luncheon, and Dorothy was by then aware of hunger. Mental effort over a sheet of paper or a typewriter seemed able to hollow out the stomach as much as climbing a mountain.

First thing in the afternoon the mail arrived. No longer would it fit in the mailbox with its large red F, so the carrier brought it from the main road up to the house.

Dorothy turned to it immediately. With John's help and her secretary's, she read letters, opened books and packages, unrolled magazines and was constantly astonished by the number and variety of requests that came to her.

"Your stories and articles have built up a band of loyal supporters, Dolly," John said. "Sponsors of causes know that your name on their boards as 'director' or 'honorary member' will be an asset. People will be bound to give consideration to any movement with which you are connected."

"Well, I'm quite ready to support as many good causes as I can," Dorothy said, "particularly those that have to do with child welfare, adult education and internationalism."

She turned through the letters putting them in separate piles, those to be answered personally, those for whom a dictated answer would suffice. An editor wanted an article; a politician wanted a statement to give support to his platform; a chairman of a committee wanted to enlist her aid in championing a cause; a reporter wanted an interview; a program chairman of a woman's club asked if she would be a speaker; a college president asked her to deliver the commencement address. There was an invitation to a banquet in New York, and one to a luncheon in Boston.

"John, here's something heart-warming—" Dorothy read aloud the letter signed by fourteen young women in Connersville, Indiana, who had formed a club with the motto "Books are more than literature. They are, when great and useful, life itself. They are not merely an escape. They are a fulfillment." All of them were readers and admirers of Dorothy's books and articles, so they had called themselves The Dorothy Canfield Club. They wanted Dorothy to know what they had done, that they felt proud to have her as an example of the highest type of American womanhood, and would strive to follow in her footsteps and promote her ideals.

"*That* is a letter I shall answer myself, for I heartily approve of their project and shall follow with interest all they do."

There was a letter from a young man whom Dorothy had helped with a small loan " . . . will you please write to me when you have time? Even a little letter would be welcome." Another letter asked her to use her influence to help in getting a book published.

She scrutinized the name and shook her head. "No one can do that. If the book is good a publisher will publish it; if it isn't good all the influence in the world won't do a thing."

"What would you like to do with this, Mrs. Fisher?"

"What is it?"

"It's bulky. It feels like manuscript."

"Is it from a publisher?"

"No—an individual. It's not a name I've come upon in any of your correspondence."

"Return it. Unopened."

Dorothy read aloud a letter from Sally, brimming with details of life at Oxford.

Among the packages in the mail was a copy of *Higher Education Faces the Future*, a symposium edited by Paul Schilpp to which Dorothy had contributed the chapter *New Leaders Needed*. Dorothy looked at it approvingly. "That's the piece," she reflected, "in which I developed the idea that the possession of leisure time is to man now what the discovery of fire once was—a tool he has to learn how to use."

"I remember when we were talking that out," John said. "It's not a bad idea, not a bit bad."

"Mrs. Fisher, this is something I believe you will want to answer for yourself."

"What is it?"

"A note from an Arlington boy who called yesterday morning while you were working to ask if he could set traps on your land."

Dorothy read the note to John.

"Well, if he will use the new kind of trap that kills instantly, we shouldn't object," John said.

Dorothy wrote out her answer. "We would be glad to let you put traps anywhere on our land, *if the traps are the kind that does not cause unnecessary suffering to the animals*. I'm not one of the people who objects to killing anything. I think a quick and painless death is nothing to be afraid of, for oneself, or for anybody or anything. . . . But there is plenty of misery and horror and anguish in the world, it seems to me, without adding anything to it. . . . Since there are now traps which prevent this torture of living flesh and blood, *it is no longer necessary* to use the older kinds."

They were delighted when a copy of Dorothy's book *Basque People* arrived in the mail. During the months when she and the children had been living at Guethary during the war she had become familiar with and fond of the Basques and their countryside. Writing about them, she had employed an eighteenth century device as she made her own shrewd comments through the tongue of a Basque.

"John, did you ever really realize how alike are Basques and Vermonters?"

He nodded as he turned through an envelope that contained pre-publication reviews. Holding one up he read from it, "Perhaps this says it, Dolly. It's from *Commonweal* and they call *Basque People* 'More than a collection of stories; it contains a delineation of a race.' "

She clapped her hands.

"You couldn't have portrayed the Basques as you did, Dolly, if you hadn't shared the same moral climate with them."

Letters attended to, Dorothy went out to work in her garden, clear a trail, or blaze trees for cutting. The Fishers had been told that the pine plantation could be thinned when the trees were about twenty-five years old, but that the cutting would have to be done carefully so the forest ceiling would be kept intact. The first thinnings were small and could only be used for odds and ends around the place; the next were big enough to send to the sawmill to be made into two-by-fours. Now trees that could be sawed into real boards were being removed. Dorothy gazed at a pile of logs waiting to be trucked away. Those useful giants from what had once been toothbrush-sized clusters of needles!

On days when the snow cover was good, Dorothy spent the afternoon on skis, making long cross-country expeditions, working slowly uphill then coming down from the mountain to a glowing winter sunset that flooded the valley with color. When the sap started to run, she spent all her free time in the sugar-bush helping with the boiling down of the thin colorless sap to the clear heavy amber of maple syrup. Well she knew how dangerous to elasticity was long sustained mental work if the pressure was too steady, but she had many means of release close at hand. Later in the afternoon a group of teachers might be coming to call on her; a reader of her books might have asked for an hour's visit; an English class from a high school might want to interview her, or perhaps one of the neighbors would be coming in for a talk. Dorothy would be back from field or mountain in time for the appointment, but only just in time, for she made minutes count.

After supper, sitting by the fire or under the stars, she and John would exchange thoughts about the day, drifting together from the sunny glare of its prose to the leafy shade of its poetry. A long musing silence would follow, then they would turn to their evening's work. While John built up the fire in the Franklin stove Dorothy would go around the house to see that the doors were latched against the wind. They were never locked. Hours of reading lay before them on the galleys that had arrived from the Book-of-the-Month Club.

Any member of the household could tell whether Dorothy had gone to bed by looking to see if her copy of Montaigne was still on the table. "Mother must be around somewhere," was a favorite remark of the children's. "She hasn't had her dose of Montaigne yet." He had been her companion for years and every evening she read a page or two in his rambling discursive essays. Her volume was the one her father and grandfather had used, with their marginal notes and underlinings. Montaigne's motto "Que sais-je?" had long been hers. An advisor who asked himself "What do I know?" and therefore stirred the liveliest realization of all there was to find out and think about, appealed to Dorothy more than one who thought he had found the answers.

After going to bed, Dorothy could generally fall into a sound sleep, but she often woke long before dawn and her busy mind went forward planning the day or the writing she was engaged in. One summer morning, waking shortly after three o'clock, she did not have the slightest inclination for further sleep nor could she see any sense in wasting time in bed. Moonlight filled the world beyond her window, making the mountains misty, the near fields shimmer with dew. She decided to do some mowing. Hitching her nightgown up, she crept through the sleeping house and out to the shed. Taking the scythe down from its hook, she touched the blade's edge with her finger. It was sharp. She might have known it would be. John always kept the tools ready for use. She went out and started to scythe—reveling in the beauty of the night, the gentle swinging rhythm. Her thoughts were with Uncle Zed who, so many years ago, had put a scythe in her hand and taught her how to use it.

Her work was half done and a faint suggestion of dawn had begun to show behind the mountains. Suddenly Dorothy wondered what her neighbors would say if they should see her. "They'll think I'm out of my mind!" she exclaimed.

Putting the scythe away, she went back through the still sleeping house and sat down at her desk. Her fingers found their old familiar way around her pen.

Sally arrived home early in the summer after two years at Oxford. She was to teach at the University of Vermont in September, but she was already engaged to John Paul Scott, who had also been an American student at Oxford, and had a teaching fellowship at the University of Chicago.

For years Dorothy had been meeting with her neighbors for an afternoon of sewing and reading aloud. Many of them had opened their homes to tourists during the summer months and some of the experiences they had had were cheerful and entertaining. Dorothy wrote a play called *Tourists Accommodated* which was first acted by the North District people in Arlington's Town Hall. After its publication it was widely performed by amateur groups.

Tourists had become a cash-crop to the state. Dorothy wrote what she referred to as her first and last piece of advertising for the Vermont Bureau of Publicity in the form of a booklet, *Summer Homes*. She called it an open letter and in it suggested that interested people come to Vermont and talk things over "with people of your own kind—ministers, doctors. . . . And don't try to go too fast. It's a personal relationship you are establishing." She reminded those who were thinking of retirement that Vermont was a place where older people had always been esteemed. People searching for a country home would have a welcome waiting for them in Vermont and to be welcomed had always been to her one of the great human joys.

Among the photographs in the book was one of Dorothy in her garden. Behind her stood the small old house that had been growing with the years. Near it was the little white-painted sign HERE IS WHERE THE FISHERS LIVE. People who saw it at the end of a journey saw it as well as an indication of the positive and permanent values the Fishers stood for.

The rooted countryman in Dorothy's play had been speaking for her when he said, "It's going out for a little excursion from the place where you really belong that's fun. But you have to have the place where you really belong."

In June of 1933 Sally and John Paul Scott were married. Dorothy and Jimmy left for Austria soon after the wedding. John was to follow them when he had completed some carpentry he was doing in the house. Dorothy kept the home circle of family and friends glowingly informed of all they were doing in a series of letters—

Mondsee, Austria
July 1933

Dear Family at home:

I'm sitting at a little pine table, looking out on a landscape composed of monstrous oak, elm, horse-chestnut and spruce trees, two excellent tennis courts, some green fields, and assorted Austrian country people sauntering back and forth.

Jimmy lies across the room from my table on a funny old-fashioned red plush sofa. He is reading a big serious text book on economics, reading interesting bits aloud to me from time to time, and fortifying himself by munching hazel nuts and dried currants (a combination known in Germany and here as "student food")....

Mondsee turns out to be a small place (1600) inhabitants, a market town for the countryside, on a lovely lake with green mountains rising all around. Two autos owned in town. A big fourteenth century church, and a plain old castle (more like a barracks), the Austro-American music summer school run by the same management as the "Institute of Economics"—or "World Affairs" to which we have come. . . . It is restful in the extreme to me not to be responsible in any way or shape for what goes on—the afternoon lectures are fine, the place lovely, and Jimmy and I are having just the utterly quiet uninterrupted time for reading and study that we wanted. It is great fun to be studying the same subject, and comparing notes as to impressions of it and of the people we meet, and—since we don't do it in public we feel justified—we have many a midriff-shaking laugh together over the extraordinary Americans we see at mealtime and others. . . .

We reserve judgment as to what may be coming next, and enjoy the quiet, the sunshine, the lovely scenery, and each other—to the last degree. Also enjoying the study of economics. I do feel ever so much less of an imbecile about it already, and expect by the end of the summer to be able to follow what happens with really less bewilderment and confusion. And my guess is that lots is going to happen! . . .

. . . The lecturer for last week's afternoon lectures was an economic specialist who had been attending the economic conference in London and came straight here from there. His lectures were extremely interesting although *harrowing!* The picture he painted, based on statistics, all of it apparently, of the present state of economic life in the Western world, certainly did freeze one's blood. The details of the "Economic war" now being waged in Europe, between the different countries is unbelievable! It certainly does look like the beginning of the break-up into the Dark Ages, after the ruin of the Pax Romana period. . . .

Yesterday morning I had a letter from the Henry Canbys, just arrived at Salzburg. Henry and I had to get together on books that had been sent us from the Book-of-the-Month office. So Jimmy and I took the narrow guage railroad to Salzburg, where we had supper. Trout. But the flavor can't compare with our Vermont trout— much coarser and tougher and less delicate eating.

Then the Canby boys drove Jimmy and me back here in their car to go to a fine string quartet concert that was held at the castle. . . .

Then we all—nearly literally all—went down stairs and across the street to "the" cafe, only one in town, and had things to eat and drink and then I came home to go to bed and sent the Canby boys back towards Salzburg, and left Jimmy to stay on as long as he liked with the gang, to dance and eat and holler around as becomes their age. . . .

Jimmy has rushed around organizingly (amusing me by seeing myself as others see me!) and has brought into existence, single-handedly but after a lot of pulling of wires and placating of the authorities, and so on, an evening course in—well, philosophic talks about music, its history and development, etc. . . . Detailed analysis of some Bach fugues and Beethoven sonatas are promised us later. Jimmy beams. . . .

. . . The much expected telegram announcing John's arrival in Salzburg came last Thursday. . . . You can imagine how good he looked to us! And how we ran and snatched at him and at his valise as he got out, and when he said wasn't it irregular just walking out with his valise so, without passing it through the usual gate, Jimmy told him gayly, "Nothing is 'irregular' in Austria! You're not in Germany!" And in a minute we were starting back up here, talking a streak about what had been happening on both sides since we'd rolled down the hill on June 23 from our own home. We think he looks well, and he returns the compliment, especially for Jimmy who is in one of his "radiant" phases, enjoying everything and profiting by everything. . . .

Weekends are the only times for expeditions, in a program so packed with things to do as this, so last Saturday, although the barometer was not promising, we all set off for the ascent of the Schafberg, the tallest mountain immediately on the lake—about six thousand feet high. . . .

And the next day, yesterday, the rain still continuing, we were sitting quietly in the hotel, reading away on Book-of-the-Month proofsheets, which follow us here, when Jimmy came dashing in to say that a grand peasant dance was going on at such-and-such an inn and wouldn't we like to go? We did, and saw such a spectacle of vitality and life-enjoying zest as seldom comes one's way! . . .

After a time, Jimmy—who knows everybody in town now and is in everything—stood up and said he'd donate a beer-horn to the party. The leader then came over, took off his pointed green felt hat with a bow and rattled off a lot of ritual compliments to Jimmy, to which Jimmy, standing very straight and smiling and vastly enjoying all the fun, made the right answer—whatever it was—and then they all threw their hats in the air and shouted, "Hurrah," and a girl brought in an actual literal horn—a huge ox-horn, mounted in silver and wreathed with laurel leaves. Jimmy took a first drink of this, to the accompaniment of cheers, and passed it to us, who went through the motions of drinking—John laughing and saying to me in an aside, "Well, anybody who lives with you has a various life, that's a sure thing!" And then the horn was passed from hand to hand on the dancing floor. Then another dance was formed— . . .

Our plans—rather vague so far—are about like this: next Saturday we all go down to Salzburg to hear some of the music festival—*Fidelio*, Max Reinhardt's *Everyman*, and Gluck's *Orpheus*. Then Jimmy comes back here to go on with work, and John and I to Passau, from which we will go down the Danube to Vienna . . . then to Innsbruck for a week around the high mountains. . . .

We think we have engaged passage on the Majestic sailing from Cherbourg, September 7, which will land me in New York in time for the September Book-of-the-Month meeting. And home probably by the 17th of September.

Shortly after the return home, Dorothy's novel *Bonfire* was published. Again the background was a Vermont village, and the story was that of the interplay of human lives. John, reading the book, was even more impressed by the force of the opening chapter than he had been when he read it in manuscript.

"Dolly, if any young author contemplating fiction for a life work were to ask my advice, I'd tell him to make a study of the first chapter in *Bonfire*."

"Would you, John? Why?"

"To observe how you have needed only sixteen pages to set up the atmosphere, the scene, and introduce a whole village-full of leading and secondary characters. Dolly, the book is like a Breughel market place, filled with active, brightly clad figures, not one is blurred or scamped and each one is utterly and entirely different from the other. People are going to wonder if anywhere on earth there is a community so packed with fascinating people as your town of Clifford."

"Stuff and nonsense!" Dorothy replied. "Anywhere, everywhere, there's just as much humanity, absorbingly interesting humanity, if we have eyes to see it."

"But that's exactly my point, most of us haven't the right kind of eyes." John picked up the book and turned to a particular page. "Remember what your Miss Bessie says—'No matter where we go, there's plenty of what we want to fill our dippers with. But we can't fetch up any more than our dippers will hold.' When you offer your readers a drink from the spring of life, Dolly, you scoop it up in a ''n'awful' big dipper!"

The critics confirmed John's enthusiasm. Many reviewers thought *Bonfire* was the strongest and most consistent of all Dorothy's novels. "Finest. . . . Most distinguished . . . Most richly felt and finely written. . . . Most enduring prose. . . . Salty humor, proportion, mellow forthrightness" were some of the things they said. The *Virginia Quarterly* commented,

Its strength lies in Dorothy Canfield's understanding sympathy for and knowledge of her locale, and her ability to evoke all the richness of life bound up in a small community.

And Harry Scherman, as warm a friend as he was sagacious a critic, said,

In this, as in her other novels, Dorothy Canfield shows a prime virtue that is sadly uncommon among modern novelists: her understanding of the people she writes about goes so deep that it can be rooted in real kindness, without being in the slightest degree uncritical or less probing and profound. So, the observant reader realizes in a glow, after reading this book, that human experience has been disclosed to him, not in moral blacks and whites, but as the ever-different and yet ever-the-same human experience, something that in its myriad aspects will be fascinating to tell about, to watch and reflect upon, till the crack of doom; and something good in almost any aspect if, whether in suffering it, in being amused by it, or merely in contemplating it with sympathy, we find our wisdom deepened.

A few weeks after the book was published, Dorothy was lecturing at a college before a mixed audience of young men and women. During the question period following her talk a young man rose.

"Mrs. Fisher—"

"Yes?"

"How do you stand it when a reviewer pans one of your books? It would slay me. How can you make yourself feel about it so it doesn't kill you?"

"Well, of course," she began, "no writer would pretend that it is pleasant to read a severely unfavorable criticism of a book he has worked on for years and put his whole heart into. But nobody can expect to be liked by everyone. You know well enough that not everybody who knows you likes you. The very fact that some do, means that others with different tastes don't—" Dorothy stopped talking, halted by a strange sick expression on the face of the virile, upstanding young man. It had never occurred to him, at nineteen, that anyone could dislike him.

Dorothy looked around the room from one sober young face to another, realizing that she had broken dreadful news to them all.

Other questions came and were answered. Hands were shaken. Good-bys said. In her inner ear Dorothy heard the casual tones of a little Cockney boxing instructor. She had not thought of him for years but the sound of his voice was stronger than the sound of the strong young voices around her. "Don't 'urry," he was saying. "There's no need to 'urry." She wondered why she had thought of him. Then the picture of her father came to her mind, James Canfield, vigorous, robust, saying "—you can make criticism serve you, if you know how to appraise it."

John had been drawn more and more into town affairs and was now active on the Arlington School Board. Dorothy, who had been writing for years as a parent, wondered what new-old truths she would have to say as a grandparent. In May she went to Chicago to be with Sally and her scientist-husband until their child was born.

When Dorothy returned to Arlington, she wrote the first in a series of articles for the *Delineator*. It was called *The New Grandmother* and, as she wrote, thoughts of her little grand-daughter were uppermost in her mind. She completed most of the series during the summer, winning the editor's appreciation—

Extra thanks go to you for your miraculously early completion of two-thirds of your series. We are again breathless with the beauty of your work. . . . I say this not above a whisper but I'm wondering if you have thought of possible book publication of this startlingly new child-and-parent training material? It would be grand. And if there should be a book, would there be more articles? And would you let us publish them?

Dorothy showed the letter to John. There never seemed to be any end to what people wanted her to do.

Chapter 13

Heroic Eyes of Truth

APPRECIATION had long rolled in to Dorothy from her readers; another tide had been swelling with the years. Her recent election to membership in the National Institute of Arts and Letters acknowledged her work in the literary field; the academic honors that were coming to her recognized what she stood for in American life and letters.

In 1921, Middlebury College had awarded her an honorary degree, Doctor of Letters. The following year similar degrees were bestowed upon her by the University of Vermont and by Dartmouth College, Columbia University honored her in 1929, Northwestern in 1931, Rockford College in 1934. In 1935 three Universities honored her, beginning with her own Ohio State. Williams College linked her with her father—

For an enthusiastic, affectionate, and intelligent love of youth, such as properly belong to the daughter of a father who was not only a favorite son of Williams, but who also won from this college forty-two years ago, similar recognition; for the enrichment of our national literature with many lovable characters fashioned by imagination yet recognized as creatures of flesh and blood.

Swarthmore linked her with her son. Sitting on the platform in her cap and gown, Dorothy saw Jimmy receive the degree for which he had worked so zestfully. When the time came for the awarding of the Honorary Degrees, Dr. Harold Goddard of the English Department stepped forward.

"Mr. President," he said, "I have the honor to present for the Degree of Doctor of Letters, Dorothy Canfield Fisher, a great American novelist and stimulating writer on educational subjects. Born and reared in an academic atmosphere, she has proved by her work that the sometimes dry and dusty discipline of the Ph.D. need not smother the flame of literary genius. Her work is distinguished by a rare understanding of education problems, and keen insight into the character and ideals of the Society of Friends. On this day when the second of her two children graduates from Swarthmore, it is with peculiar pleasure that we admit her formally to the fold to which she has for many years spiritually belonged."

President Aydelotte, presenting Dorothy with the degree, said, "Dorothy Canfield Fisher: It has been given to you to interpret in your novels with beauty and insight the new civilization which is being built up in the America of the twentieth century. In recognition of that great achievement and of your devotion to the cause of education, with which literature itself is so intimately linked, I confer upon you, by the authority vested in me by the Board of Managers of Swarthmore College and by the Commonwealth of Pennsylvania, the Degree of Doctor of Letters, and admit you to all the rights and privileges belonging to that degree."

A woman who knew Dorothy only through her books recalled a Commencement address at a State Normal School and wrote a poem about it. When Dorothy saw the poem it was as heartening in its way as the citation and hood that had recently been bestowed on her.

Commencement Day
(In tribute to Dorothy Canfield Fisher)

I saw her once . . . I was eighteen and I remember
Her scarlet cape over a Paris gown,
The flashing wit, the new ideas

With which she challenged students
On Commencement Day.

I have forgotten what I learned from books
That spring at Lynton,
But one brief contact with a glowing personality
Has vividly illumined all her lines
Upon the printed page for more than twenty years.

How simple and direct have been her themes!
A twig is bent—a mighty tree inclines;
A stream fed by its tributaries finds new depths
And flows into the harbor; now the cup of life
Is brimming; now the soul chafes at restriction
Like a squirrel in a cage.

How fine her artistry!
Always for me now a distant ribbon river
Like a legato binds the melody;
In old musicians' violins the seraph seeks
His odd abiding place; Arnold and Molly pass
In speeding cars; crossed foils say "Sylvia"
And in these stark depression days
I have seen proud Valeries going up
Unconquered by a foe.
The last house on *all* country roads
Is old man Warner's, and what joy is mine
When any Matey finds her Adrian!

Her books are ageless.
Back and forth across the loom of Life
Slips the swift shuttle of Humanity
Bearing the colors of its hopes and dreams
To interlock the weft of Time and make in patterns
That the Weaver knows, garments of harmony
For future days.

The world needs women like her—strong, courageous souls
Restorative as the Green Mountain air, homey and real
As little Arlington, yet planetary-minded with a poet's dream.

I saw her once . . . I was eighteen and I remember
Her scarlet cape over a Paris gown,
The flashing wit, the new ideas
With which she challenged students
On Commencement Day.

Dorothy Ann Gardyne

Dorothy, appointed to serve on the Youth Commission, was obliged to make frequent trips to Washington. John had been elected for a second term to the State Legislature and the Arlington house was closed. Dorothy could do her work as easily in the house they rented in Montpelier for the winter. Jimmy, now at Harvard Medical School, was engaged to Eleanor Bodine. Sally was busy with her growing family.

City life was all right for a while, Dorothy thought, but she breathed more deeply when she got back to the country where weather counted for something. It never mattered to her what the weather did, and except that like a wood-burning stove she "drew" better when it was cold, she enjoyed every kind: whirling storms with snow smothering the mountain roads and sweeping in mid-ocean swells over her woodland walks . . . dreamy days when the light over the mountains was opalescent and all nature seemed lost in a beatific trance . . . raw damp days when rain worked up from the south with slow steady sound and gradually took possession of the mouse-colored landscape . . . spring with its carpet of flowers that made walking up Red Mountain like walking through a medieval tapestry . . . autumn with leaves showering down from the big locust tree after the first hard frost, falling through the sunshine like sparks of gold.

As long as she could remember, one use for the telephone had been to draw some responsive friend's attention to beauty that might go unseen because of preoccupation with the daily round.

One morning, after a succession of gray winter days that brought neither snow nor rain to the valley but shrouded the mountain tops, Dorothy looked from her window as the sun unveiled the mountains and saw that their top portions were white with frozen cloud. "They are soaring, soaring!" she exclaimed as she hastened to the telephone.

Late one afternoon she cried eagerly over the wire, "Sally, Sally Cleghorn, have you seen the light that is coming on the mountains? We'll just have time to get up to Bromley and see it filling Peru valley."

Quickly Dorothy got the car, drove the few miles to Manchester to pick up her friend, then east and up the long climb to Big Bromley. When the road leveled off at the foot of the mountain they stopped the car and looked around them. Sunset on the distant slopes made them glow golden and rose. The valley below was darkening with heather-colored shadow that was slowly working upward. For fifteen minutes the two friends watched the wonder, wordless and happy. Then Dorothy turned the car, and drove down the long hill back to Manchester where lights were beginning to come on in the houses.

"Now it will take time for us to get used to another kind of beauty," she said.

That night at supper, telling John of what she had seen, she was reminded of a recent letter from a friend living in the Southwest, full of praise for the perfect climate found there. "But I would find it monotonous."

"I wouldn't want to miss the turning wheel of the seasons," John agreed.

"The seasons—yes, yes!" Then Dorothy's thoughts led her to wondering if the seasons of life should not be accepted as thankfully.

In June Dorothy received honorary degrees from the University of Nebraska and Mount Holyoke College. After Jimmy's marriage, she and John went to Paris for a few weeks, then into the Engadine for a walking trip. Evidences of the Nazi-Fascist shadow with its danger to freedom-loving peoples met them everywhere. Unless things changed greatly, the Fishers knew there would not be many more such trips to Europe. Dorothy felt that she had much to say to Americans, to parents particularly, but the physical act of writing was becoming difficult as neuritis had begun to attack her with pain and stiffness. When she arrived in Paris Dorothy consulted Dr. Pilliet, a well-known woman doctor, who suggested a radical change in posture. Dorothy seized on the idea as a means of keeping herself in working trim. As long as she could write and there were things to say she did not want to lose a single day of work. When she got home she carried out Dr. Pilliet's instructions—slept with several pillows instead of one, placed a cushion on her chair at the dining room table, cut the legs off her desk so it would be lower, got a stand-up desk so she could stand for periods of working time, put a cork halfway down her pen so her fingers would have a different grip. The results appeared to be miraculous. The difficulties of the past few months began to disappear. With fingers limbered and muscles more responsive, Dorothy felt herself to be again in good working order.

Dorothy's fiction writing meant more to her than any other kind of writing. It did not grow easier with the years, but seemed to require deeper, longer thinking as the situations she pondered became more universal. The neatly patterned plot, the surprise ending were of small matter to her. Her interest was, as it had always been, in people—what they did and why. If emotions pulled at the hearts of Dorothy's readers, it was because she had first been shattered by those same emotions.

Fables for Parents was waiting for them on their return from Europe. It contained many of Dorothy's recent short stories, some of them concerned with the relationships of children to parents and grandparents. The practical present, the rich nostalgic past were linked in the book by Dorothy's buoyant optimism, sympathy for others, and keen sense of social responsibility. Among the stories was the now widely read *The Murder on Jefferson Street*. When it had first been written, Paul Reynolds had sent it to various magazines without success. At Dorothy's suggestion he had sent it to the *Yale Review* which had published it immediately. Later in the year it was included in the O. Henry prize collection. Since then it had been published in many anthologies, translated into several languages, and was rapidly becoming one of Dorothy's most remembered stories.

A Danish magazine, commenting on *Fables for Parents*, said that no living author had gone deeper into the human mind and heart. "Humor, sanity, love of our race characterize her work, and she was born a true artist by the grace of God."

Dorothy had seen for herself the extent of the shadow that was creeping over Europe; she had been aware for years of prejudicial tendencies in her own country which were the opposite of what American democracy stood for. To see and think was for her to write. When her long richly-packed novel *Seasoned Timber* was published in the spring of 1939, it was the evidence of vision and thought. Vermont was her background, and the village of Clifford already familiar to her readers; but the problems she dealt with were common to mankind. The book appeared at a time when it was greatly needed. Solid and truth-telling, it was an anchor thrown into the sea of uncertainty that the threat of war was making of the world.

Lewis Gannett, reviewing the book in the *New York Times*, said that Dorothy had packed almost too much into it but that he had read every page, often swallowing hard. "Readers need the message it carries," said *The Fight*, "so the forces of freedom need these readers to join in the tremendous effort that must be made if liberty is not to end." *Equality* spoke of the qualities that distinguished Dorothy Canfield's novels adding that "in her new novel, that artistry and thoughtfulness are focussed on an American issue of such magnitude that any readers who have lingered outside her audience must and will join it."

John, after he had read *Seasoned Timber* in its published form, put the book on the shelf beside *The Brimming Cup* and *The Deepening Stream*. "They belong together, Dolly," he said. "As a trilogy, they're like an Ode to Maturity whose *leit-motif* might well be called 'Youth shows but half, trust God, see all, nor be afraid.' "

It was not only the reviewers and the bookstores that were to be instrumental in getting Dorothy's message to a widening circle of readers. A small volume, *The Election on Academy Hill*, taken from *Seasoned Timber*, was published for use in schools; it contained, as well, questions for class discussion and suggestions for further reading. When Whit Burnet edited *This Is My Best*, in which ninety-three authors presented their self-chosen best, Dorothy sent a chapter from *Seasoned Timber*. She gave her reasons for choosing *The Night on the Cobble*, which told of a man's lonely struggle to free himself from the personal and lift himself into the spacious serenity of the universal. "The chapter is thus not only a solvent of the sorrow and pain just behind him in his individual personal life," Dorothy said. "It is a spiritual preparation for what is just before him— a fiery test of his character in his role as a member of civilized human society."

To the desk in the sunny study there now came a new kind of letter. An urgent, desperate request for help from some friend in France, Italy, or Germany. Sometimes it was a letter from an

American seeking help for a European friend. Dorothy had an able pen when it came to writing to congressmen and senators, and she was known to be able to accomplish near-miracles.

"Soon," the letters said. "Help must come *soon*."

"I wonder how we can help them all," John commented.

"Well, let's see what we can *do!*"

Scholars and teachers were the most in need. Many that were helped by the Fishers to get to America, came to Arlington to express their gratitude. Even more than for the adults, who could soon put to use in the New World the careful training they had received in the Old, Dorothy felt for the children. Many of them had come from small towns and villages in Germany and Austria and were living in New York in one-room tenements while their parents earned a precarious living. She began to talk with her neighbors about the possibility of bringing a group of children to stay in farm and village homes for the summer months.

One morning a notice appeared in the *Bennington Banner*:

Everybody is invited to come to a meeting to talk about refugees and see whether there is anything we can do about living up to the Vermont tradition of sympathy for the oppressed.

The meeting was to be held in Bennington, the shire town of the county. The night on which it was called, one of the winter's worst blizzards swept the countryside. The problem of refugees might have seemed a remote one to farmers and shopkeepers, but when the meeting opened the room was full. Dorothy knew that few Vermont farmers had ever seen a person from middle-Europe, but she knew too that their roots went deep in love of liberty and hatred of persecution. Now, a way was being shown by which the smallest household could help in the world struggle against oppression. From the group assembled came the unanimous decision to invite to Bennington County during the coming summer fifty children of Austrian and German parents, exiles seeking to establish themselves in a new way of life.

Dorothy and John drove back to Arlington, sixteen miles through swirling snow, happy at the way their neighbors had met the challenge of human need.

Before the arrival of summer and the refugee children, Dorothy had a series of lectures to give in Florida at the University of Miami. John, as a member of the Rhodes Scholarship Selection Board and a recently appointed member for ten years of the State Board of Education, had several meetings to attend. When they were both free to join each other, they went on to Spokane where Dorothy spoke at a Teachers' Convention, then on to Portland. They returned home by way of the big trees in California, a visit in San Francisco and a stop at the Grand Canyon.

On their return to Arlington, they were greeted by family and friends with rapid-fire questions as to how they had liked the great scenery of the West.

"It was magnificent," Dorothy admitted, then she added, "but it was a little like seeing a king in his coronation robes."

"It's good to be home," John said.

The green-clad hills of Vermont, the simple comfort of the little house were heart's desire to them both.

Fifty-two refugee children came to Arlington in July. Their foster parents for the summer and other friendly people met the group at the station. The children were shy at first, but once settled in their new homes they delighted everyone with their sanity and sense of fun. Programs of education and entertainment had been planned ahead of time, rules for living had been worked out so the newcomers would fit comfortably into household and community activities. And, best of all, no expense was involved as the American publisher of *Mein Kampf* had turned over to the committee for the refugee children the royalties from the sales of Hitler's book.

The children were taken on various excursions and one afternoon they went to the Fishers. An outdoor supper was ready for them in a clearing on Red Mountain from which they could look down into the valley. Tanned by the sun and alive to their finger tips they played games together, then relaxed listening to stories, and closed the day by singing. Europe and its strangely distorted patterns seemed very far away.

Dorothy was proud of Bennington County that had been the first rural community in the nation to show a feeling of responsibility for the child victims of totalitarianism. The friendly note that had been struck in the southern corner of the state was echoed in August from a small village near the Canadian Border. Dorothy received a letter enclosing $2.79, a sum collected by the children who were attending a summer religious school. "Please, Mrs. Fisher," the letter said, "will you use this to help the refugee children? We haven't much money, but we still have our country to take care of us."

The money did more than help the children; it sowed a seed in Dorothy's mind which went on growing during the summer.

Other friends who had been coming for years came to stay near the Fishers in the log-cabin or the tennis-court house, both of which John had built. They were generally professional people in need of a margin of time and quiet which summer days and the pine woods could supply. Dorothy typed out a memo which she tacked on the wall of the log-cabin retreat. It conveyed all the information she could think of—places to swim, places to eat, places to get milk—and how to keep it cool in the brook; what to do with garbage—("dig a deep hole and not mind but remember that it enriches the earth and helps the trees"). She listed historic sights for the children, the two near-

est towns Bennington and Manchester where more things than
Arlington offered could be obtained.

There is a library in Arlington, an Episcopal church. Western
Union can be telephoned from our home. . . . Our house is never
locked nights. Select your door, learn how to get in, and head for
there if you find you need to telegraph. No need to wake any of
us up, just go ahead. I hope you won't ever have to. . . .
There, that's about all there is to the valley, except its pleasant
and secret places which you'll come to know yourself.
Welcome.   Welcome.
P.S. There will certainly be things we've forgotten to tell you.
Ask any of us—whichever one you catch first—about anything
that doesn't work.

Early in 1940 the seed the children had sown when they sent
their contribution to Dorothy grew to be a working idea. Many
people were alarmed by the situation of the refugee children in
the United States and almost as alarmed by the way American
children took for granted the privileges of their citizenship.
"This is an emergency measure," Dorothy explained as she discussed her idea with friends whose support she was enlisting,
"but it may reach far."
Plans were worked out for a penny collection among the
public school children of the nation and letters were sent to
interested and influential people to enlist their sanction and
support in what would be called a Children's Crusade for Children. From allowances or earned money, each child would
give voluntarily as many pennies as he was years old to help
children without a country—exiles from China, Poland, Czecho-
slovakia, Spain, Austria, Hungary, Finland. During the week
of the collection in schools, teaching would emphasize present-
day world conditions as well as American traditions and ideals.
Dorothy worked tirelessly as the idea developed. In February

she went to St. Louis to address twelve thousand members of the Association of Officers of Administration of the Public School System. At Grand Rapids she spoke before the Commissioners of Education of the forty-eight states. They were the ones who would decide whether the penny collection could be allowed. They promised her their decision in ten days. Dorothy wanted to tell Harry Scherman, who was meeting the expenses of the Crusade, what had taken place but she had only an hour before her train left and more to say than she could put in a telegram. Going to a typewriter store, she asked if she could rent a machine for half an hour for an urgent letter.

"Our machines are not for rent, madam, only for sale."

"What about that one in the window?" Dorothy asked.

"We can't take it out of the window for you. It is a demonstration machine."

"All right then, I'll sit in the window—just let me buy some paper and pay you for the use of the machine."

Dorothy sat in the window of the typewriter store, tapping away at her fastest clip.

When the promised decision came, it was favorable.

The idea spread like a wave, and though some opposition developed among groups opposed to aid to foreigners, it only made the Crusaders work harder. Offices were donated. Writers offered to speak and write for the Crusade. Professors and union leaders gave their help. All religions and races showed equal interest. A jury of award was appointed to decide on the distribution of the money—Mrs. Roosevelt, Monsignor John A. Ryan, William Allen White, Justice Irving Lehman, Miss Caroline Woodruff, Dr. Charles B. Glen, and Dorothy Canfield.

Years ago Dorothy had written a play for the Community Players in Arlington, based on events leading up to and including the first Constitutional Convention in Philadelphia. Now, with Sally Cleghorn's help, the play was rewritten. Fellow-captains they had thought of themselves once; fellow-pilgrims they thought of themselves now as they worked together evening after evening on *Liberty and Union*. Published in pamphlet form, copies of the play were sent to the public schools to be acted as part of the campaign.

When the week of the collection arrived, pennies poured into the tin mite-boxes that had been placed in schools throughout the country. The total amount was close to $140,000.

Dorothy wrote a letter of thanks to the nation's schoolchildren, telling them how the money would be distributed among the various relief organizations. "Can you imagine what fourteen million pennies look like? We can tell you—they look like mountains of kindness, like majestic Alps of decent human feeling, like a great hope shining through the night."

In July, the National Council of Administrative Women in Education, meeting in Milwaukee, honored Dorothy with their medal. President Inez Johnson Lewis, State Commissioner of Education of Colorado, said in presentation:

Dorothy Canfield Fisher—of the splendid mind and great heart! Hers is a personality which includes a rare combination of intellect, will power, drive, and quality of soul which makes for success in her undertakings.

The children of war-torn countries in Europe caught the sympathy of Mrs. Fisher. Determined to ease their suffering, she helped to develop a movement called the Children's Crusade. Words were Mrs. Fisher's weapons—she traveled, she spoke, and she used her powerful pen. As a result of her activity, the children of our nation contributed $140,000 in pennies to assist the children of Europe.

But this sum of money was not the real objective. With true insight Mrs. Fisher saw, that if our democracy is to succeed, our children must learn to accept responsibility for the welfare of their fellows. They must learn to be sympathetic to the needs and sufferings of people in their own country and in the world. They must be quick to initiate activity which alleviates this suffering.

Consequently, the Children's Crusade provided a training ground for democratic citizenship.

Therefore, in the name of this Counctil, I award the Ella Flagg Young Medal to Dorothy Canfield Fisher, in absentia, for her contributions to the children of this nation and the suffering children of Europe.

Much as Dorothy wanted to be present, she could not be. She was, quite literally, exhausted. As once before when she had worked to help the victims of another war, she weighed less than ninety pounds. An alarming shortness of breath began to develop and Dorothy went to Boston in November for a thyroidectomy.

For thirteen years she had been reading for the Book-of-the-Month Club. Rich among the rewards of the years was the knowledge of the books that were constantly being sent out— to homes, to towns where there were no bookstores, to villages where there were no libraries. Slowly, certainly, books were becoming an organic part of the thinking of the American people. During those years she had not missed a meeting of the Selection Committee, nor had she been obliged to be away from home for more than a night as the meetings were luncheon ones. The reading had been vast, but she had always been a fast reader, and reading books in galleys was like walking on new snow to her. No one had been there before, no other opinion interfered with her own. Rarely content to read only the Class A books, she asked for the lists of books preferred by the first readers as well as those rejected. Uncle Zed had once said, when asked whether he wanted mince pie or apple, "I want everything." That was how she felt about the books that were being written and published.

The train to New York or the Hudson River night boat gave her hours for reading, as did waiting for an appointment or sitting under a hair drier. As soon as she settled down with a book she had the comfortable feeling that nobody would pay any attention to her, and when she was in New York she relished the privacy given by a big city. She could go to bed with proof sheets all around her and read with no claims of any kind upon her; she could have the *Times* at breakfast instead of in the afternoon; she could talk with friends on the telephone; attend the Selection Committee luncheon; then get the train back to Arlington with a new set of galleys under her arm.

After the years of reading, Dorothy's eyes began to protest. Even cold compresses did not relieve the pain. Other members of the Selection Committee complained of eye strain and Dorothy consulted an oculist. "Don't read so fast," he said. "Such rapid reading is straining your eyes."

"But that's the way I read."

He asked her what kind of reading she was doing and she told him that much of it was in galley proof.

"You'll have to give up reading galleys or you won't have any eyesight at all."

She asked him why and he explained that an oculist prescribes lenses for a given distance. "With galleys you are at the right distance for only a short part of a very long sheet. As the eye travels down the sheet there is only one place—about a hand's length—where the print is right for the eye."

Dorothy was shocked. Give up reading? As well give up breathing!

But the thought presented by the oculist proved beneficial for all the members of the Selection Committee. A merely mechanical matter solved the collective eye strain. Publishers agreed to cut the galleys into three pages and staple them together into a sort of imitation page proof. It was thick and bulky, but eminently more readable, and soon widely known as BOMC proofs.

With the new books there was always the thrill of discovery. One particularly big bundle that seemed to be about agriculture in China, Dorothy had set aside to read on the train. It had been put into Class B and Dorothy wondered how interesting it was going to prove. Always in her mind was the consideration of what would be most suitable for a wide audience. This book, at first glance, did not look as if it would be of general interest. She began to read as the train pulled out of Arlington. By the end of the first twelve pages she was sitting bolt upright in her seat, electrified by the book's quality. She read it all the way to New York, then sat up in her hotel bedroom until she finished it.

Early the next morning, long before any New York office was really open, she went to the Book-of-the-Month office. She found nobody but the janitor languidly sweeping, so she left a note saying, "I think this book is important and that every effort should be made to hold it over to next month because it may be that it hasn't been thoroughly read. Although it's been listed as a "B" book, it's of first-rate importance."

The book was held over until the next month, then it was chosen unanimously. Neither Dorothy nor any other member of the Selection Committee had heard of the author before, a woman by the name of Pearl Buck. But everyone agreed that *The Good Earth* was an outstanding book.

Alfred Knopf asked Dorothy to stop in at his office once when she was in New York. He showed her a book. "It's a wonderful book but I can't get anybody to read it. It isn't that they read it and don't like it. They won't open it."

Dorothy saw the name on the jacket. *Life With Father.* "I know it," she said, "and I think it's marvelous."

"So do I. But why won't people read it?'

"Anything in the world I can do to try to get it over, I will."

She convinced the Selection Committee that it deserved reading, and they were soon convinced that it deserved being sent out.

During those first thirteen years, the members of the Selection Committee learned from each other, as well as from the people to whom the books were sent. "All of us knew," Henry Seidel Canby said, "that our responsibility was as great as our opportunities."

Chapter 14

Good Neighbor

CHRISTMAS greetings came to Dorothy from all over the United States. One, from the Battenkill Valley School Children, was delivered in person. The Fishers had just sat down to Sunday evening supper when a knock was heard at the door and a rosy-cheeked little girl appeared, saying she had brought a present, "From all of us to you. From the teachers, too."

Dorothy, almost too pleased and proud to speak, gave the little girl a hearty kiss in thanks. The greeting was signed by a long list of names and when Dorothy answered it each child was sent a mimeographed copy of her letter.

One day a box came in the mail containing a medal and a citation, signed by the King of Denmark, for Dorothy's services to Danish children during the Children's Crusade. About the same time she was asked to attend a gathering in New York to be honored by the Chinese government. Dressed her best, Dorothy was expecting one of the crowded occasions she so disliked. When she reached the Waldorf-Astoria she found a small group of noted Chinese, with Pearl Buck the only other woman. In the name of the Chinese Government, Mr. Hui-Shi, the Ambassador to the United States, presented Dorothy with the Order of the Jade and spoke with gratitude of her services to mankind. After this simple but deeply moving ceremony, everyone sat down to luncheon.

"What can one *do* with a medal?" Dorothy thought, as she had on another occasion.

When at a later date the Kappa Kappa Gammas presented her with a silver bowl as their Achievement Award, Dorothy was delighted. "You can do so many things with a bowl!" she exclaimed as she looked forward to filling it with flowers, or apples, or letting it fill itself with light as it stood on a table near a lamp.

Her helping spirit was now focussed on her own community. Since the school in Arlington had burned shortly before Christmas, there was an immediate need for funds to supplement the town appropriation and the fire insurance. Arlington had long needed an adequate, modern school building. John was made chairman of the Building Committee, and Dorothy with the aid of other townswomen took over the fund raising. Letters went from her desk to all whom she thought should or might want to help the young people of Arlington. Dorothy wrote a pageant, *Man and the Wilderness*, to be acted by the schoolchildren during the summer as part of their own effort to raise money.

Work on books went steadily on. With Sally Cleghorn, Dorothy wrote *Nothing Ever Happens and How It Does*. The book contained true stories to be used by teachers in reading to children and was accompanied by a manual to prompt class discussion. What the fellow-captains, fellow-pilgrims hoped was that the stories would kindle enthusiasm for living and draw out, as Dorothy said to their readers, "by natural magnetism, many more stories from the lives of the group. Nothing is so savory as fruit from one's own orchard."

Tell Me A Story, a gaily colored picture book for little children, had been a happy task for Dorothy. In it she recalled many events of her own childhood, and the story behind Tibor Gergely's spirited illustrations was like a fairy tale. It represented a small but immensely practical part of Dorothy's untiring effort to help refugees from Europe seeking a new foothold in America. When the publishers of her book were considering the choice of an artist, Dorothy recalled some particularly charming illustrations which had once been done for a story of hers in an Austrian publication. Upon diligent enquiry she learned that the illustrator, Tibor Gergely, was now a refugee from Nazi Germany and due to arrive in New York within a matter of days. When his ship docked, he had no immediate prospect of work and all his possessions were in a suitcase, but a friend was waiting to meet him with the manuscript of Dorothy Canfield's *Tell Me A Story* and a contract from the publisher for the art work.

Dorothy was well aware that throughout history exiles from one country bore great enrichment to the cultural life of their adopted land. There were continuing opportunities for her to use her imagination and wide contacts to help intellectual emigrés become integrated with American life. Enit Kaufman, a Viennese portrait painter becoming established in New York, wanted to make a collection of portraits of Americans great in a variety of fields. In an effort to help, Dorothy wrote the accompanying biographies. Each one, with the possible exception of her own, required enormous research and the work soon proved to be exhausting and time-consuming. When *American Portraits* was published, some years later, it was an inspiring book, alive with the lives it contained. The sixty-eight people within its pages, seen through the seasoned eye of an old American and the fresh eye of a new American, had all taken victorious command of their own lives. "That," Dorothy said, "no matter what is before us in the future, is of course the basic need for all human development: the emergence in each individual of the driving power needed to bring out the best of his own native powers."

With a group of other liberal thinkers, Dorothy participated in writing *The City of Man: A Declaration on World Democ-*

racy directed chiefly Against Naziism and Fascism. It was a stirring call to world patriotism and stressed the fact that the American creed must be the American deed.

Events had been moving rapidly during those last agonizing tempestuous months of 1941. Creed became deed when on December 7th the attack on Pearl Harbor brought the United States into the war. In the rush of passionate feeling that swept the country, Dorothy did as she so often had done before— reached into her past for a steadying influence. She recalled a family story that had been told for years.

It was about Great-great-grandmother and her sister who were sitting alone in their little frontier house when a violent storm came up. Winds shook the house as a dog might a rat, tore up forest trees by their roots, and drove rain with the force of cannon balls. In the midst of the tumult, Great-great-grandmother leaned toward her sister and shouted, "I think you put too much molasses in that last batch of baked beans."

"Have you lost your *mind?*" the sister shouted back. "Don't you know we may be killed the next minute?"

"But we may not be. And if we're not, we've got years ahead of us to eat baked beans in and I want mine *cooked right.*"

"What can I do?" one person after another asked. The Fishers had asked themselves that question at the time of another war and found their answer in humanitarian service. There were many people who by doing some needed work could release men for the fighting forces, but there were women who could not leave their homes or their necessary tasks, yet who were asking themselves that question. To them Dorothy gave her own heart-deep answer in one of the first of many articles she wrote for the Writers' War Board. She urged them to put into daily life the principles of Americanism for which soldiers were risking their lives. "Try," Dorothy wrote, "to make each day in your lives another proof that America is richly worth saving."

Asked to write on "How Can Artists and Writers Help the

War Effort" for the book *America Organizes to Win the War*, Dorothy spoke of how the creative person could help others to see more widely and feel more sensitively, thus helping win the war by enabling others to have a clear idea of what was to be won. "As much as tanks and ammunition, do we need the backing of farseeing, gifted, sincere writers and poets and artists, whose occupation is always to try to see through the surface confusion of mixed-up details to the clear, enduring, immortal pattern of which each detail is a part. . . . The function of the 'real' writer . . . is to keep us from just pawing facts over and over aimlessly, like a discouraged person pawing over the pieces of a jigsaw puzzle. It is the creative writer who makes us feel the eager certainty that those facts can make sense."

As a member of the American Youth Commission, Dorothy contributed the final section "Youth and the Future" to the book *Finding Your Way in Life*. And she continued to do all that she could toward the completion of Arlington's new school.

In September 1942 the Memorial School was dedicated. John presided at the exercises at which the Governor of Vermont, the Commissioner of Education and the architect of the building were present. Dorothy, in the closing address, explained the name of the school—

Artists often say that some of their finest successes are what they call 'accidental effects.' The same thing sometimes happens in human life, for there is no finer art than the art of living. Sometimes people do things, in a moment of inspiration, finer and more beautiful than they had dreamed they could. Such a moment of inspiration came to our town, when our school became the 'Memorial School.' . . . There have been towns which decided regretfully that, since there was not enough money for both monument and school, they would give up one or the other. But somehow Arlington people rose to a moment of inspiration in which they realized that they could have both, because both are one—and so made the school itself the Memorial to the heroic dead. . . . We take pride in every child who does well in this school and because of it is better prepared to serve his country and his fellow-man, because we feel that he is a living memorial of our wish to honor those among us who have marched under our national flag. . . .

Dorothy had faced up to physical challenges in her own life with gallantry and imagination. In March 1943 when John suffered a heart attack, she faced another kind of challenge.

"Bed rest. Absolute quiet," was the doctor's prescription for John's recovery.

The trust placed in her made Dorothy eager to be at her strongest and most vital, but she was past sixty and she had never been massive as to size or strength. Dorothy took council with herself as to how best she could organize her daily life so that she might be able to tap her own reservoir of reserve power.

"And one of the preparations I made for a trial of strength and endurance, as instinctively as a student drinks a cup of strong hot coffee before starting to take a long hard examination, was to send for a reproduction of Goya's *The Forge*," she wrote in one of her regular articles for the Christian Herald.

Nobody needs to give more than one look at that masterpiece to understand the first and most obvious reason for this choice. Just to glance, as you hurry by, at the tremendous outgoing strength of the man with upraised sledge-hammer, is as challenging as a sudden bugle-call. Vitality gushes out of that throb of creative human power, sweeping away fatigue, nervous tension and the poisonous stirrings of half-subconscious self-pity which sap our ability to endure. The terrific energy of that upswung sledge-hammer, the magnificent line of strength from the foot gripping the earth so stoutly, all along up the man's muscular body to the great arm at the top of its swing—they make self-pity seem laughable. They call out wordlessly a summons to take joy in putting out all the effort that can be summoned up.

Nothing is more contagious than vitality, you think, stopping before the picture for a moment to drink in another draught of it. . . .

So much you see in the very first look at the masterpiece of this great Spanish painter. But as your eye grows more familiar with it, you begin to notice other beauties, other strengths, which also have meaning for one's everyday existence. . . . You reflect, looking with pleasure at that uncluttered wall and floor, that any objects there, no matter how beautiful in themselves, would spoil the pure concentration of your gaze on what the artist is telling you. You can hardly help thinking, more or less consciously, 'Why, that principle holds true also in the ordering and composition of one's life. Each day, as we wake in the morning, is laid in our hands for us to make shapely and useful,—or the opposite. When we clutter our lives up with too many accessories—no matter how desirable any one of them is—too many clothes or shoes or hats, too much furniture, too many committees and Leagues and athletic clubs and Lodges and Associations or too many good causes, too many parties and social doings, too much attention to eating—we are spoiling the composition of our lives.' To decide what is the chief business of our lives, and then to concentrate our powers on that— such an admonition speaks from Goya's mastery of the principles of composition. . . .

John spent ten weeks in bed. Gradually his vitality returned and by early summer he began to get around again, looking longingly toward his vegetable garden and the work on his desk that concerned the schoolchildren of the state. There had been no lessening in Dorothy's work or correspondence during the weeks of nursing and by the time John was up Dorothy was told by the doctor that she must begin to reduce her desk work. Reluctantly she agreed and began by writing a letter to the editor of the Christian Herald—

I have come to a cross-roads when I must choose one or the other way ahead. I can't take both. I used to be able to do all the

Book-of-the-Month Club reading and book reviewing, and all of an immense correspondence, and write lots of articles, and make many public addresses—and also have time and vitality enough to write stories, which are really my especial way of interpreting human life. Now I find I no longer can. I've cut out public speaking almost entirely, although the pressure on me for speaking is great and although I enjoy this contact with other Americans which I get in speaking trips. I try to cut down the time given to letter-writing by every device I can invent. But I'm afraid I may have to cut out at least some of the stream of articles which have passed from my desk for so many years . . . as I step forward into the later years of my active working life. I'm not sure enough really to write an editor about it. But I have been so much touched by the real friendliness of your attitude that I don't think of our relationship as only the professional one between author and editor. I'm sure it will be easier for you to make editorial plans if you have in the back of your mind as you look into the future for the *Herald*, the possibility that I may not continue to be among your contributors.

In reply, the editor urged her to change her mind. Dorothy answered that it was not her mind but her age that needed changing.

As with all people growing older, she knew that she had to face the need of achieving a peaceful equilibrium between what she liked and wanted to do and what she was capable of doing. All was as well as usual with her, but because of her marked physical limitations, that could never be one hundred per cent; and yet, if she was well enough to go on working, that *for her* was one hundred per cent. She wrote to her doctor in Boston, "I think I feel all right . . . so busy I don't have time to consider. . . . I get tired rather easily, but I shall soon be 66 and I am working pretty hard."

Jimmy, now a first lieutenant in the Army Medical Corps,

was raised to the rank of captain. In October he left with his battalion for the Pacific theater.

Our Young Folks, the book Dorothy had been working on for three years and which she had often referred to as one of her "chores," was published. In it she brought together the findings made by the American Youth Commission during the six years she had met with them. John Dewey's words on one of the first pages set the keynote: "What the best and wisest parent wants for his own child, that must the community want for all of its children. Any other ideal for our schools is narrow and unlovely; acted upon, it destroys democracy." It was an intensely patriotic book and Dorothy's heart beat through it—for young people, for her country. As an actual, factual presentation of the status of American youth, it was based on her own observations and feelings as well as on research work done with the educators, specialists and captains of industry of whom the Youth Commission had been comprised.

Dr. David Baumgardt, one of the first of the intellectual emigrés helped by the Fishers, reviewing it said—

The book reads like a great novel. . . . Mrs. Fisher has here combined in a unique way the virtues of the thinker and the responsible educator with those of the born artist and master narrator. . . . The book speaks out eloquently the truths which we have all felt only dimly, and by which no conscientious contemporary can be left unmoved.

Parents' Magazine had awarded Dorothy their annual medal for her earlier work on the symposium *Our Children*. For the first time in their history they again awarded their medal to the same person, and presented it to her for *Our Young Folks*. The Carnegie Corporation presented Dorothy with a plaque in recognition of her continuing work in the field of education. Frederick Keppell, Corporation President, had only one comment to make of Dorothy, "Of such is the Kingdom of Heaven."

The chore, as it had proved before, had been well worth the demands made. John could afford to smile when he read reviews that referred to Dorothy as an artist even when using prosaic materials. "It's the artist in you that keeps you from becoming just a worthy work horse, Dolly."

"Me?"

He picked up a volume of Tolstoy's stories to which she had recently written the introduction. "Listen to this," he said. " 'How does it happen that Tolstoy and not the preachers can reach our hearts with this reminder that peace and love are beautiful beyond words, and that we can have peace and love if we will deserve those blessings? The answer is simple: Tolstoy was a great artist.' You didn't realize when you were describing Tolstoy that you were describing yourself as well."

Our Young Folks brought in a stream of requests from organizations, institutes, libraries, schools for Dorothy to speak before them. John was firm. "You can't do it, Dolly. Perhaps one or two, but—"

"John, I said in that book all there was to say. Why don't people read the book instead of wanting to hear me say it all over again?"

"People like personal contact."

Dorothy looked serious. "Going around giving talks is a drain on a writer's time and energy. I'm not sure that the pressure constantly being put on writers these days to speak in public is a wholly good thing. As a point of contact between many people whom a writer could not possibly know personally, yes; but—well, I haven't thought it through enough to know quite how I feel."

John's voice, warm with pride carried a note of warning, "Not many are so willing to spend themselves for others as you are, Dolly."

A few of the requests were accepted; but only a very few.

There had been times during the war when Dorothy found it hard to write and she had been glad for demanding tasks. Since the invasion of France she had written incessantly articles and statements in which she tried to uphold civilized decent attitudes toward life. But they had been accomplished with purpose, will and concentration. A textbook series upon which she had been engaged had been accomplished with research and determination. Her heart had been torn with feeling for the dear friends in France and other occupied countries. She and John had done everything possible with letters and food packages, but that everything was little enough. After long periods of no news at all, letters came in reply; often the only message was a 25-word International Red Cross "prisoner of war" message that came through Geneva after a six months' delay.

One morning, sitting down at her desk, Dorothy felt an odd impulse buried long beneath a great deposit of anxious moral concerns—to write not because she had to but because she wanted to, to comment on human life by implication. If it was successful it would turn out to be creative fiction. She felt as if she was breathing fresh, life-giving air after the work she had been doing. The story she wanted to write was filled with horror, joy and grief. It shook her to the heart as she entered into the experience of a band of imprisoned French soldiers who thought they were being repatriated, saw their beloved land through a chance knot-hole in the walls of their boxcar, and then were returned to their German prison.

Dorothy was an old enough hand at writing to know that when a story like *The Knot-Hole* was in the building it meant living at two levels of life. For hours she would live with the men in the boxcar as she attempted to put thoughts into words and words onto paper. Called from her morning's work to luncheon and then to necessary afternoon appointments, she realized acutely the technique of shifting from the deepest level of consciousness and emotion back to the surface level at which one moved with others through daily life. Writing, revising, revising and then writing a fresh approach was the most intense kind of living for her and the words connected with it went on in her mind while she heard her voice discussing the supper menu or giving instructions to a high school boy to cut brush on the mountain.

When *The Knot-Hole* was finished it seemed to Dorothy more like a groan of anguish than a story. Mr. Reynolds, who had long been her agent, sent it to several magazines before the *Yale Review* accepted it. It stirred deep feeling, drew wide comment, and was included in the volume *The Best Short Stories of the Year*.

To Dorothy's desk came a constant wave of magazines, not all were subscribed to though she liked to keep in touch with important points of view. Some came from editors because they contained reviews of her books, articles by her or about her. Often Dorothy never knew which magazine had printed one of her stories until a copy was sent her. Often she never saw the stories in print, though the checks she received gave her the satisfaction of knowing that they had been published. Reviews and articles were read and enjoyed, sometimes clipped and put in a drawer; but there was no careful adding of them to files and records. Students engaged in writing on some aspect of Dorothy's life, librarians beginning to compile bibliographies, often wrote for information, and Dorothy readily supplied what was at hand, but it was by no means all that had been written through the years.

Often a request came from a publisher, accompanied by a set of galleys, for a statement to help publicize a new book. If Dorothy liked the book, she was glad to speak out for it. Experience had shown her that criticism could be kind and still constructive.

Daily there were letters to be dictated to heads of government departments and educators, emergency committees formed for some worthy purpose, editors, readers of her books, people who wanted advice on how to be writers; but while space on the cylinder of her dictating machine remained she would stop for the pleasure and refreshment of a quick, jaunty, newsy letter to some member of the family. The spool clicked to a finish. Special messages would be added by hand after the letter was typed.

Letters were written constantly to Arlington boys in the service. Sending them the village news, she asked for their news in return. "Do write often and help us keep up the bridge that stretches from us here in this green valley out to you, representative of the heroic youth of our day for us," she wrote. She told them that she would save the letters they wrote to her, as she did Sally's and Jimmy's, to give back to them on their return. They would be glad to have them as a record of the time away. To a friend of Jimmy's, half the world away and desperately lonely, she offered the playhouse in the pines which he had built with Jimmy when they were children. In it she had written many a story.

Have it to camp out in . . . think of it with blue jays walking around it, squirrels darting in and out, waiting for you to come back and have some woodland life any time you want.

It was a long time before letters began to reach Arlington from the place in the Philippines where Jimmy was stationed. His battalion was now a Ranger Commando unit, and though Jimmy was a military surgeon he was kept as busy treating the natives as the soldiers. His long, detailed, descriptive letters were read by Dorothy and John devouringly, then circulated among members of the family.

She gave careful help freely to many young writers. Richard

Wright, whose first book *Native Son* had been a successful Book-of-the-Month choice, was one. For his second book, *Black Boy*, Dorothy proudly wrote an introduction—

More than eighty-five years ago, Oliver Wendell Holmes nobly said: 'It is so much easier to consign a soul to perdition or to say prayers to save it, than to take the blame on ourselves for letting it grow up in neglect and run to ruin. The English law began, only in the late eighteenth century, to get hold of the idea that crime is not necessarily a sin. The limitations of human responsibility have never been properly studied.'

If Dr. Holmes were alive now, he would be proud, as I am proud, of the chance to help bring to the thoughtful attention of intelligent, morally responsible Americans, the honest, dreadful, heart-breaking story of a Negro childhood and youth, as set down by that rarely gifted American author, Richard Wright.

And she did all she could to support financially every good cause, every worthwhile effort, but she found that her impulses had to be restrained as the years went on. "My earning capacity is naturally not what it was when I was younger, and I am obliged to earn by constantly repeated personal effort whatever money I contribute to good causes," she wrote once in explanation.

The three churches in Arlington did not lack her support. She wrote to the warden of St. James' Episcopal, to the minister of The Federated Church at East Arlington, and to the priest of St. Columban's saying that she was dividing her support of the three and sending to each one a check which represented a yearly contribution of a dollar a Sunday—

I am not just the descendant of the Canfields. I am a citizen of Arlington. And conscientious citizens ought, I feel, to help support churches, those representatives and reminders of the spiritual life of man. . . . I'll try to do the same next year if my earning ability doesn't drop, as everybody's does, more or less, with the recurrence of too many birthdays. . . . I am, as you know, especially interested in the guidance of young people, and I'd be glad to have this small contribution used in some special work with them. But you will know much better than I, of course, where it will do the most good—perhaps this winter, in helping pay the coal bill! I'll leave its use entirely to you.

The old Canfield house on the main street of Arlington had been given to the town by Dorothy and John as a Community House. The Library was established in one wing and the different rooms were used throughout the week by different organizations. On Sunday afternoons a Friends Meeting gathered in one of the rooms. Dorothy often met with them. Listening sensitively, openly to the silence, then to what some person speaking might have to say, she would often take up the thought, extending and illuminating it from her own experience and insight.

The war was still being fought but a number of people were working to develop American participation in international organization when the war belonged to the past. Dorothy was intensely interested in the United Nations Association and went to Burlington to attend a mass meeting in its support. She wrote a long letter to the family circle—

We are starting well ahead of time, to try to reach a much wider American public. Everybody realizes that one of the great difficulties for the lack of support of the League of Nations idea was that only intellectuals or near-intellectuals were kept informed about it. The filling-station man and his brother were left out. This time we are trying to make it a popular movement in the French and Italian meaning of the word "popular" as belonging to the people. . . . The cause of peace is an emotional one and must be approached, I think, through the emotions just as much as war. . . .

I got up to Burlington about half-past five, the train being late as usual, just had time to take a bath and get something to eat and put on something spectacular—for me that is—my long white evening dress and brilliant scarlet sari trimmed with gold braid which Bodie gave me some years ago. It makes a very striking costume—much too striking for any Vermont party as a rule. But we were going to have lots of flags and I was to be the only woman on the platform so I thought it might be a good idea and so it turned out.

There was a parade . . . a splendid parade! Three brass bands scattered at intervals, 46 pretty lively high-school girls carrying the banners of the United Nations, and dressed in costumes vaguely approximating the costumes of the countries they represented, as many nurses in their uniforms as could be spared from the hospitals, the Coast Guard from Lake Champlain, the American Legion, all the Girl Scout and Boy Scout troops that could be brought together, the sidewalks were pretty full too, as they always are when there's a brass band and flags. And I was delighted, although still very uncertain how many of that crowd would go to the Armory. I told Senator Burton who had flown all the way from Washington just to speak there, that we weren't sure whether we'd have anybody to speak of at the meeting, and he agreed with me that even if there were only a few it would be worth having as a beginning. Because I think nothing like this has been attempted as yet. After the parade had passed we all got into cars and drove around to the Armory, and took up our stand in the lobby of the Armory with the 46 girls (or were there 48) waving their flags in front of us. Then the band struck up and we all marched in and what do you think! the Armory was practically full. . . .

Dorothy told John about it after her return to the little house. "I feel better pleased than I have in a long time, John."

"Well, Dolly, it looks as if something had been started."

"Yes," she said with conviction, "something has indeed been started."

Chapter 15

Impact

Snow fell heavily during the first weeks of 1945, and cold kept the white depths intact. Toward the end of January, Jimmy's wife came to Arlington for a few days for some skiing. Dorothy watched her from the house, gracefully turning and gliding over the pasture slopes, then Dorothy wrote a long letter to Jimmy, bringing him up to date with all the news. Conscious that time was moving faster for her than for him, she ended her letter—

Dear dear *dear* son, so much love goes out to you from this snow-heaped old home of yours—love and pride, and—now!—real hopes that I'm going to live to see you return to us.

Early in February, the papers throughout the United States carried the first encouraging news that had come in a long time from the Philippines. The account was sketchy as full reports had not yet come through, but one hundred and twenty-one men of a Ranger battalion had made a successful attack on the Cabanatuan Prison Camp and freed five hundred American prisoners of war. Captain James Fisher had been one of the Rangers. Dorothy and John read every scrap of news and eagerly waited for the full report.

Two weeks later official word reached them, saying that their son had been mortally wounded.

The Commanding Officer of the 6th Ranger Battalion and the Executive Officer sent words of condolence and praise to John and Dorothy, but the letter that came closest to their hearts was written by Jimmy's Staff Sergeant.

Somewhere in the Phillippines
February 4, 1945

Dear Mrs. Fisher:

This letter is perhaps the one letter I hoped never to have to write. I realize fully the futility of any attempt I might make to mitigate your grief, for my own emotions are the measure of how much greater yours must be. In the comparatively short time he had been with this unit, no other individual has ever gained the unqualified respect and admiration of the entire personnel, commissioned and enlisted, as did Captain Jim. In a small unit, such as he commanded, where each man's affairs are common knowledge, he was just one of the boys. We knew and loved him as our Commanding Officer, and again as the man with the hammer and the saw who was always in the process of constructing something. In short, he represented the finest type of soldier any soldier hopes to meet, a soldier's soldier.

Captain Fisher called me in on the evening of the 27th of January and told me that this organization had been given the mission of attacking a Japanese Concentration Camp some 20 odd miles inside enemy lines, and freeing some 500 American prisoners there. A total of five Medical Personnel would be required. The Captain, Corporal Estensen, Corporal Haynes, Corporal Ramsey and I chose to go. The following morning we left our area by truck and on reaching the lines lay down to get what sleep we could while waiting for darkness. The unit left at dusk and began the intricate job of sneaking more than a hundred men through enemy lines. Dawn found us in hiding in a native barrio 20 miles inside Japanese lines and about 7 miles from our objective. That evening at dusk we pushed on again with every intention of making our strike that evening. However, our Scouts reported a large force of tanks and a great number of troops encamped at our objective, so we again went into hiding in a native barrio three miles from the Prisoners of War Camp.

The following night we moved on and into the attack. The attack began at 1945 and its opening found the Captain, Corporal Ramsey and myself on the left flank directly behind the unit attacking the Japanese garrison. When it became apparent that the assault was going well, the Captain ordered us to move to the right and approach the main gate through which the prisoners were fleeing. The night was very dark and during the movement of some two or three hundred yards, all of us temporarily lost contact with each other. At the gate there was naturally considerable confusion for the prisoners were all volubly excited and the G.I.s were trying to herd, lead or carry them to safety.

I searched a few moments here for the Captain, and then, knowing the type of courage with which he was endowed, headed for the gate, for I was certain he would be going through. I had made perhaps half a dozen steps toward the gate when a knee mortar shell dropped in front of me about ten feet to the left of the gate and ten feet in front of the wire. I hit the ground fast, but a moment later someone hollered "Man down" and I ran forward a few feet where a man lay on the ground. It was too dark to see who the man was, but I went to work immediately. I asked him where he was hit. He answered "Stomach." I dressed the wound, and in the meantime Sergeant Bossard came up and I asked him to find the Captain, for I knew the man was badly injured. It came as a definite shock when the man on the ground said, "This is Captain Fisher."

Private First Class Myerhoff, and First Sergeant Bossard prepared to carry the Captain back when I had to leave to take care of another man who was down. However, I got back to see the Captain several times during the march and was carrying his litter at the time we reached the bull carts. He went on into the barrio from which we had departed earlier in the evening while my orders kept me with the line of march until all prisoners and men were in the village. When I returned, the Captain was being operated upon by two Filipino doctors, man and wife, and by two American doctors from the Prisoners of War Camp. . . . The rest of the unit moved on and crossed into our lines early the next morning, leaving several Prisoners of War and the wounded in the care of two doctors and five Rangers. We had hoped to be permitted to remain in hiding in this village but were ordered out at 0200. So carrying our wounded with native help, we moved back another four miles to the first village in which we stopped, and dawn found us again in hiding.

Captain Fisher died at 1100 on the 31st of January. Blood plasma and vein to vein transfusion were tried to keep him alive but it was futile. His last remark was an expression of hope that the few of us that remained would make it back safely across the lines. A military funeral was held for him, Father Kennedy of New York City, a Prisoner of War, reading the service. The Captain sleeps at the foot of a large tree in a small grove at the edge of the barrio. This place has been unofficially designated by the Filipinos as "Dr. Fisher Park." A monument will be placed in the village by the battalion, in his honor, and native wood carvers, once the Japanese are forced out of the area, will carve the information contained on the identification tags on the tree. We crossed the lines that night. . . .

It is useless for me to attempt any words that might bring you peace, for our own sense of loss is acute. In the loss of Captain Fisher, each of us in the detachment feels the loss of an adviser, a friend, and a Commanding Officer who in our hearts is irreplaceable.

> Respectfully,
> John W. Nelson

John and Dorothy were stunned. All around them were memories of Jimmy—in the village, in forest and field, on the slopes of Red Mountain, along the Battenkill, in the old house which still rang with echoes of his voice, his light elastic step.

Letters poured in from friends and family, from unknown people whose love Dorothy had won through her work and John with his service to the state, from Jimmy's college friends and army comrades. Dr. Russell, who had brought Jimmy into the world thirty-one years before, said, "He had the nicest disposition of any human being." Jimmy's friends came to see Dorothy and John; people who had lost sons in the war came to see them; but no one seen, no words said, could make tragedy less tragic.

Grief might never lessen for them but shock would pass, and both Dorothy and John knew that nothing could diminish the beauty of Jimmy's life or the heroism of his death. Dorothy had learned to live with deafness; she would learn to live with sorrow. There was only one monument that she and John felt they could raise worthy of Jimmy's memory and that was to be useful as long as each one could. "We are struggling with what strength we have to reconstruct our lives without Jimmy," she wrote to a friend. "To the eye I am the same gray-haired, deaf writer as ever, bent over the desk, the weary old hand still driving the old pen."

In March she went to New York for the Book-of-the-Month Club meeting. John returned to his desk to continue his campaign for an increase in the minimum salary for Vermont schoolteachers. Together they made plans for a Memorial Field at the Arlington High School and for a bronze plaque to mark Jimmy's far-distant grave.

A few months later, when the atomic bomb was dropped on Hiroshima, Dorothy was asked by the *Herald Tribune* for a statement. In sorrow, but with pride and faith, she spoke out—

Six miles away from the trial of the first atomic bomb, the impact of the explosion knocked men down as though by a blow from a giant fist. All of us, by the same fist, have been knocked down, spiritually and mentally, by that terrific event.

Yet those six-miles-away observers, felled to the ground, were not killed. Not yet. Shaken and trembling, they were able to rise and face human life once more. *Once* more. And we too must face human life once more, appalled by the collective remorse, and fear of the future which after two examples of the horrible destructiveness of the bomb, lies crushingly on the heart of every responsible man and woman.

Our impulse is to cry out, "no, no, no, we have no 'comments' to make, no plans to suggest. Nothing in our human experience has prepared us to meet this crisis."

But there is no escape from the responsibility laid on us. There is no one else to take it on, save the human race, which, collectively, discovered the atomic bomb. . . .

It is not true that the atomic bomb is something new to man, and hence something of which our experience teaches us nothing. It is new only in degree. It is no more than a development of the clubs of the first men who fought each other. Then the man with a club could conquer the man without a club. . . .

What we honestly want is what the best plain people all over the world want, "to work together without fear or hate."

Not morally, or idealistically, but actually, factually, in brass-tack reality, it is true that we cannot advance into the future unless we hold hard to two things we know about ourselves: first, that every one of us is born with destructive, fighting-rat potentialities, but that they can be, by and large, controlled and kept down by human effort; and second, that human beings can be trained into that disciplined ability to think and work together, constructively, so brilliantly proved to be a human possibility by the story of the invention and manufacture of the atomic bomb.

A few days later the war was over. Dorothy's and John's thoughts went out to all those who, with them, knew what the cost of victory had been. There was comfort to them both in the thought that no other parents would now lose their sons.

When Father Kennedy, the Jesuit priest who had been with

Jimmy at his death, came to visit the Fishers he told them of the Layugs. Before the raid on the Cabanatuan prison Dr. Layug had said to Captain Fisher that he and his wife dreamed some-day of going to the United States for advanced medical work before taking up civilian practice on Luzon, and Captain Fisher had said that if they all lived through the attack, he would do his best to help them get to America. After the attack, it was the Layugs who had stayed with the wounded man, caring for him at great risk to their own lives.

The Fishers had one compelling desire and that was to locate Dr. Carlos Layug and his wife, wherever they might be, and try to carry out Jimmy's wish to help them. That would be a living memorial in keeping with their golden-hearted son's spirit of service.

Months later when the Layugs were finally traced and the idea was communicated to them, they were overwhelmed with joy and incredulity. There were many letters to be written, and much long-distance planning to be done on both sides of the Pacific, but the idea went forward and arrangements were made for the Layugs to come to Harvard Medical School for a year of post-graduate study. When they might arrive was still subject to uncertainty, but that they would arrive was sure. Both the Layugs in the Philippines and the Fishers in Vermont looked forward eagerly to their meeting.

During the past few years, Dorothy had been attempting to resign from many of the committees she had served on, the activities she had been interested in. "I must cut down some of the ballast on the old ship so it can make a little headway," she said. But her trusteeship on the board of Howard University in Washington she wanted to hold as long as possible. Mrs. Eleanor Roosevelt was the only other white woman on the board. Dorothy returned from meetings stimulated and inspired by her contact with vigorous, intelligent young men and women; but often downcast and thoroughly ashamed as she was forced to realize how difficult it was for Howard graduates to obtain recognition for their minds because of the color of their skin. It was a long time since she had written *The Bent Twig* but like a play enacted in her mind she recalled the scene in which Judith and Sylvia were defending the Fingál girls. "There's no use telling children something that they never see put into practice," their father was saying, and then came their mother's uncompromising reply, "It's not impossible, I suppose, to change our lives."

In Dorothy's mail, the letters that came from readers of her books often included many from servicemen. Some time after the war she received a letter from a Negro ex-soldier recently returned from front-line duty. It was disillusiond and bitter. Dorothy gave it compassionate attention and searched her mind to discover what she, as an old white woman who had always lived in security, could possibly say to a young Negro filled with resentment about racial discrimination. "What can I do?" she asked herself.

Invariably the answer was, "I'll do what I can."

The letter from the young Negro was postmarked Richmond, Indiana. Dorothy knew there was a Quaker College in Richmond whose doors would be open to anyone seeking an education. She wrote a letter to the ex-soldier, asking him to try Earlham College. She told him that while a college education would do no direct good to a Negro against social discrimination in the South, she had observed that college-educated Negroes had a more tolerable situation in American life than uneducated ones. In the same mail she wrote another letter to a friend of theirs who had retired from teaching and was living in Richmond. She asked him to give a friendly hand to the young Negro.

Dorothy might want to give up committees, but they would

not give her up. When asked to serve as Honorary Chairman on a Committee of Amnesty working to get release for men in prison as conscientious objectors she did, throwing her heart and pen into what she could do to preserve one of the basic American liberties—freedom of conscience. When the release was signed, shortly before Christmas, it was heartily supported by the Attorney General of the United States. "All of the mobilization and all of the war effort will have been in vain," he said, "if, when all is finished, we discover that in the process we have destroyed the very freedom for which we fought."

Ohio State University, celebrating the Fiftieth Anniversary of their Home Economics Department, wrote to Dorothy asking for a statement. She complied with a warmth of remembering. It was her father, when president, who had given academic standing to what had previously been considered mere woman's work. During the years since he had taken his stand, Home Economics had become a respected part of college curricula. Dorothy had been in that first class at Ohio State and felt that it had done much to give to her life as a homemaker interest, variety, delight and satisfaction. "Helping me," she exclaimed, "hence my family, to long years of happiness."

Dorothy wrote a creed for the initiation of senior girls in the Home Economics Association at the University of Nebraska—

I believe with all my heart that the study of Home Economics is the study of the art of living. During my college years I have acquired many facts and skills, and much understanding and insight concerning the meaning of home living. I faithfully pledge myself to make what I have learned as useful as possible to humanity. I also pledge myself never to forget that skill in the material processes of daily living is only a means to the great and noble end of helping to create harmonious and happy relations among men, women, and children in their homes and in the larger community.

And she accepted the request that came from Howard University to deliver their Commencement Address.

"You're doing the work of six people now, Dolly," John reminded her.

"Perhaps so, but, John, there are some requests I can't refuse. Nothing I can do, nothing any of us can do, will ever be enough to help redress the hardships and injustices which form so much of the Negro's lot."

John looked at her proudly. "All I can say, Dolly, is that those students are lucky to start out into the world with your words ringing in their ears."

Nor could she refuse an invitation to address the nurses of the Post-Graduate Hospital in New York at their "capping." Urging them to light the torch of their hearts from Florence Nightingale's flame, she said—

Remember the purveyors of the British army who thought everything had been all right until that woman came, asking questions. *Ask questions*, you too, of apathy and inertia, ask questions about poverty and bad housing and poor living conditions for children, as Florence Nightingale asked questions about the medical supplies that were there, kept from the sick by bureaucratic red tape. . . .

Remember the helpless humanness of Florence Nightingale's later stubborn opposition to the registering and licensing of nurses, and her refusal to look at microbes because if she looked at them she would see them and she didn't believe in them. Take this as a warning against sagging back into reactionary passivity, yourselves. . . .

Few professions can find both mighty warnings and mighty inspiration in the personality of their founder. You have both. I wish you joy as you go onward into your profession, and I hope you will have Florence Nightingale's axe in one hand, and her lamp in the other, and in your hearts a humble memory of her mistakes.

And she could not say no to a request to address a gathering of teachers at the Social Sciences Convention when they were meeting in Boston. They were the front-line fighters in the effort to civilize the coming generation. A home, Dorothy reminded them, had its basis in the dignity of the individuals within it—

And anybody who thinks that a good home can be produced by a human being immature and undeveloped in character, insults the sacred name of home. . . .

And that final axiom, "A man doesn't want a career-woman with interests to conflict with his, when he gets home after a hard day's work. He wants a wife." What are you teachers doing, I wonder, to protect growing American girls and boys from the poisonous false reasoning in this familiar exhortation? . . .

"He wants a wife" runs the rest of the fish-hook phrase, I'll say he does! He *wants* a wife, in the old meaning of the word, of *need*. Only what do you mean, "wife"? I think you ought to show you mean a woman, full grown, capable through experience, of understanding what steady effort is needed for earning a living, a woman, with that sense of the true proportion of things which can only grow out of experience of reality. . . .

Just add to that condition some honest realization that men and women can love each other all the more if they respect each other fully.

It was not easy for Dorothy to be in Boston. The city was filled with memories for her—memories of Jimmy at Medical School, as an intern, as a married man. In so many places she seemed to meet the Jimmy she knew so well. She wrote a friend, "Luckily Boston is a big city, and nobody pays any attention to anybody's looks in big cities, so nobody noticed a small, gray-haired woman trying to see her way here and there through tears."

More than a year had elapsed since the Fishers had begun

to make plans to bring the Layugs to the United States. There had been many setbacks and almost endless difficulties had been involved, but through everything the plan had moved forward. In July, Dr. Carlos Layug and his wife arrived. They came first to Arlington for a visit of a few days with the Fishers. John and Dorothy were delighted with them. They were so young and friendly, so thoroughly adaptable and eager to profit in every way possible by the opportunity that had been given them. The Fishers drove them to Boston and stayed with them until they were settled in their living quarters and ready to embark on their work at Harvard. Before leaving, Dorothy told the Layugs that now they would be looking forward to Christmas vacation and to having the Filipinos spend it with them in Arlington. Driving home, John and Dorothy felt heart-warmed by their friendship with two young people from the other side of the world, and profoundly grateful that the Layugs who were so naturally dear to them were to be the living symbols of what they wanted to do for Jimmy.

Sally, with her four children, was now living in Bar Harbor, Maine. Her husband was co-director of a biological laboratory doing research into the group behavior of animals. In December Dorothy made them a flying visit, later writing a letter to the family circle about her journey—

It is rather a complicated trip from here to Bar Harbor, as trips are apt to be in country which was settled long before the railroads were thought of. The steel rails don't exactly run where you would like to have them. I left home at eleven in the morning last Sunday, went by bus to Bennington, changed there for Williamstown, got off the bus there and took a taxi to the railway station, took a train to Boston, changed there (with a three-hour wait) went on by sleeper to Ellsworth, Maine arriving there at seven in the morning, took a bus from there to Bar Harbor, and arrived at the bus terminal station there where Sally met me with their car. . . .

Like any other country woman, I snatched up just before I left the house, a fresh roasting fowl which had just come in from the neighbor of whom we buy our poultry, wrapped it up in a paper bag and took it along under my arm with me. . . .

I also took along, as I always do, some Book-of-the-Month proof-sheets to read, since that work goes on incessantly every day of my life. . . . I can't read very well on the train because my eyes are none too good in these years, but I can read at every station when the train is standing still. This is not a bad way, because as soon as the train begins to move and jiggle the page, I shut my eyes and think over what I have been reading. By the time I had been to Bar Harbor and back, I had fully made up my mind about those two books!

. . . The train was late and Sally and Vivian had been up as long as I had in the train, to be sure to be awake and dressed by the time I arrived. So they had had their breakfast, but Sally sat down for another visit with me while I had my coffee—very welcome after that long trip. I had seen the children so lately that the younger ones, David and John Paul, recognized me and there was no period of shyness to get over. They are both dark-eyed, vital little boys, David no longer the least bit like a baby, and John Paul who has always been particularly masculine and sturdy in his physique, looking like a little football player.

Jean and Vivian were off in a very few minutes for their school, looking bright-eyed and rosy-cheeked as everybody does in that cool, moist, seaside climate. . . .

When Sally and I settled down for a really domestic visit, I began to prepare the Vermont fowl I had brought, for a fricassee. . . .

The evening meal—or indeed any meal in Sally's household—reminds one a little of one of the Jordaen pictures, you remember how jovial and noisy they are, with somebody playing a horn and with the rest of the people singing and the younger children play-ing with the dog, and such an atmosphere of hearty appetite for food and living bursting from the canvas. The dog and the cat whom you always see in the Jordaen pictures are there too, roam-ing around the table, very well-mannered but quite present. Jean

furnishes the music, for—at least while I was there—practically
every moment she was in the house when she was not upstairs
reading, she was at the piano playing fluently one Christmas song
after another, I suppose both in her school and church they are
practicing Christmas music for the Christmas celebration close at
hand. Since the piano is just on the other side of the open door
to the dining room, the noise of her spirited playing comes through
clearly and makes everybody at the table raise his voice—this suits
a deaf grandmother very well indeed, as you can imagine. And just
the noise is inspiriting you know if it is good natured noise—John
Paul raising his voice to a shout to make himself heard, little David
who doesn't speak a word of English yet but who is very fluent
in his own baby talk, contributing his share, and the grown-ups
making themselves understood as best they can.

In the midst of this cheerful turmoil, I suddenly had a thrust
to the heart such as comes to all of us in the later years after sorrow
has reached us. For Jean began to play loudly and cheerfully as
she played all the other things, the French carol of the three kings,
a song which in my mind and memory is intimately connected with
Jimmy, since it was the first song he ever learned to sing. It was
while Sally was so sick with typhoid fever in Paris, and Jimmy had
kindly been taken by Denise Macquer's sister because I was so
concentrated on the care of Sally. Every morning I raced over
along the Boulevard de Clichy to take Jimmy to his nursery school,
and this morning he came out to me calling out that he had learned
to sing a song and sang the first phrases "Ce matin, j'ai rencontre
les Mages," and then in an instant, those of you who are old enough
and experienced enough know how this is, everything around me
melted away and I stood again on that cold, ugly, cheerless, French
boulevard, looking down into my little son's beautiful, soft, brown
eyes and hearing his voice exactly as though he stood there again
beside me.

And then the struggle, familiar to all you older people in the
circle I am sure, quickly to repress the tears, not to darken the
cheerful present moment by one's own sadness, the effort—vain as
always—not to go on to the inevitable next picture to see those

same soft brown eyes closing in death, half-way around the globe, his tall soldier comrades weeping around him, his voice sending the last touching message, "Tell-tell them I always tried to do my best." And then the slow fading of that like a Bach air heard in the midst of a lively Haydn symphony fading away—and the happy, vital family around me seen again—the interval having been so brief that not a sentence had been finished, not a gesture had been completed, and the piano sounding loudly in my ears something quite different "God rest ye merry, gentlemen." (No, this is not fanciful or literary expression. There is really great beauty as well as great suffering in the thought of such a life as Jimmy's was and such a death, glorious because he died in the attempt to help others who were in terrible danger.)

That house is crammed-full with that big family, with no extra room so that night I slept on the davenport in their living room, very comfortably. . . .

. . . And then the trip through the long state of Massachusetts to Williamstown, and the joyful reunion with John who was waiting for me there, our own landscape covered with a fresh fall of white velvet which made the drive home like a drive through fairyland. . . .

Chapter 16

Rooted Deep in Life

DOROTHY was celebrating her seventieth birthday. Felicitations from many parts of the world poured into her study. One of the most cheering was an article in the *Educational Forum* by David Baumgardt, *Dorothy Canfield Fisher on her Seventieth Birthday*. Dr. Baumgardt quoted a remark made by an acquaintance of his about Dorothy, "I am afraid that in Vermont and all over the United States she is, perhaps, more thoroughly loved than understood."

"If there must be a choice between love and understanding," Dr. Baumgardt replied, "how good that once in a while a great writer is more loved than understood, since almost without exception the opposite is true, either because great men are not lovable to those who see them daily, or because the home town and state think it may suffice to respect their great sons and daughters and dispense with the special effort of loving them during their lifetime."

In the article, Dr. Baumgardt analyzed nine of Dorothy's books. He spoke of the "radius of her vast civic and humanitarian activities. . . . There is no human need alien to her. . . . But she herself likes to give the impression of doing nothing but taking a modest share in necessary labors for public welfare. Therefore, people are not infrequently 'misled' by herself to see her only the lovable friend and fellow worker, overlooking the artist. . . . I see another danger, the danger that her greatness as a creative mind may be obscured by the affection given her as an American citizen, educator and international humanitarian."

He felt that there was more in Dorothy's novels than people had fully seen and his article was a two-way present: to Dorothy, appreciation; to the American reading public, evaluation.

Dorothy, taking a look at her years, recalled what she had heard one of her old Canfield cousins say, "When you get to be my age you take whatever comes without fussing." At seventy, she felt like a carpenter whose kit of tools had begun to give out on him—her ears had gone long ago, her eyes had been failing, her hands were often stiff and painful; but she kept going. That was what mattered. She could hold a pen, though at times it was difficult, and she could tap the keys of her typewriter. She had never used the touch system, though she had always typed with great speed; now to ease the strain on a few fingers she taught herself the system that would bring all ten into use. She knew well that there was no magic drug, no recipe or ritual which could restore what had been used in living, but self-control, patience and perseverance were as unfailing as ever.

There were, as always, some simple restorative methods which she had found useful in counteracting the fatigue brought on by long hours at her desk. Getting up from her chair in the downstairs study, she would step out on her little porch and stand still facing the mountain world. Then she would draw nine long breaths to lessen nervous tension. The oxygen that filled her lungs restored a sense of well-being as the view of distant mountains lifted her spirit. Clasping her arms behind her head, she felt relaxation slide over her like cool water. Then she would bend down, pick up an armful of wood for her Franklin stove, and go indoors, ready again for work.

"The chimney must be warm for the fire to keep going," she would say, adding to the familiar saying one of her favorite rejoinders, "And that must be symbolical of something."

And there were friends to turn to when the inner spring seemed slow in bubbling. A hasty note sent to someone in the circle that had been widening through the years with a request "to pull something out of the bag for your old Dorothy who needs a boost" would bring a letter in return that could feed and quicken her.

And there was music. Never had there been a period in her life when she had not been aware of its miraculous power. "There are times," John said, "that Beethoven seems the only force to keep one going." There were many such times, Dorothy knew, and she knew too that they would increase rather than diminish.

The narrowing in of the years, the limitations of the body, could all be accepted; but it seemed impossible to fit sorrow into any pattern of acceptance. Often, often she heard the echo of Jimmy's voice, saw him walking up the road, coming out of the woods, unself-conscious and inwardly serene. The house, the fields, the mountain paths were full of Jimmys of all ages come back from memories. She was glad for the work always waiting on her desk; she was thankful that there was a constant need to earn. Memory filled to overflowing the empty place in her heart, but memory was a poignant force. "Love knows the secret of grief," she wrote to a friend, feeling that she had a divination of the meaning of the words.

She endeavored with every modern device to make the most of her working hours. A simplified air-cooling system was installed in her study during the summer for never did she want to lose a day of work. Dictating machines served her well, and the telephone. Telegrams frequently carried her first reactions to the Book-of-the-Month Club office in New York—

I find ——— ——— adequate treatment of subject but not nearly interesting enough to put in Class A.

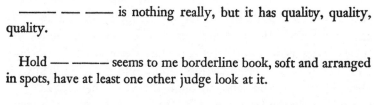

—— —— —— is nothing really, but it has quality, quality, quality.

Hold —— ——— seems to me borderline book, soft and arranged in spots, have at least one other judge look at it.

Vote to send ——————— out as valuable aid to public opinion.

I read —— ——— with an aching heart and most complete feeling of its being a true picture.

Among the letters that were brought to her study in the bulging Gladstone bag were often some from members objecting to Club selections; people who liked Dorothy's books felt betrayed when they found they did not agree with her. At times they protested violently, threatening to withdraw their memberships. Dorothy's answers, always given at length, were so tactful and satisfying that she had long been the appointed member of the Selection Committee to deal with complaints. Never was she at a loss to explain why she felt as she did. If the book in question was life portrayed, wasn't it better to know about it, she asked, providing the book was good for what it was supposed to be? That was the test, not the pleasantness of the subject matter. Surely a reading public should be able to read books dealing with all phases of life, "Or else, why read?"

Every day, immediately after luncheon, she settled down to attend to the mail. Many letters gave pure enjoyment, some gave cause for pondering; but all had to be answered. There were three letters with special requests—one was from Tsuda College in Japan, another from the American Library in Madrid, and the third from a Junior College in Switzerland. Dorothy put them aside for later dictation. She smiled when she opened a letter and read, "You have lived, for I am sure that you must have experienced most of it yourself, a noble book."

Another letter contained a request from a committee "just for your name." But it was never that, Dorothy reflected, and set the letter aside. Only after searching thought on the purpose and worth of the organization would she give her name. A letter from a person who, through the years, had read everything Dorothy had written, said, "I know of no author, ancient or modern, who has done so much to enable her readers to see life steadily and see it whole." An editor asked for a particular article for his magazine. Dorothy knew that she could not possibly do it, but the idea was such a good one that she wanted to suggest it to a younger writer-friend who would do it justice. Hastily she scribbled a notation on the envelope.

"Listen to this, John." Dorothy read, " 'Dad says he ran across your name on a list of extreme liberals still being "allowed" to write in this country. I have a strong impulse to congratulate you.' "

John chuckled as he looked up from the plan for the small building project which he was contemplating.

Two letters were handed to Dorothy by her secretary. One was from a Writers Conference asking her to lecture at the summer session. Dorothy read it and looked ahead on her calendar to see whether her time was free. The other was from a Writers Group asking her to become a member. She dashed off a word on the envelope and handed it back to her secretary. Some things were easy to refuse. She had always felt that writers writing books had neither time nor vitality left to attend gatherings of writers.

"Why, oh why," she exclaimed "do some people want to get together and talk about words instead of getting down to the hard work of trying to produce them!"

"All your life you have done much to make people better," a letter said, and another "What tangible home-happenings have resulted from your years of family writings, Book-of-the-Month Club choices, novels and children's books that grow into

young lives—all of them never ending in creating liveable un-
derstandings." One letter contained a clipping from a newspaper saying that in a recent poll Mrs. Eleanor Roosevelt had
placed Dorothy Canfield Fisher among the ten women in the
country who had most influenced the everyday lives of women.

"John, here's a letter from the Dorothy Canfield Club in
Connersville, Indiana, giving a report of their winter's activities
and ever so many friendly personal details about their members."

"Mrs. Fisher, here is a request for a statement on the words
you take to live by."

"But there are so many—" Dorothy took the letter and read
it. "I'll answer this myself, after I've had time to think more
fully." Words that had given valor to her living came to mind
like lights coming on in a valley at twilight, but none seemed to
ring more loudly just then than Edmund Burke's. "Never despair. But if you do, work on in despair." Out of hopeless pain
Burke had sounded that trumpet note. His heart had been
broken by the death of his son, and all around him he thought
he saw civilization crumbling. Many great thinkers had handed
down courage, Dorothy reflected, but what *help* there was in
Burke's words. He knew despair as many people did, dragging
on through day after dreary day, but he said, "Work on."

The remaining half-dozen letters seemed to require personal
answers and Dorothy read them thoughtfully. "Being a new
author I haven't the slightest idea who to go to for help so I am
writing you." ". . . though the story could have occurred in real
life, I would like to know whether it actually did occur. I want
to be able to answer people who say 'But this is only a
story.' . . . " "I want to thank you for the encouragement you
have given me. Six years ago you told me to keep on writing.
'It will make you so much more of a mother,' you said. . . .
Now my first article has been accepted. I am enclosing a snapshot of my family. . . ." An American woman visiting in a
foreign country had been asked for books about ordinary

people in the United States. "It delighted me that I could hand her your books. . . . Thank you for the delight and inspiration you have been to me and thousands of others like me—mothers and housewives, living on farms and suburban streets, and trying to make a home in which children may truly grow."

The last letter but one was from a woman who had been so moved by Dorothy's World War I stories that she and her husband had given a year to Near East Relief. Helped by Dorothy's books to keep a more widely human perspective when her three sons were involved in World War II, it had suddenly occurred to her to write and thank Dorothy for the breadth of human kindliness and understanding in her writing. "Your books confirm my conviction that all that matters deeply in this funny old world are things of the spirit. I hope I meet you some day."

The postmark, the handwriting and the suspicion of good news caused Dorothy to save one letter for the last. It was from Harold Goddard's daughter to say that her father's book *The Meaning of Shakespeare* had just been published and that a copy was in the mail to Dorothy. Blake's words "Joy and woe are woven fine" began the letter. It closed with the sentence "Thank you for being such an angel!" Between the two lay the story of five long years. Dorothy thought back to the time when she had first learned of Dr. Goddard's work on Shakespeare. He was, then, a professor of English at Swarthmore College and had been loved by more than one generation of students, her own Sally and Jimmy among them. The manuscript of his book had failed to interest any publisher and his daughter had asked Dorothy for advice. Dorothy had read it and been moved not only by its scholarliness but by the spiritual penetration with which he linked his material to the present day. Letters, telegrams, meetings with editors were all part of her faith in the book and desire to see it published, but nowhere could she find any interest in it. Two years passed, then three. Dr. Goddard's wife died; his own time was known to be short.

Then, as Dorothy remembered, one of life's miracles happened. The manuscript was sent to the University of Chicago Press and the editor received it as if it had been written for him. Only a matter of hours before Dr. Goddard's death was the news given him that his book would be published. "I'm happy," had been his last words.

Dorothy pushed everything else aside and started to write a hasty memo. Publication was one step for a book. She wanted now to do everything in her power to help the book receive the reviews it deserved.

One by one the letters that needed prompt attention were given it. Some Dorothy answered briefly in longhand, others were answered by dictation. To her sister-comrade Sally Cleghorn, went a pencilled page. "I have stopped in the midst of my busy weaving of many threads to pleasure myself by writing out this Blake poem to send to you . . . how the words come leaping to the fingers' end when your eyes will read them." To a young friend announcing her engagement she wrote, "My heart goes out to you. People often say the heart goes out in sorrow—mine does, but how it leaps to share a deep and satisfying joy."

Dorothy throve on news, receiving it, giving it, news of human happenings, of physical health, of joys and sorrows, the events of living, the small details. Everything that concerned her friends was of interest to her. "Tell me what happens at Meeting . . . tell me of the children . . . tell me about yourself, dear fellow-pilgrim." She told in return of library meetings and the work the school board had to find teachers for the next year. "Our news is chiefly of hard work," she wrote as she described the progress of the pages on her desk or the Book-of-the-Month Club reading—so much of it just then that she was surrounded by reports that overflowed her lap and were spread out on floor, couch and table.

She told of a fire that had started among some papers on

John's desk. Called from her study, she had gone running, grabbing a dressing gown and dipping it in water as she passed the bathroom, then slamming it on the desk. She told of finding a place for an old houseworker who had helped in different ways ever since the Fishers had lived in Arlington. "It's like transplanting an old tree and it takes patience, caution and ingenuity." Her words danced over the page as she wrote of the trip to Burlington when John received an LL.D., the highest honor the University of Vermont could confer, for the value of his service to the public school system. "And you'd better believe I was the most pleased spectator at *that* commencement!"

She wrote of the weather, always a part of life's savor to her. "The weather has turned—what tourists call 'bad'—dark and rainy. I like it, and it suits my dimmed ancient owl's eyes." . . . "Today it was like a Chinese painting in the pines. The damp air was still and motionless. Curls of filmy fog drifted among the trees." . . . "Twenty below zero—and what a triumphant feeling it gives that it is not too much to stand." . . . "How pleasant it is that we share the same climate in such a neighborly way!" To one of her colleagues in the world of books she had a recurrent question, "Is there anything I can do for you? Short of my bodily presence, I'm yours to command." To a young writer in whose progress she was interested she wrote, "I feel a concern, as Quakers say, a deep, heart-felt concern, anxious to let you have the best counsel an old woman has for a young one, an old professional writer for a young one."

When her desk was clear she was free to do what she liked with what remained of the day. Sometimes she would refresh herself for a few moments by turning through a book of Rembrandt paintings, or by taking a deep draught from Wordsworth, then she would go outdoors. With the stout pole in hand which her father had used on his climbing expeditions in Europe, she went up one of the mountain paths.

The sound of axes ringing through the pines drew Dorothy

to the pasture line where one of their neighbors was cutting some marked trees to use as boards for a house he was building. During the war years thinning among the pines had been neglected. When Arlington boys returned from army duty, some of them were kept from building their own homes by the high cost of lumber. The Fishers agreed to let them have pines from their plantation for the work of thinning. During the cold weather the sound of axes was like a special kind of music, and the sight of trucks loaded with sturdy brown trunks was immensely satisfying. And there were plenty of pines left, their forty-foot trunks lifting green crowns into spacious new room to grow.

"What will they be ten, fifteen years from now?" Dorothy wondered as she gazed up at them. She would be very ancient then, she knew, but the thought of what she might see made her old age something to look forward to.

Feeling rested to the core of her being, she started back to the house. The sense of peacefulness that pervaded her was not release from the pressure of work, it was a strong pulsing benediction from life itself. On her way she stopped for long meditative pauses on a bench near the brook, an old carriage seat on a rise of land, or a wooden chair that faced a clearing from which she could watch the last light on Equinox. Stimulating as a conversation with a friend was a thinking bout with herself.

Work in her flower garden during the spring and summer was something that had always given her new life, but she had been gradually cutting down its size as part of her attempt to get the necessary efforts of life reduced to the point where she could cope with them. She planted seeds thick, so weeds would find no ground to grow, then when she thinned there were plenty of seedlings to give away. By early summer her garden was a blaze of color, glowing with hollyhocks, and delphinium, poppies, Canterbury bells, Sweet William, zinnias. She called it her Posy-bed and loved it for what she said it was—a typical old lady's garden, a tangle of the strongest perennials growing in full hot sunshine. It provided a center of color in the midst of the green that was everywhere pervasive. Coming out of the pine woods after a walk, the splash of color was always a stimulus to her eyes. "But it's not a garden to be looked at too closely," she cautioned people, "and it seldom is except by the old lady to whom it belongs—and who often leaves it alone to do its sturdy best for considerable periods of time when she is busy about other things."

Four-Square was published, the first fiction to appear from her pen in ten years. Reviewers and public welcomed it. Mary Ross wrote in the *Herald Tribune*, "Reading this book makes you feel better about people and the world." Clifton Fadiman, now a colleague on the Selection Committee, said, "The accent that falls upon the ear is not that of a story that has been written, but of a tale that is being told."

The seventeen short stories in the book had all appeared previously, but Dorothy had rewritten each one for inclusion in *Four-Square*. She felt better able to handle the written word, as the years went on, because of the collaboration given her in thoughtful letters by many of her readers. They were an invisible presence around her desk and she addressed herself to them—

Of course I don't profit from every one. Sometimes it is apparent that a reader dislikes my work because it is not something I could never make it—that is, the work of another kind of person. Nothing to be done about that. Once in a while my fear is that a reader likes something in a story which I didn't know was there and wouldn't have left in, if I had seen it. But often a considered criticism accurately casts a light on a place which can be improved. And how heart-warming and reassuring is a reader's perception of an inner meaning I was not sure I had succeeded in writing between the lines. . . .

I don't share the feeling of those writers who say they write solely for themselves. It doesn't seem to me that I am unlike people who read my books—how should I be? What I write is an invitation to those with whom time has proved that I have much in common to join me in reflecting on the human life we all lead. . . . Here is the place to acknowledge with comradely appreciation the spoken explicit, and unspoken implicit co-operation given me by readers in the revision and re-writing of these stories.

Another group of her stories she rewrote for younger readers, *Something Old, Something New: Stories of People Who Are America.*

"You may try to make believe you're not in your stories, Dolly," John said, "but some of your great-greats are certainly in you."

"Well, for goodness' sakes, why shouldn't they be?"

Vermont's past was in her blood, as its bracing air was in her lungs.

When *Holiday* magazine asked her to write an article on Vermont, Dorothy called it her happiest task. "I never had a more rewarding assignment in all my long writing career. When *Holiday* said grandly, 'Go ahead, take what space you need,' my heart leaped up at the glorious words. I had about 180 years of Vermont lore in my head (figuratively speaking), and being allowed to say what I felt should be said without an incessant anxious counting of words was a happy experience—new to me for all my fifty years of writing for magazines."

Falling back on the fact of her seventy years, she wrote freely and fully. "Old people cannot condense," she said in a letter to a friend, "they must be free and leisurely if they are to express at all."

Then the California Oil Company asked her to write the text to go with a color photograph of a Vermont village and limited her to five hundred words. As was often her way, she asked a question. "What is there for Americans in a small quiet Vermont village?" Her concluding words held her answer—

The landscape has the lovable look we all recognize in a house which has been so long lived in that it has stopped being a house and has become a home. It is as a reminder that this our strange, wild globe can become a true home for humanity, that it is worth looking at Vermont villages.

For the magazine *Woman's Day*, Dorothy compiled a list of stories to read and tell to children. *The Kingdom of Childhood* became a treasured possession of many boys and girls who had long thought of Dorothy as a friend. Now, asked by a publisher to write a book in a series for young readers, she gave a prompt reply.

"*A* book? Why, I want to write two."

The first was *Paul Revere and the Minute Men*, the second *Our Independence and the Constitution*.

Dorothy had made more than one attempt to resign from the Selection Committee, but always she had been dissuaded. She liked the work as much as she liked being able to do the things the generous salary made possible, but her eyes were beginning to give her serious trouble and the monthly trips to New York were a strain. In October 1950, she and John worked together for the last time on a set of bound galleys. Sitting by the fire, with no more sound than the turning of a page or a yawn from one of the cats, they read throughout the evening.

During twenty-five years, Dorothy had missed only two meetings of the Selection Committee. Reading and discussing the books as they arrived at the Arlington house, John had constantly marveled at Dorothy's wisdom and astuteness. Often she had seemed to care for one point more than for the whole book, but invariably the point proved to be the book. There were other times when John had tried to pin her down, but she had persisted in seeing the broad, over-all implications. She never fussed over little things and was always willing to give benefit of doubt. The same native shrewdness and artistic balance that kept her from being taken over by the ceaseless requests in her enormous correspondence, kept her from being overwhelmed by the tide of new books. With an ear as keen for the meaty phrase as it was for the eternal values, she read and thought and came to her decision. Between them they had met the demands of reading an average of one book every other day for the time Dorothy had served on the Selection Committee.

"This is an even more prodigious achievement than may appear," Harry Scherman wrote in the Book-of-the-Month Club News. "These books, close to 4000 in number, were not merely read. They have been thought about prayerfully, compared with one another, discussed with others who had read them, appraised with a wonderful judgment; but also with an unerring eye always for anything meretricious or false. Over the years it has been a constant joy to her confreres to observe her rare critical faculties being exercised. No one in the past quarter century has worked with more devotion and conscience, and with such good effect, in the cause of American letters."

After her resignation Clifton Fadiman wrote to Dorothy, "You are often in our thoughts: partly as a beloved person; partly as a paradigm of conduct, something sorely needed by my generation."

Chapter 17
Full Circle

PEOPLE urged her to put her philosophy between the covers of a book.

"Haven't I been doing that in everything I've written for these more than fifty years?" she replied.

"Well, then, when will you write your autobiography?"

Dorothy shook her head.

In February 1951 she went to New York to attend a dinner of the Women's National Book Association. There, she was presented with the Constance Lindsay Skinner Award, a medal given annually to a woman in recognition of her contribution to the world of books. Few had participated so fully in that world as had Dorothy Canfield Fisher.

"It's a great responsibility," a neighbor remarked after her return, "being loved by folks as you are."

Marlboro College, Vermont, of which Dorothy was a founding trustee, gave her an Honorary Doctor of Letters in June. The citation read—

. . . distinguished author, interpreter to the country of Vermont virtues, participating citizen of the nation who exemplifies and expounds the strength and nobility of its democratic spirit, delightful deflater of stuffed shirts and pretense; the high purpose, dignity and beauty of her life and writings have made her universally honored and beloved.

In Emporia, Kansas, the William Allen White Library had recently been dedicated, but Kansans wanted to do something more to memorialize one of their great men. The establishment of a yearly Children's Book Award that would combine Mr. White's love of children and books was discussed and Dorothy's advice was sought. In her reply, which was immediate, she said, "I know Will would like the idea of such an award. Who wouldn't?"

Endeavoring to release some of the pressure of desk work, Dorothy had a form printed to acknowledge some of the letters that came to her.

Arlington, Vermont

This printed note is to give you the reason for my not answering you with such a full personal letter as, until now, I have always written. For some time I have been trying to find a good way to manage the fact that my correspondence increases almost in proportion to the inevitable slowing down and lessening of vitality which comes to people as they get older.

I don't like this plan very well—to send an impersonal statement and a telegram-brief message. But for the time being it must serve. I greatly hope you will understand that it doesn't mean any lack of interest in your letter or appreciation of your writing it.

She found, however, that she could not bring herself to use the form. Answers to letters were dictated as usual, or written in longhand. The unused forms made excellent material for lighting the kindling in her Franklin stove.

Years ago she had agreed to write a book about Vermont, while making sure that there was no deadline. Now she began to work over the notes she had been collecting, feeling that to tell the truth about one state might cast an occasional ray of light on the larger truth about human life. Her book was not to be a history of facts and dates, but an interpretation of what led up to the history and how events shaped the character and personality of the people. In the midst of work on it, she was asked to write a book for young people on the Declaration of Human Rights which had been adopted by the United Nations. It seemed, as she said, "almost alarmingly important," and so she agreed to do it at once.

When this manuscript neared completion, she sent copies of it to groups of boys and girls in different parts of the country for their comments and suggestions. Her relief was great at the thought that soon she might be able to clear her desk of its heap of papers and return to the Vermont book. "I don't expect to survive," she wrote a friend. "This is one of the most complicated pieces of literary keeping-five-balls-in-the-air-at-one-time I ever took on."

Dorothy dedicated *A Fair World for All: the Meaning of the Declaration of Human Rights*, to the people of her home town—

. . . because since the foundation of the town in 1764, they have, like many another peaceable, hard-working community all around the globe, proved in the factual field of everyday life the truth of the idea on which the United Nations is based—that men and women, each one full to the brim of human nature, can, by the act of living together, create for all more safety, more opportunity, and more hope.

Shortly after publication several hundred books were sent to Dorothy to be autographed. She unwrapped them carefully, wrote in them, and wrapped them for return to the publisher, but she called it a piece of foolishness. "What difference does it make *how* anybody writes his name!" she exclaimed.

When she returned to work on the Vermont book the words came to her mind warm, idiomatic, gay, alternately terse and lengthy, sometimes winged, generally comfortably earthy.

Published a year later, *Vermont Tradition* was aptly subtitled *The Biography of an Outlook on Life.*

"It is because you see her in it all the way through: she's talking to you," Harry Scherman said.

It was a long, richly packed book of informal unorthodox history; a spirited statement of faith in democracy. In it Dorothy spoke freely and with force her principles, her hope, her joy in living.

"Why, this *is* your autobiography, isn't it?" David Baumgardt said. "Anyone reading this will know all that you are willing to tell the public about your attitude towards life."

The *Herald Tribune* asked Dorothy to tell its readers what she had been doing recently. She did. She had been on a journey into the Vermont tradition, she said—

. . . in between happy mountain scramblings in snow, in early spring flowers, along with beautifully quiet, snowed-in, mid-winter days, and as beautifully sociable mid-summer days by seeing the world on wheels bringing old friends to our door, I've been living—absorbed, down-cast, exalted, hopeful, despairing, breathlessly interested—through the 17th century, the 18th, the 19th, and the first half of the 20th as they shaped the lives of ordinary Vermonters—of Americans today. And what do you think—the 20th was the hardest to understand and report on. That's what I've been doing with myself, that's where I've been. . . . Now I'm off with brush-hook and hatchet to lay out the path through our swamp-lot, neglected too long while I laid out the path of the older generation of my folks, and other Vermonters' folks—your folks too, wherever you live—through English and Colonial life which has brought us to where we are.

Again the letters came in baskets-full.

Unknown people sent their love, saying, "But what you write creates a feeling of deep affection." Her readers were often surprised to know how quietly she lived. "I always think of you as living right at the heart of life, right in the middle of everything—that is, everything important, perhaps one must live quietly to live there."

The first of December the country was shocked to hear that Dorothy Canfield Fisher had suffered a stroke of paralysis. A few days later hopeful reports began to come from the house on the slope of Red Mountain. Dorothy wanted her friends to know that she was comfortable, that she appreciated the solicitude reaching her by letter and telegram. Sally came to be with her mother. Writing to the family circle, she reported that though her mother was confined to bed she was radiating warmth and vitality and was as much the center of the house as she had always been.

As soon as Dorothy could, she dictated a long letter giving the details of her illness and the triumphant steps of her recovery.

January 8, 1954

Here it is now a week after New Year's, and I am downstairs walking around (slowly and cautiously but without a cane and without limping), looking around happily at the heaps of bright cards, and the flowers (always so miraculous in Vermont in December) and the Christmas candy-boxes and the pretty knitted things, Christmas presents not yet put away, and the dear, welcome, loving letters. I begin to wonder how I am going to reach you, of my special inner circle, responsible for this Christmas cheer. How can I send you thanks and a bulletin of health and Arlington news? . . . I'm well enough now to dictate into my invaluable electric dictation machine with no manual fatigue.

Here is the chronology of what happened;—The last of November my nephew and his wife were at the brick farmhouse. . . . John and I went down to spend the evening with them. . . . I never felt better in my life. When we came home, I went cheerfully to bed and had a fine night's sleep.

The next morning I woke, feeling just as usual (I think it is worth setting down how suddenly that interruption to the brain nerve center can happen), got up, staggered a little, thought I must be still half asleep, went on into the bathroom, tried to take a shower, couldn't seem to manage the faucets or the curtain, decided to get dressed, had unconquerable difficulties with hooks and eyes and buttons, dragged some clothes on, sideways, began to realize there was really something the matter with me, managed to take the few steps to the couch in John's study just across the landing from the bathroom, and lay down on that. Laddie, the big young collie dog, delighted to see somebody awake, leaped joyfully up beside me and, with collie enthusiasm, started to lick my face. I tried to raise my left hand to push him back, and found I couldn't lift that arm at all. It just lay dead on the bed and so did my left leg.

Then I knew what had happened—probably more accurately than some of you would. For a stroke of paralysis (as it is picturesquely called in ordinary language up here) is not only a common enough occurrence with elderly people, but extra familiar among Canfields. . . . The inert left arm and leg told me the story clearly. . . .

So when John got Dr. Russell here (he's been our doctor for more than 40 years and knows the family history), we had some data to talk over. His medical examination showed cerebral hemorrhage without any doubt. But which kind? My great-grandmother's variety or Uncle Zed's? There was no high blood pressure at all. I've always been just about normal in blood pressure and I still was. And I could move the toes on my left foot. So there was a pretty good chance, both the doctor and I thought. . . .

Dr. Russell's guess was that I'd be bedridden at least six weeks or two months. . . .

Hospitalization was not required. Quiet rest and care were needed and they were at hand. A capable nurse, who was a neighbor of the Fishers, came in daily. The devoted house-keeper of many years kept the household running.

And there is John—oh, *John—!*

So I don't need to tell you that the little old house, after one earthquake upheaval of emotional shock, moved on steadily and quietly.

I passed the first two weeks still on the couch, now made up as a bed, in the room just over our dining room. Up there, I could hear beautifully the music which John played on our good-quality record-player. The dining room is, as some of you remember who know it, panelled in old wood as dry as a violin. It makes a wonderful soundbox. What magnificence came triumphantly up, vibrating through those wood panels. All the Bach Mass in B Minor, all the Beethoven quartets, some of the quartets of Haydn . . . the exquisite Mozart quintet . . . and Mozart's "Haydn quartets," the lovely, lovely Schubert trio . . . the St. John Passion. It was wonderful to float in that timelessness of the sick-room with no more breaks in its wide expanse of the quiet hours than in the wide ocean on a calm crossing. I was certainly not to be pitied, even if there had been a break in the nerve connection between my brain and my left arm and leg.

The hours wheeled smoothly. . . .

Letters—precious, loving letters poured in and affectionate tele-grams, John read aloud to me in the evenings, finishing up *Adam Bede*, which he had begun before, and in which we were really abashed to find so much more greatness and significance and pene-trating realism, and honesty in complex character-portrayal than we had seen when we read it years ago in our youth. And then he began *The Brothers Karamazov* and you'd better believe we're still at that,—after George Eliot and *Adam Bede* something like plung-ing into Bartok or Shostakovitch after Beethoven. . . .

Another vivid interest and pleasure that I have had in these weeks of quiet—I've had time really to look *in detail* at the very fine pictures in that large volume of Hieronymus Bosch's work which was given me some years ago by David Baumgardt. I'd looked at them, of course, a good many times before. But never with the prolonged scrutiny under a magnifying glass with nothing pressing to do, so that I can between these long gazes, lean back and reflect, reflect, reflect (as I so love to do with a subject which is beyond my immediate understanding, like Bosch's work) on the deeper meanings of what I'd been looking at. It's given me ten thousand things to think of and just about as many questions left unanswered.

And Sally came! Our dear Sally! The first visit, all by herself, without any of her family, since she was married twenty years ago. We three had all the time for talking there was, with no children around. She looked splendidly well and vital, brought good news of the four children, all doing well and happy, of her having finished a new book for children, her eleventh, and we had a marvelous chance to hear every detail of all their news so that it was almost like a glimpse of her Bar Harbor home. . . .

While all these things were going on, the broken nerve connections between my brain and the muscles were mending themselves. I began to be able to manage those inert members with more and more comfort as the days went by. It didn't take anything like as long as had been thought. Dr. Russell could hardly believe his eyes. But he was as pleased as I was. . . . We let Mother Nature do her best, and I think she did very handsomely. For, except for three fingers on my left hand, still paralyzed, the nerve connections are all right. I'm weak, weak, weak, but prepared to wait patiently for the inner springs to fill up from whatever their mysterious sources are. As I dictate this, not six weeks after the first shock, I'm just in from a trip in the jeep with John up on the mountain.

It wasn't a very long trip, and I got into the jeep with the utmost caution, you'd better believe. And John drove cautiously. . . .

I've no idea, of course, what's before me now. Who does know what's before him? But as you can see, it hasn't been a very violent or melodramatic experience. Uncle Zed stood by, as he has in many another experience of my life. *You all stood by!* I have felt—no mystical dreamy imaginings about it!—almost materially and literally upheld and steadied by the thought of you, brought so closely

near by your loving messages—written and unwritten, many of
them from so far! And now that the paralysis has (almost) gone,
leaving me with this extraordinary lack of vitality, I still thankfully
lean on you.

By June she was well enough to walk in the Academic Procession at Smith College. It was her first public appearance after
her recovery. The citation which again made her a Doctor of
Letters read—

Though born in Kansas, and educated in Ohio, New York, and
Paris, she is by ancestry, by residence, and by conviction a citizen
of the state whose profile she has most skillfully depicted. Her
position as a first citizen of Vermont she has made secure, not only
by her distinction as author, but also by her active support of the
continuing effectiveness of its local institutions, particularly that
foundation of democratic society, the public school.

John, reading it with pride, found in his mind something that
Oliver Wendell Holmes had once said, "Identification with a
locality is a surer passport to immortality than cosmopolitan-
ism." The tree that grew tall and cast far shade had roots that
went deep. Deep.

A letter from Earlham College came to Dorothy's desk. Probably an invitation to speak, she thought, realizing wistfully that
such engagements were no longer for her. Opening it she saw
that it was not the usual pleasantly-phrased request for an address, but an invitation to Earlham's One Hundred and Ninth
Annual Commencement. A personal note was tucked inside—

Thank you for making this possible. Without your friendly,
sincere advice, it never would have happened. The faith you showed
in me so long ago has really done wonders.

Her mind went back to the letter that had come to her from

the young Negro soldier just out of the service. She knew he had been admitted to Earlham as letters had maintained a friendly contact, but this! Taking up her pen to write him she recalled a sentence in one of his letters, "I have learned with the Quakers that there are better ways than hate to resist injustice."

Dorothy went over the mountain trails often in the jeep with John. Soon she was walking them herself. Dr. Russell asked her to be careful not to fall.

"Why?" she demanded. "Am I more brittle now? I used to fall and nothing ever happened to me."

Dr. Russell looked at her humorously. "Well, what do you want to fall for anyway?" Then he turned to John. "Don't let her get pointed up hill, too often that is."

"Is that," John smiled slyly, "symbolical of something?"

When the Arlington Historical Society was in need of funds so that Dr. Russell's collection of Vermontiana might be permanently cared for, Dorothy wrote a little book entitled *Memories of My Home Town*. A thousand copies were printed, to sell for a dollar each, with the proceeds going to the Historical Society. Dorothy doubted if anyone outside the state would be interested in the recollections of one old lady but she hoped that through the years the paper-bound books might continue to sell and bring in a few dollars. Within a month there was not a copy to be purchased anywhere and Dorothy was asked by a trade publisher to add to the length of the book as he wanted to include it in a series on the American scene.

A deeper excursion into the past was made. Dorothy added to her childhood memories and current local stories, tales of neighborliness and solid good sense, fragments of history and common responsibility, linked with her warm feeling for all kinds of people. When *Memories of Arlington, Vermont* was published a year or two later, one of Dorothy's former colleagues on the Selection Committee termed it "a book to make one happy and proud to belong, if not to the same town, at least to the same country and the same race that produced it."

Once every summer for some years past, Dorothy had spent an evening at Bennington College with the foreign-exchange students, young men and women who had come to the United States as Fulbright scholars. Under a State Department plan, they spent their first month getting acquainted with each other and America at Bennington. Dorothy had supper with them, then talked with them in her easy friendly way, inviting their questions.

A serious young Hindu asked, "What has been the effect on the Vermont community of their religious institutions?"

Dorothy took a long breath before she answered. "There has not been much. The Vermont life has been mainly secular."

"Mrs. Fisher," a young man from Zanzibar stood up to ask, "what is your motive in writing novels?"

"I've tried to make some sense out of human life," Dorothy replied. "I've puzzled over how it is that some people can live together, others can't. Discoveries made about a marriage relation are not enormously different than what can be seen in international relations. If I can put my idea into a story and present human life so it makes sense, shows reason, I think it's going to do some good."

Dorothy looked from one to another of the group. "I hope," she said, "that you will all be writers—in your notebooks, in your letters home. Tell people in the countries you come from what your reactions are to situations here. Don't keep everything to yourself. Share it. That's the only way ignorance can be dealt with, and it's ignorance that keeps us apart."

A dark-haired, pansy-eyed young woman from the Philippines raised her hand, "Mrs. Fisher, how old are you?"

With a smile and a lift of her head, Dorothy said, "Old enough to be your grandmother. I'm in my seventy-eighth year."

"I just wanted to know how long I would have to live to learn what you have."

The next afternoon Dorothy received in her mail a letter from the little Filipino. It had been written five minutes after she had returned to her dormitory and she wrote—

Dear Grandma Fisher,—

Your talk answered a lot of questions I've been bothered about for quite some time. . . . It certainly takes an older person to make one see things from a second point of view. I never fully realized how idle my mind has been, how much time I've wasted. . . . I did think once in awhile but I found it very convenient to dismiss provocative thoughts. . . . Your talk, in fact you yourself, how you have managed to be able to see, hear, feel, keep alive in spite of the years—has made me feel ashamed of myself. . . . Listening to your talk about the 'motives' that have compelled you to write has given me the impression that writing is something simple— something like following an urge to talk about something. . . . Many impressions overwhelm me. Maybe I should wait until my mind clears a little, but I do want to write something. . . . Thank you for establishing our relationship. I never had a grandmother and I'm glad she turned out to be a writer, and a famous one at that.

The letter touched Dorothy, not only because of the warm ties that would ever exist for her with the Filipinos, but because something in the master craftsman sensed the yearning in a promising apprentice. Out of a full life and with a brimming heart she answered Rosie—

You say you've never had a grandmother before I came along; but I have granddaughters, one of them about your age I think, and you certainly seem like another one, brought in by one of the great new tides which are sweeping around our human world.

Your letter written in such impulsive haste, gives this experienced old writer the most complete proof that you *are gifted for writing* and self-expression. Your letter was as vivid a glimpse of you as if you had stepped into my little work-room here on the side of Red Mountain. There can be no doubt about that. You can certainly write, if—

But you remember my saying how very badly most of the people made music who were taught (in the period before the great musicians could reach our ears through modern inventions). The reason of course was not that none of them were gifted. Probably a normal number were. But since music was regarded as just a pleasant social accomplishment, they had no idea of the amount of vigorous mental effort needed to become real musicians. It's the same thing with writing. Lots of people have native gifts—not many as clearly marked as Rosie's—but too often they only use the gifts they were born with and do not add the special skill which comes only with long self-discipline. Grandmothers should be truth-telling as well as affectionate, so I'll have to set down a reminder to you that a great deal of effort on your part will be needed so to shape and master this native gift of yours, as to make it what it may easily be, an instrument for lifting the plane of human understanding.

A pretty big job for Rosie? Yes, you can see by my white hairs and other evidences of age that it's hard work. But worth-while effort towards a worth-while goal is just about the most satisfying job anybody can find in life. So I don't hesitate to make this statement about hard work in all its rigor.

How are you going to do it? Here in the midst of ten thousand crowding new impressions, you'll have to find out how to order them till they make some kind of clearer understanding of life, life with its joys and its difficulties, with its hardships and brilliant sunlight passages of happiness, will be understandable, more understandable, that is, to you and to the people you write for.

That is a very generalized report on writing, isn't it. But before I finish this letter to my new Filipino granddaughter, I'll set down just a few simple suggestions that are a little like the homely recipes which are passed on by an older cook to a young person just beginning. One of them is to keep some kind of a journal, every day, while you are on this global adventure of yours. If you don't, you will find at the end that it has all run together in a sort of blur. Just make it a practice to have pencil and paper conveniently at hand in your bedroom, so that before you go to bed every night, you jot down at top speed while they are fresh in your mind, some of the impressions of the day—every day will be crowded with impressions—while they are in the foreground of your mind. . . . If it's only a few words of characterization, *set something down,* as an artist makes notes in his sketch book of something he wants to make a picture of, later on when he has time. . . .

There, does that give you an idea, dear Rosie, of some of the techniques of writers. They have learned that one impression drives out a good deal of the one before it and so, quickly, quickly they set down a little sketch of what they have just heard, or seen, or felt.

This makes, in the end, a volume or storehouse of memories which are not at all in the usual meaning of the word "creative writing," but which form the raw material for the creative writing I hope you are going to do.

There, that's enough sermonizing even from a grandmother who by tradition, loves to moralize for the younger generation. . . .

Grandma Fisher.

In 1956 Dorothy's *A Harvest of Stories* from *A Half Century of Writing* was published. Of the reviews that heaped her desk, the one in the *Christian Herald* brought deep pleasure—

Dorothy Canfield has lived a full life and lived it with love and understanding of her fellow men. Her intimate associations have been with the humble and the great, with the young and the old. She writes of war-time France and the day-to-day struggle with community living. She writes of the fabled Basque country. . . .

The life of this woman is an almost fabulous chronicle of abundant and yet more abundant living and her stories are like "apples of gold in pictures of silver."

There were many days now when, as Dorothy said to a friend, "the old shell of the body seems to become a little harder to inhabit"; but all of her came vibrantly alive when she was asked to do something for children. With the Vermont Council on World Affairs she sponsored an essay contest for schoolchildren to help stimulate interest in the United Nations. A committee representing the Vermont Congress of Parents and Teachers and the Free Public Library Commission, inspired by what had been done for reading in Kansas since the establishment of the White Award, wanted to establish a similar one in Vermont. The purpose was threefold: to recognize an author's work, to encourage children to read more and better books, and to honor one of the state's great citizens, a woman as loved as she was distinguished. When the plan was taken to Dorothy she heartily approved. Any plan that would encourage reading appealed to her, and she felt deeply honored that the award should bear her name.

When mention was made of a medal, she firmly said, "No."

"But, Mrs. Fisher," a committee member protested, "the award should be evidenced in some tangible way."

"How about a plaque that can be hung on the wall?" Dorothy suggested. "What can you do with a medal anyway?"

So the award that honors her, perhaps above all her awards, and that will continue through the years, was established—THE DOROTHY CANFIELD FISHER CHILDREN'S BOOK AWARD.

Dorothy's feet since childhood had been familiar with the trails that traversed Red Mountain, trails she had worked to keep open. Now, slowly, slowly, in the jeep with John at the wheel, the trails were still open for her. She remembered what it had been to scramble through brambles and over stones, to feel out-of-breath and leg-weary, to breathe again as the path leveled off and the end appeared in sight; then, through a gap in the trees, to see that it was no end at all, that the real climb was only just beginning. The steep trail to Flag Rock had always been a favorite one, giving her a wide view of the Battenkill Valley, neat, purposeful, patterned. Leaning back against granite rocks in a lap of sunshine, breathing the fragrance of sweet fern, feeling the feather-light brush of the wind and listening to the sounds from the valley, Dorothy had often looked lovingly on the weatherworn mountain ranges. There was a reason for their beauty. Geologically, they were older than the Alps. Worn down by natural forces, they were composed and at rest.

What she thought about life—her philosophy—was something like the mountains, developed by the forces that had worked on them; what she had done in life—her writing—was something like the river that flowed through the valley, fed by deep springs. There were certain basic facts about writing which she had proved for herself and which she had put into words on more than one occasion, but when she was asked to put her philosophy into words she could not do it. To condense into a paragraph or a few pages the beliefs by which she tried to govern her life was not possible. She had put them by implication into every book she had ever written.

"Some say there's no religion in Dolly's books, why, it's all through them!" John exclaimed. "For years, people have looked to her for light and leading and she has never failed them."

In the biggest of all possible ways, her life is her religion— her vigorous and productive, gallant and resourceful life in which the art of living and the art of working have been so beautifully balanced.

"These years are almost too happy, too fulfilled," she says, "but there is so little time left, so little vitality, I don't want to waste it."

Beside her stands John.

Years ago he had found in Wordsworth's poem "She Was a Phantom of Delight" an apt description of Dorothy. He did not need to take the book from the shelf to recall the words that painted a true portrait for him. They were alive in his mind, especially the last stanza which line by line said exactly what he thought of Dorothy—

> And now I see with eye serene
> The very pulse of the machine;
> A Being breathing thoughtful breath,
> A Traveller between life and death;
> The reason firm, the temperate will,
> Endurance, foresight, strength and skill;
> A perfect Woman, nobly planned,
> To warn, to comfort, and command;
> And yet a Spirit still, and bright
> With something of angelic light.

If she had any secret he should know it, but what she had was an open secret. Hers was the spiritual, tempered strength to handle creatively whatever life gave her, and in turn to give herself to be used by life. Her dreams, no less than her desires and talents, were always put at the disposal of the greatest possible good.

Dorothy and John had enjoyed working and being together; now that to a large extent the active years were over they found there was still much to enjoy. Chief among the permanent elements was their delight in each other's minds. To think and to exchange thoughts was something time could not tarnish. Music came into their home with its vitality and power; books were there with wisdom and comfort. The mountain world outside their door was as strength-giving as ever. And there was a blessing now of which they were both keenly aware, one that only years could give,—patience and the larger perspective.

Epilogue

Twelve Years Later

DOROTHY CANFIELD FISHER once said about her father, "I try to take his spirit forward into life." The ways chosen to remember her, since her death in November 1958, are carrying her spirit on into the life she loved best—the life of books.

First is the Children's Book Award, established while she was living with her help and happy consent. Similar to the *William Allen White Children's Book Award* set up in Kansas a few years earlier to honor a distinguished citizen, the *Dorothy Canfield Fisher Children's Book Award* is co-sponsored by the Vermont Congress of Parents and Teachers and the Department of Libraries. Its purpose is to encourage school children from grades four to eight to read more and better books and to discriminate in chosing worthwhile books. From a list of some thirty titles, compiled by a select group of Vermonters interested in children's reading and in library service, the young Vermonters are encouraged to read books best suited to their ability. "Those participating read and discuss as many books as possible from the Master List provided and then, in the Spring, cast their votes for the books they liked best." One child, one vote. Announcement of the winner is made in alternate years at the meeting of the Vermont Library Association (May) and at the annual meeting of the Vermont PTA (October). The award is an illuminated scroll by Julia Bottum Wager, an artist who lives in Arlington.

The Editorial Board of the Book-of-the-Month Club issued two statements. One was an eloquent estimation of her life:

DOROTHY CANFIELD FISHER

1879·1958

SHE DIED on November 9 in the little town of Arlington, Vermont, where so many Canfields lie in peace. She was 79; and those many years were richly and beautifully lived. In the course of them she had won for herself high reputation in many fields: as novelist, short-story writer, essayist, historian, writer of books for the young; as translator, lecturer, and interpreter of the Vermont tradition; as educational philosopher and as a member of Vermont's State Board of Education. For a quarter of a century, from the year of its founding, she served as a member of the editorial board of the Book-of-the-Month Club. When in 1951 she retired, only her colleagues could estimate how much her independent judgment, rigorous standards and broad scholarship had contributed to the Club's healthy growth. ✳ But when we of the Club think of her it is not her many achievements that we recall, nor the honors and distinctions that quite properly came her way. Other Americans have achieved as much and won for themselves equally respectful obituaries. But this does not necessarily mean that they will be remembered in quite the same way that Dorothy Canfield will be. For she was more than an American of great ability. She was one of the rarest and purest character. In her completely unself-conscious integrity, her courage, her humor and her practical good sense (the last almost always used to help other human beings) she harked back to and lent new luster to our highest pioneer traditions. ✳ A confirmed Vermonter, she was also a cosmopolitan in both space and time. All who knew her felt at once this combination of deep-rootedness and broad humanity; and felt themselves the larger for it. Her death leaves our country poorer. Her life enriched it.

Editorial Board: JOHN MASON BROWN
BASIL DAVENPORT
GILBERT HIGHET
JOHN P. MARQUAND
CLIFTON FADIMAN

The other, their decision of how that life could best be remembered:

AN ANNUAL MEMORIAL AWARD

ALL HER LIFE, from her girlhood to her last days, one of the deepest concerns of Dorothy Canfield Fisher was the wider and ever wider dissemination of books. That was the reason she associated herself with the Book-of-the-Month Club at its inception in 1926 and why her work on our Editorial Board became, next to writing, the most absorbing activity of her life for a quarter of a century. In discussing how we might set up a lasting memorial to this beloved friend and associate, we felt that it would be most representative if it could take the form, in some way, of books. Accordingly, it has been decided that an annual DOROTHY CANFIELD FISHER LIBRARY AWARD will be made by the Book-of-the-Month Club, with the advice and co-operation of the American Library Association. The Awards will be made, one a year, to libraries in small communities, where it is usually not easy to raise money to equip a library properly. The Awards will be in the sum of $5000 each, in the form of requested books. They will continue to be given over a period at present undetermined, but at the least for five years. The first one will be made to the library in Arlington, Vermont, where Mrs. Fisher lived most of her life. Thereafter, they will go to other libraries selected by the Book-of-the-Month Club with the advice of the American Library Association. . . . There is nothing her friends at the Book-of-the-Month Club could do, we feel sure, that would have pleased Dorothy Canfield Fisher more than this expression of their devotion to her. This sort of thing would have delighted her inmost being, just the doing of it, unconnected with her name or any other; but there is no possible name such Awards could be more fittingly associated with than that of Dorothy Canfield Fisher. That name will be on a bookplate, the first thing each reader sees, in every book.

HARRY SCHERMAN
CHAIRMAN OF THE BOARD

MEREDITH WOOD
PRESIDENT

DECEMBER 1, 1958

The awards were given over a period of six years to small libraries, wide apart geographically but closely related in their work of raising standards and motivating people to read. After the Arlington Library in 1959, the *Dorothy Canfield Fisher Library Award* was presented in successive years to the Preble County District Library in Eaton, Ohio; the Yuma City–County Library in Yuma, Arizona; the Jenkins Public Library in Jenkins, Kentucky; the Beaufort County Library in Beaufort, South Carolina; the East Central Regional Library in Paramus, New Jersey; and the final award was made to the Northeast Regional Library in Corinth, Mississippi.

When Mrs. Fisher turned over her vast file of papers, manuscripts, correspondence, memorabilia to the Wilbur Library at the University of Vermont, she said in her Deed of Gift, dated 1953, "I desire that . . . the Dorothy Canfield Collection . . . be made available to students and to persons engaged in research." The papers had begun to arrive years before the bequest was made formal, and they continue to arrive as material comes to light and personal letters can be made public. Students and scholars use the collection extensively for course papers, critical studies, doctoral dissertations. Some of the work has already been published; more will be. Indicative of the influence Mrs. Fisher has on the world of letters is the list of work accomplished and work in progress which the librarian and curator, Thomas D. Seymour Bassett, has at hand:

WORK ACCOMPLISHED

The Lady from Vermont is the only book-length publication we know of. All of the authors but Payne used our Collection.

MALCOLM D. DAGGETT. *A Heart with Courage in It.* Excerpts from the correspondence of Dorothy Canfield Fisher with Céline Sibut, 1900–1941. Typescript in the possession of the author, completed 1968.

JOSEPH PAUL LOVERING. *The Short Stories of Dorothy Canfield Fisher.* Typescript course paper in English, University of Ottawa, 1956;

24 1. *The contribution of Dorothy Canfield Fisher to the development of realism in the American novel.* Typescript Ph.D. thesis in English, University of Ottawa, 1956; 215 1.

LOIS MCALLISTER. *Dorothy Canfield Fisher: A Critical Study.* Typescript Ph.D. thesis in English, Case Western Reserve University, 1969; 357, 1.

LETA WEISS MARKS. *Dorothy Canfield Fisher: The Development of Her Educational Thought.* Typescript M.A. thesis, Trinity College, 1961; 357 1.

JACQUES MITCHELL, III. M.A. thesis in English, Florida State University, 196–?, on Dorothy Canfield Fisher's ideas about writing.

MARGARET HEALD PAYNE. *Dorothy Canfield Fisher: Bio-bibliography.* Microfilm of typescript M.S. thesis in Library Science, Florida State University, 1959; 84 1.

WORK IN PROGRESS

BETTY BANDEL (Department of English, University of Vermont). Dorothy Canfield Fisher's view of the life of the artist in America.

ERIC W. CARLSON (Department of English, University of Connecticut). A critical study of her fiction and related letters; possibly a Canfield Reader.

DAVID CARROLL DUKE (University of Tennessee Ph.D. candidate). "American Byrons," not followed up, on her activities in France during World War I.

BRUCE FLACK (Ohio State University). Activities with the American Youth Commission.

ANNA M. KEPPEL (University of Hawaii). Interest among students and historians of education in Dorothy Canfield Fisher and the Montessori method.

MERCEDES RANDALL (MRS. JOHN H.). (Columbia University). Her relations with Emily Green Balch.

DON SMYTHE, S. J. (Georgetown University). Her relations with General John Pershing.

LIVIA TILGHER (Rome, Italy). Dorothy Canfield Fisher's correspondence with her late husband, philosopher and journalist Adriano Tilgher, for an edition of his works.

IDA H. WASHINGTON (MRS. LAWRENCE M.) (Southeastern Massachusetts Technological Institute). Critical biography.

CHARITY C. WILLARD (U.S. Military Academy, West Point). Edition of her letters during World War I. (inactive)

The staff of our Special Collections has steadily added to the collection of manuscripts given by Mrs. Fisher. The principal donors have been David Baumgardt, Henry Castor, Bertha Dodge, Merle S. Haas (Mrs. Robert K.) (some 650 letters, 1918, 1927–58), Howard C. Rice, Jr., and Fannie G. Shaw.

No longer is her influence intensely personal, but it is still intensely present; as if the single heart had now become one with the great heart of humanity. Many of her ideas that were thought revolutionary have become part of our current thinking. Much of what she labored for, with the help and support of her husband, has been absorbed into an improved educational system, incorporated into social betterment. Books were her heritage, they became her bequest. Because of their importance, she was ever aware of the need to instill a hunger for reading while providing its satisfaction.

In a Bowker Lecture given at the New York Public Library in 1947 she expressed her concern. "Now, in our times, when the complexity of the human situation on the globe needs the best thinking human brains can achieve, one of the surest tools for thought—the book—is under attack, an attack the more dangerous because indirect, and, for practical purposes, invisible. . . . Every one of our millions of Americans has a vote every year. Does he read a book of value every year? That vote is a safeguard or peril, according to the personality of the voter. And there is no shaping modern human personalities to the necessary minimum of intelligence and civilized standards, without a continuous, widespread use of books of decent quality." She brought her challenging speech to a close as she urged that "Every mechanism that can be devised should be put into action to keep up the book-habit among people, and to distribute in numbers comparable to the need, books of civilized quality." She would only underscore those words today.

In the churchyard of St. James' in Arlington, where many

Canfields lie buried, are two unweathered marble stones; plain and beautifully proportioned. They are close together and their deeply cut letters tell of two lives that found each other, then found the way to enrich each other and their world:

DOROTHY CANFIELD   JOHN R. FISHER
WIFE OF JOHN R. FISHER   1883–1959
1879–1958

No other words were needed. Each one had faith in words already written, and in their continuance.

December 1970

ELIZABETH YATES

BIBLIOGRAPHY

Bibliography

Emile Angier, playwright-moralist-poet; a study. (Graduating Thesis, printed for private circulation.) Ohio State University, Columbus, Ohio, 1899.

Corneille and Racine in England. Columbia University Press, New York, 1904.

Elementary Composition. (With George R. Carpenter) The Macmillan Company, New York, 1906.

Gunhild. Henry Holt & Company, New York, 1907.

What Shall We Do Now? Frederick A. Stokes Company, New York, 1907.

The Squirrel Cage. Henry Holt & Company, New York, 1912.

A Montessori Mother. Henry Holt & Company, New York, 1912.

The Montessori Manual. Richardson, Chicago, 1913.

Mothers and Children. Henry Holt & Company, New York, 1914.

Hillsboro People. (With occasional Vermont verses by Sarah N. Cleghorn) Henry Holt & Company, New York, 1915.

L'education Montessori; Adaption française de Jacqueline Andre. Librairie Fischbacher, Paris, 1915.

The Bent Twig. Henry Holt & Company, New York, 1915.

The Real Motive. Henry Holt & Company, New York, 1916.

Self-Reliance. Bobbs-Merrill Company, Indianapolis, Indiana, 1916.

Fellow Captains. (With S. L. Cleghorn) Henry Holt & Company, New York, 1916.

Understood Betsy. Henry Holt & Company, New York, 1917.

Home Fires in France. Henry Holt & Company, New York, 1918.

The Day of Glory. Henry Holt & Company, New York, 1919.

The Brimming Cup. Harcourt, Brace & Company, New York, 1921.

Life of Christ. (Translated from the Italian of Govanni Papini) Harcourt, Brace & Company, New York, 1921.

What Grandmother Did Not Know. Pilgrim Press, Boston, Massachusetts, 1922.

Rough Hewn. Harcourt, Brace & Company, New York, 1922.

Raw Material. Harcourt, Brace & Company, New York, 1923.

The French School at Middlebury. Middlebury College, Middlebury, Vermont, 1923.

The Home-Maker. Harcourt, Brace & Company, New York, 1924.

Made-to-Order Stories. Harcourt, Brace & Company, New York, 1925.

Her Son's Wife. Harcourt, Brace & Company, New York, 1926.

Why Stop Learning? Harcourt, Brace & Company, New York, 1927.

Learn or Perish (Kappa Delta Pi Lecture). Liveright Publishing Corporation, New York, 1930.

The Deepening Stream. Harcourt, Brace & Company, New York, 1930.

Work; What It Has Meant to Men Through the Ages. (Translated from the Italian of Adriano Tilgher) Harcourt, Brace & Company, New York, 1931.

Basque People. Harcourt, Brace & Company, New York, 1931.

Vermont Summer Homes. Vermont Bureau of Publicity, Montpelier, Vermont, 1932, 1935.

Bonfire. Harcourt, Brace & Company, New York, 1933.

Moral Pushing and Pulling. (Commencement Address, Leland and Gray Seminary, Townshend, Vermont) E. L. Hildreth & Company, Brattleboro, Vermont, 1933.

Tourists Accommodated. Harcourt, Brace & Company, New York, 1934.

Wells College Phi Beta Kappa Address. Wells College, Aurora, New York, 1936.

Fables for Parents. Harcourt, Brace & Company, New York, 1937.

On A Rainy Day. (Prepared for the National Recreation Association with Sarah Fisher Scott) A. S. Barnes & Company, New York, 1938.

Seasoned Timber. Harcourt, Brace & Company, New York, 1939.

The Election on Academy Hill; a story drawn from the novel *Seasoned Timber*. Harcourt, Brace & Company, New York, 1939.

Tell Me a Story. University Publishing Company, Lincoln, Nebraska, 1940.

Nothing Ever Happens and How It Does. (With Sarah N. Cleghorn) The Beacon Press, Inc., Boston, Massachusetts, 1940.

Our Young Folks. Harcourt, Brace & Company, New York, 1943.

American Portraits. Henry Holt & Company, New York, 1946.

Book-Clubs. (R. R. Bowker Memorial Lecture) New York Public Library, New York, 1947.

Four-Square. Harcourt, Brace & Company, New York, 1949.

Something Old, Something New. Scott, Foresman & Company, Chicago, 1949.

Paul Revere and the Minute Men. Random House Inc., New York, 1950.

Our Independence and the Constitution. Random House Inc., New York, 1950.

A Fair World for All. Whittlesey House, New York, 1952.

Vermont Tradition. Little, Brown & Company, Boston, Massachusetts, 1953.

Memories of My Home Town. Privately printed, 1956.

A Harvest of Stories. Harcourt, Brace & Company, New York, 1956.

Memories of Arlington, Vermont. Duell, Sloan & Pearce, Inc., New York, 1957.

INTRODUCTIONS BY DOROTHY CANFIELD FISHER

Kent, Rockwell. *Wilderness*, G. P. Putnam's Sons, New York, 1920.

Canfield, Flavia Camp. *Around the World at Eighty*, Charles E. Tuttle Company, Rutland, Vermont, 1925.

Hard, Walter R. *A Mountain Township*, Harcourt, Brace & Company, New York, 1933.

Dinesen, Isak. *Seven Gothic Tales*, Harrison Smith & Robert Haas, Inc., New York, 1934.

Cartwright, Morse Adams. *Ten Years of Adult Education*, The Macmillan Company, New York, 1935.

Morgan, Arthur E. *The Long Road*, National Home Library Foundation, Washington, D.C., 1936.

Federal Writer's Project. *Vermont*, Houghton Mifflin Company, Boston, Massachusetts, 1937.

Wright, Richard. *Native Son*, Harper & Brothers, New York, 1940.

Schauffler, Robert H. *Fiddler's Luck*, The Island Workshop Press Co-op, Inc., New York, 1941.

Washburn, Ruth W. *Children Have Their Reasons*, D. Appleton-Century Company, Inc., New York, 1942.

Pierce, Enid Herberta, and Flanders, H. H., editors. *Green Mountain Verse, An Anthology of Contemporary Vermont Poetry*, Farrar & Rinehart, Inc., New York, 1943.

Zoff, Otto. *They Shall Inherit the Earth*, translated by Anne Garrison, John Day Company, Inc., New York, 1943.

Tolstoy, Leo. *What Men Live By*, translated by Louise and Aylmer Maude, Pantheon Books, New York, 1943.

Wimberly, Lowry C., editor. *Prairie Schooner Caravan*, University of Nebraska Press, Lincoln, Nebraska, 1943.

Mann, Klaus, and Kesten, Hermann, editors. *Heart of Europe*, L. B. Fischer Publishing Corporation, New York, 1943.

Cleghorn, Sarah N. *Poems of Peace and Freedom*, Women's International League for Peace and Freedom, New York State Branch, Rome, New York, 1945.

Wright, Richard. *Black Boy*, Harper & Brothers, New York, 1945.

Guptill, Arthur. *Norman Rockwell, Illustrator*, Watson-Guptill Publications, Inc., New York, 1946.

Poley, Irvin and Ruth. *Quaker Anecdotes*, Pendle Hill, Wallingford, Pennsylvania, 1946.

Abernethy, Jean, editor. *Meditations for Women*, Abingdon-Cokesbury Press, Nashville, Tennessee, 1947.

Newton, Earle. *The Vermont Story*, Vermont Historical Society, Vermont, 1949.

Broomell, Anna P. *The Friendly Story Caravan*, J. B. Lippincott Company, Philadelphia, Pennsylvania, 1949.

Eaton, Allen H. *Handicrafts of New England*, Harper & Brothers, New York, 1949.

Kershner, Howard E. *Quaker Service in Modern War: Spain and France, 1939–1940*, Prentice-Hall, Inc., New York, 1950.

Poley, Irvin and Ruth. *Friendly Anecdotes*, Harper & Brothers, New York, 1950.

Mangione, Jerre G. *Mount Allegro*, Alfred A. Knopf, Inc., New York, 1952.

Thomas, Will. *The Seeking*, A. A. Wyn, Inc., New York, 1953.

Yates, Elizabeth. *Prudence Crandall, Woman of Courage*, E. P. Dutton, & Company, Inc., New York, 1956.

FURTHER READING

Overton, Grant. *The Women Who Make Our Novels,* The Macmillan Company, New York, 1919.

Williams, Blanche Colton. *Our Short Story Writers,* Moffat, Yard & Company, New York, 1920.

Cleghorn, Sarah. *Threescore,* Random House, Inc., New York, 1936.

Kunitz, Han A., and Haycraft, Howard, editors. *Twentieth Century Authors,* The H. W. Wilson Company, New York, 1942.

Witham, W. Tasker. *Panorama of American Literature,* Frederick Ungar Publishing Company, New York, 1947.

Baumgardt, David. "Dorothy Canfield Fisher on her Seventieth Birthday," *Educational Forum,* Kappa Delta Pi, Tiffin, Ohio, 1950.

"You Meet Such Interesting People," *Publishers' Weekly,* Vol. CLIX, No. 2, p. 145, January 13, 1951.

"Take a Bow," *Publishers' Weekly,* Vol. CLIX, No. 8, p. 1042, February 24, 1951.

Warfel, Harry R. *American Novelists of Today,* American Book Company, New York, 1951.

Wagenknecht, Edward. *Cavalcade of the American Novel,* Henry Holt & Company, New York, 1952.

In addition to many hundreds of magazine articles and book reviews, as well as plays, pageants and addresses, from 1903 throughout her writing career, Dorothy Canfield Fisher's work is included in many anthologies, text books, readers, etc., among them—

Phelps, William Lyon. *What I Like in Prose,* Charles Scribner's Sons, New York, 1933.

Agar, H. and others. *The City of Man,* The Viking Press, Inc., New York, 1940.

Roosevelt, Franklin D., and others. *America Organizes to Win the War,* Harcourt, Brace & Company, New York, 1942.

Weston, Sidney A. *Finding Your Way In Life*, Association Press, New York, 1942.

Watkins, Ann. *Taken At The Flood*, Harper & Brothers, New York, 1946.

Woods, Eugene J., editor. *I Wish I'd Written That*, McGraw-Hill Book Company, Inc., New York, 1946.

Burnett, Whit, editor. *This is My Best*, Dial Press, Inc., New York, 1942.

Bader, Arno L., and Wells, Carlton S. *Essays for Our Time*, Harper & Brothers, New York, 1947.

Foley, M., editor. *Best American Short Stories, 1949–1952*, Houghton Mifflin Company, Boston, Massachusetts, 1952.

Ghiselin, Brewster, editor. *The Creative Process*, Mentor Books, New York, 1952, formerly published as *Americans All*, edited by Benjamin Heydrick, Harcourt, Brace & Company, New York, 1941.